W

NOV   2006

What Paul Meant

GARRY WILLS

What Paul Meant

VIKING

VIKING
Published by the Penguin Group
Penguin Group (USA) Inc., 375 Hudson Street,
New York, New York 10014, U.S.A.
Penguin Group (Canada), 90 Eglinton Avenue East, Suite 700, Toronto,
Ontario, Canada M4P 2Y3 (a division of Pearson Penguin Canada Inc.)
Penguin Books Ltd, 80 Strand, London WC2R 0RL, England
Penguin Ireland, 25 St. Stephen's Green, Dublin 2, Ireland
(a division of Penguin Books Ltd)
Penguin Books Australia Ltd, 250 Camberwell Road, Camberwell,
Victoria 3124, Australia (a division of Pearson Australia Group Pty Ltd)
Penguin Books India Pvt Ltd, 11 Community Centre,
Panchsheel Park, New Delhi – 110 017, India
Penguin Group (NZ), Cnr Airborne and Rosedale Roads, Albany,
Auckland 1310, New Zealand (a division of Pearson New Zealand Ltd)
Penguin Books (South Africa) (Pty) Ltd, 24 Sturdee Avenue,
Rosebank, Johannesburg 2196, South Africa
Penguin Books Ltd, Registered Offices: 80 Strand, London WC2R 0RL, England

First published in 2006 by Viking Penguin, a member of Penguin Group (USA) Inc.

1 3 5 7 9 10 8 6 4 2

ISBN 0-670-03793-1

Printed in the United States of America
Set in Aldus
Designed by Francesca Belanger

TO THE CATHOLIC WORKERS

who know what Jesus meant

Contents

What Paul Meant

Introduction: "The Bad News Man"

✝

MANY PEOPLE THINK that Judas was the supreme betrayer of Jesus. But others say Paul has a better right to that title. Judas gave Jesus' body over to death. Paul, it is claimed, buried his spirit. He substituted his own high-flown but also dark theology for the simple teachings of the itinerant preacher from Galilee. Thomas Jefferson wrote to his friend William Short that Paul was the "first corrupter of the doctrines of Jesus." Bernard Shaw said the same thing in the preface to his play *Androcles and the Lion:* "There has never been a more monstrous imposition perpetrated than the imposition of the limitations of Paul's soul upon the soul of Jesus." This represented a triumph over the four evangelists ("good news bearers") by what Nietzsche called Paul in *The Antichrist*—"the Dysangelist" (Bad News Bearer), a man with "a genius for hatred." Shaw told a correspondent in 1928 that "it would have been better for the world if Paul had never been born."

What causes such harsh judgments on Paul? It is said he threw the human mind into prisons of sinful doom and predestination, subjecting human beings to a "law in their members," trapping them in "the flesh," so that neither moral effort nor religious code can free them from this bondage. Paul inspired pessimisms as influential as those of Augustine and Luther and Pascal (Nietzsche called Paul "the Jewish Pascal"). In line with such tidings of great gloom, Paul's letters have become the place to go, over the centuries, for attacks on women, marriage, gays, and Jews—especially Jews. The great German scholar Adolf von Harnack proclaimed—in *What Is Christianity?*—that Paul "confidently regarded the Gospel as a new force abolishing the religion of the [Jewish] Law." Jews, naturally, have been less than happy with that judgment, suspecting that the deep anti-Semitism of Christianity comes in large part from Paul. The attitude of some Jews, complained Richard Rubenstein, can be summed up as "Jesus, yes; Paul, never!"[1]

The Outsider

HOW WAS PAUL able to subvert, so early and so thoroughly, the message of Jesus? Those who believe he did so can argue that he was bound to, since there was no reason for him to know or understand Jesus, a figure he never met. In fact, during the earthly career of Jesus, Paul was never in the same country with him. Jesus came from Judaea and never moved outside it. Paul came from Cilicia (specifically, from Tarsus) and became a follower of Jesus in Syria (specifically, Damascus). Paul did not even go to Judaea for three years after he professed allegiance to Jesus, and he remained there for only two weeks. After this first visit, he stayed away for another fourteen years (Gal 2.1). He was, by his own account, not even recognizable there: "I was not known by my features *(prosōpon)* to the Judaean gatherings in Messiah" (Gal 1.22). Even when he tried to prove that he was a Jew among Jews, he did not claim Judaean birth or upbringing (Phil 3.4–6). In fact, he often took occasion to stress how distant he was, how independent, from the gatherings in Jerusalem.

Then how could Paul know much about what Jesus did or said in the land where he was born and lived? In fact, Paul's letters have few explicit mentions of Jesus' acts or words on earth. His acquaintance with the Jewish homeland being small, he concentrates on the risen Jesus, who appeared to him in the Diaspora. That is where, according to his critics, he picked up the components he would weave together into a new religion, reflecting his own psychological makeup and Greek education more than the rich events unfolded in the life of Jesus. The great scripture scholar Rudolf Bultmann wrote that "the teaching of the historical Jesus plays no role, or practically none, in Paul . . . in fact, his letters barely show any traces of the influence of the Palestinian tradition concerning the history and preaching of Jesus."[2]

With no credentials for knowing Jesus outside his own

private revelations, Paul dared to disagree with and criticize the original Twelve; and Peter, their leader; and James the brother of the Lord, who presided over the gathering in Jerusalem. He called Peter a hypocrite, one of those "who maintained a pretense" and "did not hew to the clearly marked meaning of the revelation" (Gal 2.13–14). He defended himself against "a party of Peter" in Corinth (1 Cor 1.12). He thought Peter had been misled by James (Gal 2.12) and he refers to the two of them as "apparent pillars" of the gathering in Jerusalem (Gal 2.9).

As befits one setting up his own religion, Paul became—in the eyes of early critics—"the father of heresies." All through Christian history Paul has been a sign of division, a stone on which many stumble. Apocryphal writings by Peter and James would charge Paul, in the second century, with being a tool of Satan. On the other side, Marcionites from that period claimed that only Paul and the Pauline "Luke" were authentically inspired authors. This kind of conflict was extended into the medieval use of Paul by various "antinomians." The problem reached its climax in the Reformation, a fight over what Paul meant in which, at times, there seemed to be little concern over what Jesus meant. It was not enough, then, for some to claim with Wilhelm Wrede that Paul was "the second founder of Christianity," second only to Jesus. He became the *only* founder of Christianity, leaving the misunderstood Jesus without any religion of his own.

The Letters

WHAT MADE PAUL such an apple of discord? The problem has its origin in his own words. It is sometimes said that the historical Jesus is hard to find because he left no writings of his own. Paul is hard to find precisely because he did leave writings. The letters attributed to him in the canonical New Testament seem to fall apart in our hands as we try to read them. Almost half of them (six of the thirteen) are no longer accepted by the mass of scholars as authentically his. Even some of the seven genuine ones are called composites, made up of several letters (or parts of letters), since they contradict one another or even themselves.[3] One or more letters may have been added after a first one on a papyrus roll, and then all recopied as a single letter when the rolls were recopied. Our seven genuine letters may thus be an amalgam of anywhere from eight to a dozen letters (or parts of letters). There are, besides, lost letters that Paul explicitly refers to or readers plausibly surmise. There may have been many earlier letters, written before Paul became so well known, before his network of correspondents increasingly saw the worth of what he wrote ("His letters, they say, are impressive and strong," 2 Cor 10.10), and before communities took care to preserve their own archives. There were probably later letters suppressed or destroyed because they were an embarrassment to the gatherings—whence the blackout on Paul's later days and death. So we have a spotty collection of writings, with many a known or unknown gap.

Even when one winnows down the few extant missives to an agreed-on authentic core, the letters remain dark or elusive. Within half a century or so of their composition, the "Peter" of the New Testament was calling them difficult and potentially misleading on the subject of the end time.

> Keep in mind that our rescue comes from the Lord's staying with us, as Paul, the brother we love, wrote to you out of the wisdom imparted to him. He has made the same point in all the letters he wrote on this subject. There are things in them hard to understand, which the unlettered and unsteady twist about—as with the rest of his writings—to their private and pernicious sense. (2 Pet 3.15–16)

It is not surprising that people should have trouble reading the letters of Paul. They are occasional writings, fired off to deal with local crises. He dictated them in the midst of various struggles, often to answer problems or refute opponents not clearly specified in his responses. We hear his raised voice without knowing what the other side was shouting. Some of the acerbic terms he uses were echoed back against now-invisible critics who first used them. Wayne Meeks rightly says: "We never see pure Pauline thought being developed at leisure by its own inner logic; rather, we see Paul always thinking under pressure, usually in the heat of immediate controversy."[4] The result is sometimes a lava flow of heated language, words tumbling out in self-defense or urgent exhortation. Paul is not a cool and remote philosopher but an embattled messenger—at times, as Nietzsche said, "disagreeable to himself and to others." He is a mystic and a deep theologian, but also a voluble street fighter, a man busy on many fronts, often harried, sometimes exasperated. To take on Paul is to plunge into a melee, as Donald Harman Akenson emphasizes:

> Saul, as revealed in his letters, was a feral creature. He would appear in one town or city after another, sometimes leaving footprints the size of craters, at other times, no marks at all, save a half-sentence in a later letter as the only mark of his coming and going. To the historical observer he is maddening, for he appears when least expected and he ducks out of sight just when we think he will be most useful.[5]

Keeping up with this theological Scarlet Pimpernel can be a strenuous endeavor. To quote Akenson again:

> At times, Saul reminds one of a vice-principal of a large urban high school who has to teach a daily class in calculus to the college-bound stream, then, as head of discipline he

breaks up a fight in the hall, and next he finds he has to fill in for a shop teacher who has gone home with a migraine. After school he coaches the offensive line of the football team, and finally at night he has to appear before a special session of the city council and give a polished argument for continued funding of the art and music classes. So we honor the canon of Saul's letters by accepting their sometimes-distracted, sometimes-staccato quality as part of the warrant of their authenticity, the words of a man on a mission.[6]

As one would expect of a man facing in so many directions to cope with so many tasks, Paul treated different situations with different approaches. He had to keep explaining his different treatment of Jesus' followers who were circumcised and those who were not. He gave different advice on observance of the Jewish food code to the Galatians and to the Romans. He refused to accept financial support from the Corinthians but welcomed it from the Galatians. He is frank about the flexibility of his mission strategies:

> While I am not anyone's slave, I have made myself everyone's slave, to win over more of them. For Jews I have been a Jew, to win over Jews. For those observing the Law I have been under the Law, though not subject to it, to win over those under the Law. To those free of the Law I have been free of the Law—not in fact free of God's law, but

under Messiah's law—to win over those free of the Law. I am weak with the weak, to win over the weak. To all people I am all things, so I may in all ways rescue some of them. All I do, I do for the sake of the revelation, that I may act along with the revelation. (1 Cor 9.19–23)

He gives plausible reasons (as we shall see) for these and other twists and turns. But their variety does not make him easy to follow.

The Best Witness

NO WONDER many people would just as soon avoid Paul's psychodrama and go "back" to the pure Gospels, which do not argue about understanding Jesus but just present him. Taking that shortcut was the obvious thing to do in the Middle Ages, when it was thought that the Gospels were written by the original followers of Jesus, who were eyewitnesses to what they set down. This led to the view that there was a primitive church, true to Jesus' simple teachings, which was later contaminated by Paul's doubts and theories and wrangling. (This is the Thomas Jefferson thesis.) But scholarly enquiry has destroyed the idea that the Gospels have a simple biographical basis. They are sophisticated theological constructs, none written by their putative authors, all drawing on second- or third- or fourth-hand accounts—and *all written from a quarter of a century to half a century after Paul's letters.* If we want to see what the original Jesus communities looked like, the first and best witness to this is Paul, the earliest writer of what would become in time the New Testament. In fact, his authentic letters are the only parts of the New Testament of which we can say that we know who wrote them. The Gospels, coming later, try to make sense of a history that already contained the conflicts Paul reveals to us. Those who believe in a providential revelation through the New Testament must deal with the fact that Providence preserved the first batch of inspired writings with the signature of Paul. His letters were written roughly two decades after the death of Jesus. Other New Testament letters attributed to Paul or to other authors (Peter, James, and John) are written two to five decades after his, and imitate the forms of his.

It was Paul who brought the good news to many communities. He still brings it to us. I shall argue that what Paul meant was not something other than or contrary to what Jesus meant, but that we can best find out the latter by studying the former. His letters stand closer to Jesus than do any other words in the New Testament. They were the first to be penned, the first to be saved. That fact must be remembered when we look at the Acts of the Apostles, the work of someone calling himself Luke. That book describes the travels and teachings of Paul, integrating them into the activities of other early members of the Jesus movement. The letters used to be interpreted in terms of the chronology and issues discussed in Acts. But that later account is often at odds with the earlier and authentic letters—for a very good reason. Luke does not cite or refer to any of the letters. In fact, *he does not seem to know they exist.* If he does, he treats them as a nuisance best ignored. That in itself is enough to destroy the image "Luke" presents of having known Paul, and even of having traveled or worked with him.

There are other grounds for treating Acts with great caution when it purports to be telling the story of Paul. Luke is writing after the Romans destroyed the Temple in Jerusalem (70 CE), a catastrophe that was still decades off when Paul wrote. Luke's contemporaries are trying to work out the troubled relations with their parent body of Jews, the displaced worshipers from the Temple and in the synagogues. With Luke and his contemporaries, there is the beginning of a separate church with a primitive because inchoate structure, in which various communities are becoming connected in a more systematic way. This proto-church is a body to which people are being converted, and Luke treats Paul as one of them. He also presents him as part of the Jerusalem community before it was dispersed, in accord with Luke's unifying program. He makes Paul's career show many good relations with Rome—he even makes Paul a Roman citizen—and he presents Paul's relations with Jews who do not believe in Jesus as more hostile than they are in the letters. That reflects the bitter circumstances of Luke's own traumatized time, the time when the Jews' world was upended with the obliteration of the Temple.

Luke's situation was not that of Paul. Paul never thinks of himself as a convert to some new religion. He preaches the Jewish God, Yahweh, and the Jewish Messiah. He preaches in synagogues. When he brings others to believe in Jesus, he teaches them from the Jewish holy writings, which were the only "Bible" of the day—his letters would not be joined together with later documents to create a separate "New Testament" till long after his death. Though relations between Jews who believed in Jesus and those who did not were becoming strained and even combative in Paul's time, he says there can be no permanent break. History is moving fast toward its conclusion, and the only conclusion he recognizes is the one God has arranged for his covenanted people. "Has God rejected his own people? Far from it" (Rom 11.1).

[Rather than thinking God had rejected his people] I could prefer to be outcast from Messiah myself if it would help my brothers, the forebears of my flesh, who are the Israelites. Theirs is the sonship, and the splendor, and the covenants and the gift of the Law, the rites, and the promises. From them are the patriarchs, and from them, by fleshly descent is the Messiah, the God above all, be he forever praised. (Rom 9.3–5)

Other peoples are to be included in God's final plan, but the original people cannot be excluded. How this was to happen was mysterious, but Paul and his fellow believers in the Diaspora were hurriedly trying to work the matter out. We shall see that he was not alone in his efforts, or the first to set up communities of believers in Jesus throughout the Diaspora. He worked from pre-existing bases, learning from and teaching his fellow emissaries of the Lord. Even when he arrives in cities new to him, he often meets and works with fellow believers from Rome and elsewhere, places that already had "gatherings in Jesus," as he put it.

All of this is hard to understand if we go back to Paul through later assumptions with a familiar (but anachronistic) framework. That is why this book will forswear the use of terms for things that did not exist in Paul's world—terms like *church* or *Christians, priests* or *sacraments*. (For reaching back to Paul's "pre-churchy" language, see my Appendix.) When Paul addresses the *ekklesiai*, the "gatherings in Jesus," he is writing to those who met in the homes of particular men or women, in the same town or in several towns. He addresses himself to the whole gathering, in each case, not to some leader or leaders. Some towns had more than one such home-gathering. There was no hierarchy among the gatherings, one having more authority over another. The housekeepers, whether male or female or both, were the informal leaders of the gathering. Emissaries—for this sense of *apostle*, see my

Appendix—moved from gathering to gathering, normally in teams, often husband-and-wife teams (Rom 16.6–15), like the team of Peter and his wife, or of the Lord's brothers and their wives (1 Cor 9.5). Paul usually had several partners in his team—most of his letters are written with cosenders, and he often refers to coworkers, women as well as men.

New gatherings were hived off from pre-existing ones, sometimes by the work of emissaries like Paul's team, sometimes by the gathering's own natural reach outward toward friends or relatives or associates, either in the same town or in other ones. The proliferation of these gatherings was astonishingly rapid. They had grown out from Palestine even before Paul came to believe in Jesus. They were already present in the country where he was living (Syria). He began his work as a junior partner (with Barnabas) in an emissary team operating from a pre-existing gathering at Antioch. The story of Paul is never that of an individual, some religious genius hatching his own religion out of his own head. We find in his letters hymns that communities had formed and sung before he set them down in an epistle. He constantly appeals to traditions handed on to him, to be handed on to others. It is as a testimony to the vital explosion of belief in Jesus all across the Diaspora that Paul assumes his importance.

He takes us closer in time to Jesus than does any other person or group or body of writings. The best way to find out what Jesus meant to his early followers is to see what Paul meant to his fellow believers, many of whom had seen Jesus in his earthly lifetime or after his Resurrection, without having written their stories down for us. Paul did write. But he was writing about a shared experience, not a single and idiosyncratic one. If Paul was such a foe and underminer of Jesus, why was he accepted so soon and broadly by those who knew Jesus? The answer is that Paul was not a counterforce to Jesus but one of the early believers who together bore witness to him. The Jesus gatherings in the Diaspora proved more fertile and lasting than those in Judaea itself, not because of any one man's brilliance, energy, or deceptions, but because they were more vitally expressive of what Jesus meant. Paul was part of this explosion of belief. His letters are dispatches from that hurricane of activity.

The Pauline Writings

THIRTEEN LETTERS are attributed to Paul in the New Testament, and for centuries they were all accepted as his. But modern scholarship has reached a consensus that some were definitely not written by him and others are of dubious authenticity. Only seven are now accepted as certainly by him. The seven in their probable order of composition are

1 Thess   Letter to the Thessalonians
Gal   Letter to the Galatians

Phil	Letter to the Philippians
Phlm	Letter to Philemon
1 Cor	First Letter to the Corinthians
2 Cor	Second Letter to the Corinthians
Rom	Letter to the Romans

Two letters seem to be written by followers of Paul who had a profound understanding of what could be made of his teaching:

Col	Letter to the Colossians
Eph	Letter to the Ephesians

One letter seems a clumsy restatement of a genuine one:

2 Thess	Purported Letter to the Thessalonians

Three later letters are written in circumstances and from standpoints clearly not Paul's:

Tit	Letter to Titus
1 Tim	First Letter to Timothy
2 Tim	Second Letter to Timothy

For understanding what Paul meant, one must rely on the letters accepted by almost all scholars as authentic. This book will use only those seven letters.

NOTES

1. Richard L. Rubenstein, *My Brother Paul* (Harper & Row, 1972), p. 114.

2. Rudolf Bultmann, *Theology of the New Testament*, translated by Kentrick Grobel (Scribner, 1955), pp. 35, 188.

3. It is widely agreed that the Second Letter to the Corinthians combines two separate missives, and some find as many as six original components tucked into it. Two letters are also found in the First Letter to the Thessalonians and the First Letter to the Corinthians, while three or more have been found in the Letter to the Romans. Thus the seven authentic writings of Paul may be made up of a dozen or more works by him.

4. Wayne A. Meeks, *The Writings of St. Paul* (W. W. Norton & Company, 1972), p. 438.

5. Donald Harman Akenson, *Saint Saul: A Skeleton Key to the Historical Jesus* (Oxford University Press, 2000), p. 129.

6. Ibid., p. 134.

1. Paul and the Risen Jesus

☩

THE MOST IMPORTANT EVENT of Paul's life, that which determined everything else, was his encounter with the risen Jesus. He puts this in a social context, as part of the Resurrection experience that other followers of Jesus shared. His own account of this epochal occurrence does not accord with the most famous story of Paul's "conversion," that given in the Acts of the Apostles (9.1–9). But that story, told by one "Luke," was written half a century after what it purports to describe, and we shall find that it has many holes in it. Here are Paul's own words, close to the event:

> My urgent concern was to pass on to you what was passed on to me—that Christ died for our sins, in accord with the sacred writings, that he was buried, that he arose on the third day, in accord with the sacred writings, that he appeared to Kephas, then to the Twelve. After that, he appeared at the same time to more than five hundred of the Brothers, most of whom are still with us, though some have died. And after that he appeared to James, then to all the emissaries.[1] Finally, as by a delayed birth, he appeared to me, though I am the least of the emissaries, one

not even worthy to be called an emissary, since I perse-cuted God's gathering. (1 Cor 15.3–9)

Paul puts his own experience in the context of the Gospel rev-elation, of the tradition passed on to him, which it is his ur-gent concern to pass on to others, in company with the other emissaries, his superiors.

The principal thing to notice here is that Jesus *appeared* to Paul—*ōphthē*, "he was *seen.*" In Luke's account of Paul's en-counter with Jesus, Paul sees nothing—a sudden flash of light proves literally blinding, so that he merely hears a voice. This is technically not an apparition but a *photism* (a light flash) accompanied by an *audition* (a disembodied voice). In the Gospel stories of meetings with the risen Jesus, genuine ap-paritions occur—the Lord not only appears to men and women but he converses with those who see him, he gives in-structions, he answers questions.[2] Paul, putting his own record along with theirs, implies that his experience was like theirs—that he spoke with Jesus. That is the credential he of-fers to others who also possess it. He asks to be tested by all those he has identified as his fellow witnesses to the risen Lord. "Am I not an emissary? *Have I not seen Jesus our Lord?*" (1 Cor 9.1). That is why he can report that he had his calling as an emissary to the nations directly from Jesus: "I, Paul, made an emissary not in any human way, or through any man, but through Jesus-Messiah and his Father, God, who raised him from the dead" (Gal 1.1).

Of all those who saw the risen Lord, Paul is the only one whose own words we possess. The other accounts are second- or third- or fourth-hand, written down four or five decades after the Resurrection. Yet Paul, at the time he wrote, met many of those who shared his privilege—people who could have challenged his claim. No doubt he shared his own story with them, they all "compared notes."

And of all this large company of witnesses to the Resurrection, only Paul has described (so far as that is possible) what a risen body is like. The others remark on an elusive or uncanny aspect to their encounters. They often do not at first recognize Jesus. He seems paradoxically physical (eating food) yet ghostly (gliding through a door), ordinary (a gardener, a traveler) yet transfigured.[3] Paul, who knows what he is talking about, says that the risen body does not fit any of our expectations. Only he, of those who have seen such a body, tells us what it is like:

Will someone ask, in what way are the dead raised, and in what kind of body do they fare? Do not be a fool. Even a seed you sow does not come to life until it dies. And what you sow is not the plant it will become; it is a mere seed—of wheat, perhaps, or of some other grain. God gives it the plant he has decreed, a different plant according to what seed is sown. And all flesh is not the same, but that of humans, or of beasts, or of birds, or of fish. There are, moreover, heavenly bodies and earthly bodies, and the splendor of the heavenly bodies is one thing, the splendor of earthly bodies another. There is one splendor for the sun, another for the moon, and another for the stars—since star from star differs in splendor.

That is how it is with the resurrection of the dead. Sown in disintegration, it is raised in integrity. Sown in disgrace, it is raised in splendor. Sown in frailty, it is raised in strength. What is sown as a sensate body is raised as a spiritual body. If there is a sensate body, there is also a spiritual body. For it is written: "The first man, Adam, became a living soul." But the last Adam became a life-giving spirit. Yet the spiritual comes not first; rather the sensate is first, and then the spiritual. The first man came from the clay of earth; the second came from heaven. As the first man was of clay, so are the others claylike. And as the last man was from heaven, so are all his fellows heavenly. And as we have borne the likeness of the man of clay, so shall we bear the likeness of the man from heaven.

So, brothers, I assure you, flesh and blood cannot have any inheritance in God's reign, any more than disintegration can have any inheritance in integrity. That is the secret thing I am telling you. Though we all may not die, we shall all be altered at a stroke, at an eyeblink, at a last trumpet blast, and the dead will awaken in integrity and we shall be altered. Then must disintegration be clothed in integrity, and death be clothed in deathlessness. When such death is clothed in deathlessness, the word will apply: Death, what victory have you? What stab, Death, is left you? (1 Cor 15.35–55)

Paul inevitably associated what other risen bodies would be like from his encounter with that of Jesus. "He will transfigure our body's lowliness into the pattern of his dazzling body" (Phil 3.21). "By looking with unveiled faces at the glory of the Lord mirrored back on us, we are transformed into that image, from splendor to splendor, by the working of the Lord's Spirit" (2 Cor 3.18). When Paul talks of seeing the splendor of Jesus' face, it is often assumed or asserted that he is registering the internal assent of faith, but there is no reason we should artificially keep his statement apart from his report that he had actually seen the Lord's face: "The God who said, 'Let light shine out of the dark,' has shone a light in our heart to understand the splendor of God that is the features *(prosōpon)* of Messiah" (1 Cor 4.6). Paul is our expert on the risen body, and he shows a fascination with it. He writes about the longing for it.

When this transitory housing we inhabit is dissolved, we know another housing is prepared for us by God, a lasting casement in the heavens not made by hand. We naturally chafe in our present casing, yearning for the heavenly one to be put on over it, lest we be caught naked but for our first habiliment—we chafe while pent in this narrow enclosure, though not wanting to put it off until it is enclosed in the new casing, so that the mortal shall be absorbed into the immortal. God has prompted us to this yearning, and has given us the Spirit as a surety of its fulfillment. Bracing ourselves on all sides, then, realizing that while we are held in by our bodies we are held off from the Lord, we fare on, believing beyond what we see, bracing ourselves as I say and taking heart to leave the body's home and enter the Lord's home, making it our point of pride to win his favor, however disembodied or re-embodied. (2 Cor 5.1–9)

Paul is attributing to others his own yearning to be freed into the higher state where Jesus has led the way. "For me, living is Christ and dying a boon. . . . I feel an urgency for dissolution, to be with Christ" (Phil 1.21, 23).

The tug between the present body and what he had seen of the future one played into Paul's mystical experience of prayer. This is something he would not have mentioned in his letters had Corinthian spiritualists not boasted of their ecstatic states as a warrant for their aberrations. Paul refutes their arguments, but also says that such experiences do not excuse their conduct. He is a bit embarrassed at having to engage in such competitive spiritual credentialing, so he modestly puts his claim in the third person.

> I am forced to boast. Though it does me little good, I will venture on the subject of visions and revelations from the Lord. I know a man in Messiah who, fourteen years ago—whether in his body or out of it I know not, God knows—was swept up high as the third heaven. And I know that this very man—whether in his body or out of it, I know not—was swept up into Paradise, where he heard unspeakable words, words it is impossible for a man to pronounce. About such a man I might boast, but about myself I may boast only of weaknesses. (2 Cor 12.1–5)

Apparently describing the same time, he assured the glossolalists of Corinth: "Thank God I can speak in tongues more than all of you—though I would rather speak five intelligible words in the gathering, to be understood by others, than speak thousands of words in tongues" (1 Cor 14.18–19).

By dating his ecstasies back to a specific time, Paul no doubt refers to the key period in his life, that in which he received his call from Jesus. As soon as Jesus appeared to him, he went to Arabia—to the desert just over the eastern border of Syria (the country Damascus is in).

> I would have you know, Brothers, that the revelation I revealed to you came not in the ordinary human way, for I

did not receive it from a man by way of teaching. Rather, it was directly revealed to me by Jesus-Messiah. For you have heard how I led my life under the Jewish Law, that I was extreme in my persecution of God's gathering, trying to extirpate it, how I surpassed many of my contemporaries in adherence to Jewish Law, more highly devoted to the traditions I received from the ancestors. But when the time came for what God had destined me to from the womb, summoning me by his favor, he directly revealed his Son to me, that I might proclaim him to the nations. At this point I consulted no flesh-and-blood person. Nor did I go to Jerusalem, to see emissaries called before me. I went off, instead, to Arabia, whence I later returned to Damascus. (Gal 1.11–17)

Why would Paul go even farther off from Jerusalem—to Arabia? Some have said he was acting at once on the commission to preach to "the nations." But that underestimates the wrenching experience that turned him from a fierce assault on "the Brothers" as enemies of the Law. He had to come to grips with all his earlier misconceptions. He had to reconcile somehow his reading of Jewish destiny and its improbable fulfillment in Jesus as Messiah. We also have to suppose that Jesus, in his appearance to him, directed Paul toward a kind of desert experience of intense prayer and study. All the later citations of the sacred writings that Paul made while dictating his letters "on the road" could not have come from ad hoc unrolling of the bulky papyruses of the Bible. He had to puzzle out, under divine guidance, where he had been wrong in his reading of the prophets, what new light was cast on them by the words Jesus spoke to him. This deep involvement let him quote scripture extensively from memory (it is noticed that he is often slightly "off" the precise wording). There is no reason to suppose that Jesus appeared to him only once. He appeared to others several times and in several places (Mt 28.10, Jn 21.1). In fact, Paul tells us of a later apparition (Gal 2.2), when he decided to go to Jerusalem, not summoned or sent by men, but "directed by an apparition" (*apokalypsis*, the same word he uses of Jesus' apparition to him at Gal 1.12 and 1.16).

Paul, by withdrawing into Arabia, away from his home and prior associations, was able to develop what would continue to be his passionate intimacy with Jesus. "It is no longer I who live—Messiah lives in me" (Gal 2.20). "It is in Messiah-Jesus that I take pride for service to God, though I dare not say this is anything but Jesus himself working through me to bring the nations to his service" (Rom 15.17–18). "I made up my mind not to display any learning to you, only Messiah, and him as crucified" (1 Cor 2.2). "Be imitators of me, as I am of Messiah" (1 Cor 11.1). "I bear on my body Jesus' wounds" (Gal 6.17). Paul's identification with Jesus was not just a personal matter. It was what he saw as the essence of belief for all his Brothers. This is what made them "the Holy," the persons "in Jesus." Baptism had incorporated them into the Messianic fulfillment of history. "We were buried with him by this baptism into his death, so that, just as Messiah rose from the dead to the splendor of his Father, we should fare forward in a life entirely new" (Rom 6.3–4). "Anyone in Messiah is a new order of being, the ancient things have passed away, and—see!—the new ones begin" (2 Cor 5.17).

In Paul's dizzying early days of communication with Jesus, he had to reconcile his earlier devotion to the Jewish Law with his experience of the risen Jesus—and he came to recognize the latter as the fulfillment of the former. Jesus is the Promised One: "Messiah is the Law's completion" (Rom 10.4). In most English translations of Paul's letters, "Christ" is taken as a name, not a title. "Jesus Christ" is made to sound like a full name (praenomen and cognomen). But *Khristos* in Greek is a title, like *Kyrios* (Lord). It is the Greek form of Hebrew "Messiah." Both words mean "Anointed." Paul sometimes refers to Jesus as the Messiah, or just Messiah, or Jesus-Messiah, or Messiah-Jesus. But it is always his *title* that is at stake, and we should keep this as much to the forefront of our minds as it was to his, since it is what unites the risen Jesus with his Jewish destiny.[4] That is why the basic revelation of faith for Paul was always that Jesus died for our sins and rose again, *in accord with the sacred writings* (1 Cor 15.3–4).

The experience of the risen Jesus was not only the pivotal event in Paul's own life. It was for him the center of salvation history, for the Jews and for the world. It is what he preaches.

Without it, he would have nothing to say and the gatherings would have nothing to bring them into existence.

> If it is our revelation that Messiah was raised from the dead, how can some of you say that there is no resurrection from the dead? If there is no resurrection from the dead, how could Messiah have been raised? If Messiah was not raised, our revelation is an empty thing, as is your faith, and we are guilty of false testimony about God, since we were God's witnesses that he had raised Messiah, which he could not have done if the dead cannot be raised. If in fact the dead are not raised, the Messiah was not raised; and if Messiah was not raised, your faith is pointless, and you are still in sin's thrall. More that that, those who died in Messiah have simply perished. If our hope in Messiah is only for this present life, we are the most pitiable of all human beings. But Messiah truly was raised, the first harvest of all who die. As death came through one man, so resurrection comes through one man. (1 Cor 15.12–21)

He cannot repeat this message of the Resurrection often or urgently enough.

> We look toward his Son's appearance from the heavens, the one he raised from the dead, Jesus our rescuer from the impending wrath. (1 Thess 1.10)

[I am] an emissary from Jesus-Messiah, and from God his Father, who raised him from the dead. (Gal 1.1)

. . . to experience him and the energy of his Resurrection and the oneness with his sufferings, shaping myself to the pattern of his death, to have a share in his Resurrection from the dead. (Phil 3.10–11)

. . . knowing that he who raised Jesus the Lord will raise us along with him, and bring us to his side. (2 Cor 4.14)

Baptized into Messiah-Jesus, we were baptized into his death. We were buried with him by this baptism into his death, so that, just as Messiah rose from the dead to the splendor of his Father, so we may fare forward in a life entirely new. (Rom 6.3–4)

Luke's Story

IT IS IMPORTANT to get Paul's own words firmly in mind when considering his relation to the risen Jesus, since—as has already been mentioned—his own version is not the famous one. That comes from the Acts of the Apostles, and it is so sensational that there can be no wonder that it has eclipsed his own words. The Acts of the Apostles has been called a theological novel, and it does share some traits with the Hellenistic novels being written at the same time as Acts—wandering preachers, miracles, sea adventures, long rhetorical speeches.

The story of Paul's "conversion" is so good that the author of Acts repeats it three times, each time with variations. In one version, bystanders fall down when Paul does (Ac 26.14). In another, they stay standing (9.7). In one, the bystanders see a light, but hear no voice (22.9). In another, they hear a voice but see nothing (9.7). In short, in one version people get the photism without the audition, in the other one they get the audition without the photism—but Paul, Luke assures us, got them both. By the third version, what the voice says is considerably expanded in length as well as intention (26.16–18).

Luke is a theological artist. He creates for a purpose, and the purpose can shift from one part of his story to the next. He wrote the Gospel that bears his name, and the beautiful accounts he created of Jesus' birth and presentation in the Temple, with their accompanying canticles, show how good he was at presenting doctrine as narrative. His theological purpose in dealing with Paul will be considered later, but the first thing to note about his accounts is their distance not only from Paul's words but from legal possibility and historical probability. The best known of the three versions is the first one in the book. Paul had already appeared in Jerusalem as Saul (his Hebrew name), where Luke says he was a student of the great Pharisee scholar Gamaliel (Ac 22.3). Though Gamaliel was known to oppose zealots, Saul joined the hotheads who stoned Stephen, the first martyr for Jesus. He kept the executioners' coats as he condoned their violence (Ac 7.57). Not content with that, Saul decided to go and do likewise, first in Judaea: "Saul raided the gathering, going house to house, dragging men and women off to prison" (Ac 8.3). Then he moved out to a foreign land:

Saul, snorting even greater threats of murder against the Lord's followers, went to the high priest with a request for letters to the synagogues in Damascus, to identify those of the Path, male or female, and bring them back in chains to Jerusalem. But as he neared Damascus, a sudden flash from heaven lightened all about him, and he heard a voice as he fell to the ground, saying, "Saul, Saul, why are you persecuting me?" And he asked, "Who, Lord, are you?" And he: "I am Jesus, the one you are persecuting. But get up and go into the town, and you will be told what you must do." His companions on the trip had stood there speechless, hearing a voice but seeing no one. Saul then got up from the ground but, on opening his eyes, was able to see nothing. So they led him by the hand into town. For three days he saw nothing, nor did he eat or drink.

There was a follower in Damascus named Ananias, and to him the Lord called, "Ananias," in a vision. He responded, "Here, Lord." And the Lord said: "Get up and go to Straight Street, and look for a man named Saul of Tarsus in the house of Judas. He is praying there, you see, since he has seen in a vision one called Ananias coming to lay hands on him and restore his sight." But Ananias said, "Lord, many people have told me about this man, all the suffering he has brought on your Holy Ones in Jerusalem, and that he has a mandate from the high priests to arrest all who call upon your name." The Lord told him: "Off with you, this is the instrument I have fitted for carrying my name to the nations, to kings, and to Israel's sons, and I will make clear to him what he must suffer for that name of mine."

So Ananias went and entered the house, and said as he put hands on him, "Saul, Brother, the Lord has sent me—Jesus, who appeared to you on the road as you traveled—so that you may see again and be filled with the Holy Spirit. And instantly what seemed like scales fell from his eyes, and he could see. He rose and was baptized, and ate and became strong. (Ac 9.1–19)

The problems with this account are many.

1. We know from Paul that he was "not known by my features to the Judaean gatherings in Messiah" (Gal 1.22). How could that be, if he had been a student in Jerusalem of the high-profile Pharisee scholar Gamaliel? More important, how could a man who had gone house to house arresting the Brothers be unknown to them?
2. If Paul had been a pupil of the famous Gamaliel, he would surely have said so when he boasted of his Pharisaical training (Gal 1.14, Phil 3.5).

3. The role Luke assigns to the otherwise unknown Ananias, here made Paul's sponsor in the faith though Paul never mentions him, is directly contradicted by Paul's own words about the appearance of Jesus to him: "At this point I consulted no flesh-and-blood person" (Gal 1.16). Luke is just as much at odds with this passage: "I would have you know, Brothers, that the revelation I revealed to you came not in the ordinary human way, for I did not receive it from a man by way of teaching. Rather, it was directly revealed to me by Jesus-Messiah (Gal 1.11–12).

4. Jerusalem was under Roman occupation, and the authorities did not like to have religious fanatics stirring up trouble. Why would they let Saul go around "snorting threats of murder" and hauling people out of their houses? Why would the Brothers not draw the Romans' attention to their plight? Luke does not present the Romans as hostile to Christians.

5. How was Paul able to force his way into homes and kidnap people? Luke seems to imagine that he used Temple police for the task, but he is evasive on the actual commissioning of terrorism. In line with his generally hostile attitude to the Jews, he says in one place that the high priest sanctioned Paul's campaign (Ac 9.2). But elsewhere he attributes it to the Sanhedrin (Ac 22.5). Still again, it is the body of chief priests who are behind him (Ac 26.12).

6. More to the point, Jews under the occupation were not allowed to put men to death. That is why Jesus had to be turned over to the Romans for execution (Jn 18.31).[5] Yet Luke later puts these words in Paul's mouth: "I not only put many of the Holy in prison, under orders from the chief priests, but I voted for their death sentences" (Ac 26.10). If the Jews had been able to execute men (and they were not), only the Sanhedrin could have carried out the sentence, and the idea that Paul was a member of the Sanhedrin is absurd. (Remember, he was not even known by his features in Judaea.)

7. To cap all the other impossibilities, the high priest could not have authorized Paul to search out and arrest people *in another country.* Damascus was in Syria, whose Roman rulers would hardly recognize an authority that was not even valid in Judaea. The archpriest would want to avoid trouble with the Romans, not court it by challenges to the peace. Saul could not have kidnapped masses of people from a foreign authority.

8. Finally, since Luke has improbably brought Paul down to Judaea for his education and persecuting activity, he has to move him back toward Damascus, where Paul says that Jesus appeared to him. That is how we get a photism "on the road to Damascus." Paul does not get to his destination under his own power—he has to be led into the town by companions ministering to his blind state.

Luke tells a great story, and it has entered the world's imagination. We hear all the time of "road to Damascus" experiences. This is the most famous conversion story in Christian history, rivaled only by Augustine's conversion in the garden, when he, too, receives an audition telling him to pick up a book and read. Both these stories are used as paradigmatic of conversion in classic accounts of the subject like William James's *The Varieties of Religious Experience* or Arthur Darby Nock's *Conversion*. This is unfortunate, since the event is not really a conversion, as even Luke will emphasize in his second and third tellings of it. But what is important here is to see how far the whole thing is from Paul's description of his dealings with Jesus. Paul tells us nothing of falling to the ground, being blinded, needing an Ananias to restore his sight—any more than we hear of such dramatic things happening when the risen Jesus appeared to Peter or James or the other followers. Luke's fiction has replaced far more interesting fact. Here as elsewhere we must look intently at Paul's own words to see what he actually meant. Luke will prove a continuing obstacle to this effort.

NOTES

1. A. M. Hunter argues that this part of Paul's letter is just what he declares at the outset, a credal formula he took from the tradition and is handing on. The wording, the prominence of the Jerusalem leader

James, the Aramaic form *Kephas,* Hunter argues, point to an origin in the Jerusalem church. *Paul and His Predecessors* (SCM Press, 1961), pp. 15–18, 117–18.

2. Mt 28.9–10, 17–19, Mk 16.12–18, Lk 24.13–49, Jn 20.14–18, 19–23, 26–29, 21.4–23.

3. A simpleminded objection to Paul's account of Jesus' apparition was that he would not have known how to recognize that it was actually Jesus, since he never saw him before the crucifixion. According to the Gospel accounts, even those who had lived with him had no advantage here. The risen body is a mystery not so easily explained; but Jesus surely knew how to make himself known.

4. For the importance of translating *Khristos* as "Messiah," see N. T. Wright, *The Resurrection of the Son of God* (Fortress Press, 2003), pp. 554–83.

5. The execution of Stephen, if it really occurred as Luke describes it, is explained as occurring during a "prefectural interstice," when Pontius Pilate was recalled to Rome in 36 CE and no replacement had taken office. See Raymond E. Brown, *The Death of the Messiah: From Gethsemane to the Grave* (Doubleday, 1993), p. 370. But Luke's whole treatment of Stephen is a theological construct in which the trial and execution are modeled closely on the trial and death of Jesus. Stephen too predicts the fall of the Temple, says that God is not confined to a single house of worship, is tried by Jewish authorities using false witnesses, says, "Receive my spirit," cries "with a loud voice," and prays, "Father, forgive them this sin" (Ac 6.13, 7.59–60). The whole scene is treated theologically, not historically.

2. Paul and the Pre-Resurrection Jesus

✝

GIVEN PAUL'S concentration on the risen Jesus he had encountered, some people take it for granted that he knew little about—or cared little to find out about—Jesus in the life he led before Paul was even aware of his existence. This view is strengthened by the assumption that Paul, a Jew of the Diaspora, seems not concerned with what occurred in Judaea. He emphasizes his distance from the Jewish center. This attitude apparently disturbed Luke, the author of the Acts of the Apostles, who tried to establish as many Pauline ties to Jerusalem as possible, bringing him there early to be trained by the great scholar Gamaliel. Some defenders of Luke have claimed that only in Jerusalem could Paul have acquired the knowledge he boasted of as a Pharisee, as one who outstripped his contemporaries in devout observance of the Law.

This argument underestimates the importance of the Diaspora in the first century of the Common Era. There were between 5 and 6 million Jews in the Diaspora, more than lived in Judaea. They made up more than 10 percent of most major cities in the Roman Empire—180,000 in Alexandria alone, and 50,000 in Rome.[1] The Greek word *diaspora* means "a scattering," and the Jews were scattered thick and wide. Though most Pharisees would no doubt have preferred to stay near the Temple and the full rites of their faith, scholarly men of the Law had reasons, like other influential Jews, to move around in the network of commercial, familial, and educational opportunities afforded by the rich Diaspora culture. We are told in the Gospel of Matthew (23.15) that the Pharisees were active missionaries. At a time of brisk travel, when there was intense traffic to and from Judaea, there is no reason Paul could not have had a full Pharisaical training in Tarsus, or later in Damascus, his two homes, neither of them far from Judaea, and both of them centers of trade and communication.

If Pharisaism was widespread in the Diaspora, so—almost overnight—was the Jesus movement widespread in Syria and Cilicia. There were already Brothers in Damascus and Antioch soon after Jesus' death—otherwise, how could Paul have persecuted them in the one place, and joined them in the other? And how, precisely, did he try to "extirpate" them (Gal 1.13)? Not, as Luke claimed, by arresting them and putting them to death. What instruments were available to him as a Jew in the Roman province of Syria? Where, for that matter, did he encounter the early Brothers? The obvious place is the synagogue. The Brothers had not broken with the synagogue in the early days. As a strict observer of the Law, Paul would resent those claiming to have seen the risen Jesus. False Messiahs were a constant threat to the upholders of the established

Law and to good relations with the Roman rulers. The Brothers were not merely outside the authorized observances. They would upset the crucial population of "Godfearers," those sympathetic outsiders who attended synagogues in considerable numbers as potential converts. These people, we shall see, proved important for Paul's future ministry, but in his observant days he would have feared the effect of the Brothers on these "fellow travelers," who might be drawn away from their initial attraction to the Jewish faith.

How could Paul prevent this? Obviously, by using the weapons we shall see him employ against opponents in the letters that have come down to us—fierce argument, fine distinctions of scriptural interpretation, sardonic humor, and denunciation. He would refute the intruders, ridicule them, drive them out, deprive them of a base in Damascus. That would indeed be an "extirpation." We can easily imagine him doing this against the Brotherhood after we have seen him doing it within that company. Here is how Wayne Meeks describes Paul at work on those he opposes in the Corinthian gathering:

> A wealth of rhetorical devices clothes this appeal: curses and threats on the one hand, reminders of blessings on the other, ironic rebukes, shaming and sarcasm. All are ways of suggesting to the addressees that they are in danger of committing irreparable folly and of recalling them to their earlier sound judgment.[2]

It is true that Jews had won the right in some cities to discipline their own members—that is how Paul later came to be flogged five times by Jews. But this was a community action, calling for community support, and Paul never says that anyone but himself was involved in his "persecuting" activities. He did not have the authority to flog, any more than to arrest or put to death. It is true that, once he became a Brother, he threatened to visit his fellows in Corinth with a club (1 Cor 4.21), but that was comic bluster—provoked by the people in Corinth who had called him weak. His real weapon was always language, and the community responded with an acknowledgment that he had wounded them with a letter (2 Cor 7.8).

If in Damascus Paul's major form of persecution was exposure of what he felt were false claims, then he had to study those claims well before he came to accept them. What was he objecting to in the Brothers' presence at the synagogue? Not—yet—the observance of kosher laws or the necessity of circumcision. Those points of difference were not at stake—he would raise them once he became a Brother himself. The first witnesses to Jesus were circumcised men, and observant. Their initial difference from other Jews was that they proclaimed the resurrection of a crucified man, the very thing Paul would later call "an affront *(skandalon)* to Jews" (1 Cor 1.23). In other words, what would become the center of his own faith, the risen Jesus, was the thing he felt at first he had to oppose and "extirpate." Jesus' appearance to him would be the supreme refutation of all his own refutations of the Brothers.

Once Paul joined the Brothers, he had many of his new fellows to tell him about Jesus' life. Those five hundred witnesses to the Resurrection were obviously a mobile bunch. Three members of his missionary teams—Barnabas, Silvanus, and Mark—had probably come from Jerusalem as part of the first spread of the faith from the original followers.[3] Some who had joined the Holy before Paul did would cross and recross his path—the married team, for instance, of Prisca and Aquila he encountered and worked with in Corinth and Ephesus and Rome. By the time he wrote to Rome, where he had never been himself, Paul would greet over two dozen of the Holy who had gone there. Followers of Jesus were pullulating everywhere.

How did these active missionaries communicate the knowledge of their Lord? There were no Gospels yet. If any writings existed, they have perished, though they may have left traces in Paul's own letters and in later writings. Some hymns may have been written down. But we are dealing with a predominantly *oral* culture, one in which transmission viva voce was highly developed, along with the mnemonic skills such a culture entails. Jesus had spoken to many crowds, on many occasions. He had answered many questions, retold many parables. There was a rich store of memories from different people who had seen him in different contexts. The variations of what seem the same events or sayings in the Gospels are probably a thin harvesting of a wide variety of accounts originally circulated.

Paul did not have to go to Jerusalem to hear such accounts—though he could have confirmed many things when he met Peter and the others there. For that matter, he did not have to go to Jerusalem to talk with Peter. They would be active together in the gatherings at Antioch, and Peter's associates (if not Peter himself) were influential in Corinth. The Lord's brothers, too, were out traveling with their wives (1 Cor 9.5). Paul had frequent occasion to talk with people who had known Jesus in his lifetime, some whose names we know, many whose names we do not—and he had even more opportunities to talk with followers of those first associates who had committed oral traditions to their minds and hearts. He lived during his first days as a Brother in the gatherings of Damascus and Antioch, where he learned the rituals and traditions of his new faith. He had to learn before he could teach, and close study of his work shows that he did just that.[4]

But if Paul knew a great deal about the life of Jesus, why does he recount so little from it in his letters? There are several reasons for this. The letters are not expositions of the meaning of Jesus' life—though Paul could have engaged in that when he was with the gatherings he helped form. The letters are addressed to specific problems, and he uses material from Jesus' life only when that is needed for addressing those problems. When such citation of Jesus' words is called for, he has the right words at his command—on the Lord's Meal *(Kyriakon Deipnon),* for instance, or on a case of divorce in the gathering, or on observance of kosher, or on the acceptance of financial support by an emissary. It has been argued that in these direct citations Paul's versions are probably closer to what Jesus said than are later records of it in the Gospels.

On the Lord's Meal, for instance, his report is not only the first—written decades before any of the Gospel versions—but probably the closest to what Jesus actually said. We should not fall into the fallacy of thinking that a saying of Jesus in one of the Gospels is "the original," which Paul only approximates in what seems to be a paraphrase of it. The truth could be the other way around. Out of the rich store of oral accounts that would be reflected in the Gospels, that which Paul received may be closer to Jesus' own words than are the variants in the Gospels.

Of the many places where Paul echoes the teaching of Jesus, consider just some:

1. When the Brothers in Rome differed over observance of kosher, Paul used the authority of Jesus to compose their differences: "I know, *relying on Lord Jesus,* that nothing is unclean of itself. Only if a man supposes it unclean does it become unclean for him" (Rom 14.14). Is that

Paul's fumbling toward what Jesus says in the Gospel of Matthew, answering those who accused him of flouting the purity code? "Understand what you hear from me: What a man takes into his mouth does not make him unclean. What comes out of his mouth—that is what makes him unclean" (Mt 15.10–11). Jesus in the Gospels frequently says that purity is a matter of the heart and intention, not of ritual observance: "Make sure your heart is not a darkness. If your whole body is suffused with light, no part of it is left in darkness, it will be light-giving, as when a lamp lights you with its brightness" (Lk 11.35–36). Paul gives us our first version of this teaching. He is not, necessarily, parroting what would not be written for years to come.

2. When the Brothers in Corinth made the meal of love an occasion for conflict, Paul reminded them of the instruction he had given them earlier on what Jesus said at that meal:

> What I received from the Lord I passed on to you—that the Lord Jesus, on the night he was betrayed, took bread and, after blessing it, broke it and said: "This is my body, which is for you. Do the same to keep the memory of me." Just so with a cup, after finishing dinner: "This cup is the new bond, in my blood. Do the same, as you drink it, to keep my memory." For as many times as you eat this bread

or drink this cup, you announce the death of the
Lord, before his return. (1 Cor 11.23–26)

How did Paul learn this "from the Lord"? In a vision?
He does not say that. He uses the language of
tradition—what was handed to me I handed on—the
same formula he had used for the basic creed he recites
at 1 Corinthians 15.3. Where did he learn the tradition
of the Lord's Meal? Obviously in the first gatherings
where he took part in the Lord's Meal, in Damascus, in
Antioch, where followers from Jerusalem had brought
the revelation before Paul joined them. Those gatherings
were as close as we can get to the actual night being
commemorated. Paul is closer to that night than any
of the three Gospels that quote Jesus' words. The Gospels, for that matter, differ from each other in the
details of what was said, as well as from Paul's account—
but his stands first in the tradition, and nearest to the
source.

3. At Corinth, Paul actually got himself into trouble by
quoting the words of Jesus. He had refused to let the
Brothers there support him, but when the Corinthians
learned that he had taken contributions from the gatherings in Macedonia, he had to admit: "The Lord directed
that those who reveal the revelation should be supported
(zēn) by revealing it" (1 Cor 9.14). He is referring to

directions Jesus gave when he first sent off any emissaries of the revelation. Jesus told them to take nothing with them, not even a pouch to provide for future supply, but to eat what was offered where they were welcomed, since "he who does a work deserves support *(trophē)* for it," as Matthew puts it (10.10). Or "deserves payment" *(misthos)* for it, according to Luke (10.7).

Paul could not use, because he clearly did not know, Luke's modification of the Lord's instruction. Jesus originally sent the emissaries out on a short errand to nearby villages in Judaea. Missionary efforts of a long-term and long-distance nature in urban areas made Luke present Jesus as saying (22.36) that they could take provisions on later journeys. Paul has to justify himself in another way, and it would be undiplomatic to give his real reason for not taking support in Corinth. That city was split venomously between a wealthier and a poorer faction. The gulf even made their dinner of unity a source of division, as the better-off ate and drank more lavishly than the poorer Brothers (1 Cor 11.21–22). If Paul, who wants to be the neutral reconciler, took support, it would obviously come from the wealthier Brothers, whom he is trying to correct. But to say this would itself cause enmity. Instead, he says that the Lord's directive gave a right *(exousia,* 9.15) to the emissary that Paul would rather not exercise. He even uses a play on words to make his argument. He says that carrying the revelation is itself a reward *(misthos)* for him (9.17)—so this laborer has, as directed, received his pay! What is interesting for our purposes here is that Paul knows the Lord's directive and has to acknowledge it, even as he explains his departure from it.

4. The Corinthians had an endless supply of troubles to lay before Paul. One involved a divorce in the gathering. Once again Paul begins from the words of Jesus: "To the married I pronounce—no, it is not I, but the Lord—that a wife should not be separated from her husband; or if she does separate, she must either stay single or rejoin her husband; and a husband should not divorce his wife" (1 Cor 7.10–11). Paul refers to Jesus' teaching "What God has joined, let man not sunder" (Mk 10.9, Mt 19.6). When he allows for an exception, in the case of a Brother or Sister married to an unbeliever (1 Cor 7.12), he is careful to preface his remark: "It is I saying this, not the Lord" (7.12). In the same way, when he recommends celibacy, he says that this is his position, not one he has from the Lord (1 Cor 7.6–7, 25–26, 35, 40). His care to stay with the sayings of the Lord shows that he clearly knows them, far more of them than he needs to cite for meeting special problems.

5. Another teaching Paul says he has "from the Lord" concerns the end time. Like Jesus, Paul taught that Jesus had

fulfilled the Messianic prophecies by his coming, but that the completion of his mission was still to take place. But the Thessalonians feared that their Brothers who had died would not be part of that glorious consummation. To reassure them he writes:

> For this we tell you from the Lord's word: we who remain alive shall not go in before the dead when the Lord appears. Rather, at the summons, as the archangel cries out and God's trumpet sounds, the Lord will come down from heaven, and those who died in Messiah will rise up first, then we who remain living will be swept up with them in the clouds to meet the Lord aloft. After, we shall be with him forever. Give each other comfort with these words. (1 Thess 4.15–18)

Paul has a tradition from Jesus like that caught in the Gospel of Matthew:

> Then will appear in heaven a presage of the Son of Man, and all the tribes of the earth will lament, and they will see the Son of Man arriving on heaven's clouds in power and great splendor, and he will dispatch his angels with great trumpet flourishes, and they shall gather in his chosen ones from the four

winds, from one end of the heavens to the other.
(Mt 24.30–31)

Like Jesus, Paul says that the consummation will come
unexpectedly—"in an eyeblink" (1 Cor 15.52)—and the
Brothers must be alert. It will come "like a thief in the
night" (1 Thess 5.2)—a direct parallel with Matthew
24.43 and Luke 12.39–40. Is the report in Matthew any
more authoritative than the far earlier one in Paul?

6. One saying of Jesus was particularly useful to Paul in his
   conflict with the "wise" ones of Corinth. In two of the
   Gospels, Jesus says, "I thank you, Father, Lord of heaven
   and earth, for hiding these things from the learned and
   the wise and revealing them to simple people" (Mt
   11.25, Lk 10.21). Paul brought the saying to bear on his
   argument with the learned Corinthian faction: "God's
   ignorance surpasses human learning, and the trivial
   things of God surpass human importance. . . . We speak
   of the learning of God, kept as a secret hidden away, as
   he arranged ahead of time for our glory, a secret this
   time's important ones never penetrated" (1 Cor 1.25,
   2.7–8).

7. Paul also echoes the claim of Jesus that the Temple is to
   be replaced by his body, and by the Brothers incorporated into that body, since the Spirit has his abode *(oikei)*

in them. The Spirit is no longer confined to one physical space. "Surely you must know that you are the Temple of God, and the Spirit of the Lord has his abode *(oikei)* in you. If anyone destroys the Temple of God, God will destroy him, for the Temple is holy, and you are it" (1 Cor 3.16–17; cf. 6.19, 2 Cor 6.16). "In Christ we became one body by baptism through the action of a single Spirit" (1 Cor 12.13). These passages are crucial, since it is often said that Jesus' claim in the Gospels that he is the Temple, replacing the old meeting place between God and man, is an invention that grew up only after the actual destruction of the Temple in 70 CE. But here is Paul saying the same thing almost two decades before the destruction of the physical Temple in Jerusalem. He is in perfect accord with the sayings of Jesus, and proves that this tradition was in circulation among the Brothers well before the Temple was destroyed—and even more clearly before the Gospels were written.

In the Gospels, when Jesus is rebuked for letting his followers violate the Sabbath, he responds: "In truth I tell that here you have something greater than the Temple" (Mt 12.6). When some scoff at his saying, "Destroy this Temple and in three days I will raise it again," the Gospel of John explains: "The Temple he referred to was his body" (Jn 2.19, 21). Jesus tells the Samaritan woman: "Believe me, the moment is coming when you will worship the Father neither on this mount [at the Samaritan Temple on Mount Gerizim] nor in Jerusalem. . . . The moment is coming, and is now here, when true worshipers will worship the Father in Spirit and in Truth" (Jn 4.21, 23). She says that this can occur only with the arrival of the Messiah—Paul's title for Jesus. Jesus responds to her, "I am he, I who tell you this" (4.26). Some might say John takes this from Paul, reversing what used to be said, that Paul draws on (and distorts) the Gospel. In any event, Paul is not saying things alien to what Jesus says in the later Gospels.

8. The belief that all the Brothers are members of Christ leads to the corollary that they are members of each other. "As we have in our body many members, and all the members do not perform the same function, so we, though many, are one body in Messiah, and serve as members of each other" (Rom 12.4–5). Jesus, after saying that "I am the vine, you the branches" (Jn 15.5), draws the corollary, "Love one another as I have loved you" (Jn 15.12). "I am in the Father, and you are in me, and I in you" (Jn 14.20). One Spirit pervades the vine and the body. This is the deeper meaning of the "Golden Rule" (Mt 7.12, Lk 6.31)—not simply that you should treat others as you would be treated, but treat them as if they were you (because *they are*).

9. Paul says that the essence of the Law is love, and Jesus

said the same. Here is Paul: "The entire Law is fulfilled in this one saying, Love your neighbor as yourself" (Gal 5.14). "The one who loves his neighbor has fulfilled the Law, since Commit no adultery, Steal not, Covet not—any commandment whatever—all are comprehended in this language: You shall love your neighbor as yourself. Love your neighbor and you can do no wrong. For love is what fulfills the Law" (Rom 13.8–10). And here is Jesus: "What you would have others do to you, do to them. That is the Law and the prophets" (Mt 7.12). "You shall love the Lord your God with your entire heart, your entire soul, your entire mind—that is the greatest and the first commandment. The second is its like: You will love your neighbor as yourself. From those two commands is the entirety of the Law derived" (Mt. 22.37–40).

This is the real point. Those who say that Paul's was an alien spirit superimposed on that of a loving Jesus do not see that they both taught the same message of love. Jesus told his followers to love their enemies (Mt 5.44, Lk 6.28). So did Paul: "If your enemy is hungry, give him to eat; if thirsty, give him to drink" (Rom 12.20). Jesus said, "Judge not, lest you be judged" (Lk 6.37), since only the sinless can judge others (Jn 8.7), and Paul said: "In convicting others you condemn yourself, since you are guilty of what you condemn" (Rom 2.1). And: "Who are you to be your brother's judge?" (Rom 14.10). Paul, like Jesus (Mt 7.1–2), said, "Take no revenge" (Rom 12.19). Jesus said not to resist one who wrongs you (Lk 6.28–30), and Paul directed others to submit to wrong rather than take people to court (1 Cor 6.7). In the Gospels, Jesus says, "Rescue comes from the Jews" (Jn 4.22), and Paul: "From Zion is the Rescuer" (Rom 11.26), and, "The revelation is God's miracle of rescue for one who believes—the Jew first, then the Greek" (Rom 1.16).

I am not saying that Paul had specific words of Jesus in mind for all these similarities. But he surely had grasped the key to what Jesus taught during his life on earth. Most would agree that the point of the Sermon on the Mount, of the Golden Rule, of the frequent commands to love unstintingly was deeply understood by a man who could write this:

Were I to speak the languages of all men and all angels, without having love, I were as a resonating gong or jangling cymbal. Were I to prophesy and know all secrets and every truth, were I to have faith strong enough to move mountains, without having love, I were as nothing. Were I to give away all my possessions, or give my body to be burned, without having love, it would avail me nothing.

Love is patient, is kind. It does not envy others or brag of itself. It is not swollen with self. It is not wayward or grasping. It does not flare with anger, nor harbor a grudge. It takes no joy in evil, but delights in truth. It keeps all confidences, all trust, all hope, all endurance. Love will never go out of existence. Prophecy will fail in time, languages too, and knowledge as well. For we know things only partially, or prophesy partially, and when the totality is known, the parts will vanish. It is like what I spoke as a child, knew as a child, thought as a child, argued as a child—which, now I am grown up, I put aside. In the same way we see things in a murky reflection now, but shall see them full face when what I have known in part I know fully, just as I am known. For the present, then, three things matter—believing, hoping, and loving. But supreme is loving. (1 Cor 13.1–13)

Does that sound like a man with what Nietzsche called "a genius for hatred"?

NOTES

1. Wayne Meeks, *The First Urban Christians: The Social World of the Apostle Paul,* second edition (Yale University Press, 2003), p. 34.

2. Ibid., p. 116.

3. Ibid., pp. 57, 60, 61.

4. Traces of prior Diaspora teachings are discovered in Paul by, among others, A. M. Hunter, *Paul and His Predecessors,* second edition (SMC Press, 1961), and David L. Dungan, *The Sayings of Jesus in the Churches of Paul* (Fortress Press, 1971).

3. Paul "on the Road"

✝

PAUL WAS, by any measure, a heroic traveler. It is estimated that he covered at least ten thousand miles, much of it on foot. He lived in a new age of travel, thanks to Roman roads-and-bridges engineering, as well as administrative military skills in the Pax Romana. Not that travel is ever entirely easy or safe. Brigands by land, pirates by sea, haughty officials, punishing weather, random chance, and dogging malice can never be eliminated—certainly not when one is on the road as much, and with as few resources, as Paul was. It has been said that Luke's Acts of the Apostles resembles a Hellenistic novel in its wonders and perils and hairbreadth escapes. Paul's own sober account is fairly hair-raising on its own:

> I have been more than they—more overworked, excessively beaten, more imprisoned, closer to death. Five times I was given forty-less-one lashes by the Jews, thrice clubbed, once stoned, thrice shipwrecked, a day and a night I spent in the sea—with many trudgings of the road, with river dangers, dangers from brigands, dangers from my people, dangers from outsiders, dangers by

town, dangers by country, dangers at sea, dangers from pseudo-Brothers, with toil and effort, often sleepless, with hunger and thirst, often without food, in cold, with no covering. (2 Cor 11.23–27)

That would be a heroic catalogue for the most robust of travelers. But Paul was, at least intermittently, sickly. He was laid up, the first time he went to Galatia, by an illness that could have tempted the Galatians to despise him (Gal 4.13–14): "You know that I brought you the revelation for the first time because of a bodily debility, and in this test for you, posed by my flesh, you showed no contempt or revulsion" (this latter is a strong term—"you did not spew me out," *exeptysate*). The passage is naturally read in conjunction with Paul's statement that he had a "thorn in my flesh" to keep him mindful of his weakness (2 Cor 12.7). Some plausibly argue that he was an epileptic. This is a recurring debility that can be ridiculed, as we see from the case of Julius Caesar. At any rate it was something he had to acknowledge, and which he praised others for accepting. On the other hand, it may help explain the attitude of the Corinthians who said that "his letters are impressive and strong, but in person he is physically feeble and his speech contemptible" (2 Cor 10.10). His physical debility, whatever it was, makes the catalogue of his travels become all the more heroic—as does the manual labor he performed despite this handicap. Obviously, a strong will drove a flagging body forward.

Compelling as these arduous travels are, they can be misleading. They can suggest Paul was always on the road, communicating only by letter with the Brothers he worked with and for. Actually, of course, his seven letters are exceptions to his normal way of speaking with the Brothers. He spent long and patient months with each community we know of. He began in the already established gatherings at Damascus and Antioch, and may have spent years there, where he was baptized, learning baptismal formularies and hymns echoed in his letters.[1] He often stayed in one place until driven out by Jews or Romans who considered him a troublemaker. Sometimes he left one or more of his coworkers with a community when he moved on, or sent back others to continue his activity. He maintained contact across the network of gatherings through traveling Brothers who went from one place to another on business or family errands or in special delegations to call for or supply help.

Luke has contributed to the hit-and-run atmosphere about some accounts of Paul's missionary activity. He gives the impression, for instance, that Paul stayed in Thessalonica for little more than three weeks before he had to flee persecution stirred up by Jews (Ac 17.1–10). But the Anchor Bible editor of the Letters to the Thessalonians, Abraham Malherbe, points out that Paul says he more than once received financial aid in Thessalonica sent from Philippi (Phil 4.16). Since arrangements and delivery for such aid would take weeks, if not months, he obviously spent considerable time establishing this first gathering in Greece. He refers to the manual labor he and his fellows engaged in, to support themselves while growing close to the community. He speaks in the plural, since the letter comes from Silvanus and Timothy as well as Paul:

> Our deep fondness for you made us ready to share with you not only the revelation of God but own our lives, so dear had you become to us. You remember, Brothers, our burdensome toil, working day and night so as not to impose on you while we expounded to you the revelation of God. (1 Thess 2.8–9)

That does not describe a brief visit but an intense commitment to the gathering.

Nonetheless, he was driven out by Jewish hostility (2.14). Though he was eager to see the Thessalonians again, his return was delayed, so he sent Timothy back to give his support to the young community (3.1–2). Far from being hit-and-run, his relations with the various gatherings were so close that he uses the most intimate terms to describe those relations. He feels always like the Brother he calls them, but also as tender as a nurse toward them (1 Thess 2.7), or a father (1 Thess 2.11), or a mother who has begotten them in pain (Gal 4.19). His message was one of love, which he had to practice as well as recommend. Even when he clashed with other Brothers, there is evidence he was reconciled with them—surely with Barnabas, and Apollos, and very probably with Peter. We see him angry in the letters, probably more often than people saw him showing wrath in their presence (2 Cor 10.9). Indeed, some Corinthians found him fiercer in letters, milder in person—though he tries to assure them that, in this case, it will be the opposite, that he will come in wrath if he has to come to them (1 Cor 4.21). But this storm, too, blows over.

What was he like for those who met him? Certainly he was persuasive, or he could not have won over so many people to new or enlarged gatherings. Though few people, on the evidence of the letters, would compare this fierce rhetorician with a Francis of Assisi, he must have had the kind of incandescent goodwill that makes loving ascetics so attractive. He took up menial labor among his fellows, asked for little, collected for the needs of others. Since he says he supported himself in Thessalonica, the aid he received from Philippi must have gone to help the poorer people he was calling into Brotherhood.

Tents?

WHAT KIND OF WORK did Paul labor at? It is interesting that he never tells us, only that it was hard and time-consuming ("night and day"). Luke says in the Acts that he was a tent maker, and this has generally been accepted. Some were disturbed that he would work in leather goods, which Jews did not consider quite clean. Even if he did not use pigskin, there was something contaminating to Jews about handling dead animals. Others contend that he could have worked in linen, since awnings and other shields from the sun were in great demand. Even that would have involved heavy sewing. Indeed, when Paul adds a postscript to one of his letters (which were all dictated to scribes), he draws attention to the large size of his writing (Gal 6.11). The Dominican scholar Jerome Murphy-O'Connor thinks this may be a reference to his gnarled fingers, toughened by drawing thread through heavy linen. Murphy-O'Connor believes that he was an artisan who carried his tool kit with him—though he acknowledges that Paul does not refer to his work in terms that reflect an artisan's pride. He calls it "burdensome toil" (1 Thess 2.9), and says, "We weary ourselves in hard labor with our hands" (1 Cor 4.12).

The belief in Paul's tent-making has led people to exercise their creative imaginations. Some suppose that Paul's father in Tarsus owned a tent-making business and Paul grew up knowing the trade. Luke more positively connects Paul's work with the tent-making business of his coworkers Prisca and Aquila (Ac 18.3). Luke seems to have good information about Prisca and Aquila, who were part of the Brotherhood before Paul was, and who traveled and knew many of the Brothers. So it is probably true that when Paul was with them he worked in their shop, along with other members of their firm, including slaves. In that case, Paul was probably speaking more than figuratively when he said, "I have made myself everyone's slave" (1 Cor 9.19).

But can we say, as many do, that tent making was Paul's trade everywhere he went? Remember that he and Silvanus and Timothy were working night and day in Thessalonica. Were they all tent makers? Could they expect to find enough tent-connected contracts for all of them wherever they went? Since Paul made much of his own labor and commended it to others, it is unlikely that his coworkers would have shirked toil. It seems far more likely that Paul and his fellows took up whatever jobs they could get in each community, however menial. For one thing, this would give them a place in the community while they made their initial contacts and began their instruction of people they found there.

If the members of the team could find work only in different shops or work yards, so much the better—they would have multiple points of engagement with others. Wayne Meeks makes the case that Paul's communities, though they covered a broad social span (omitting only the very top and the very bottom of society), had a core of mainly artisans and small-scale merchants. Working and teaching among them was Paul's way of becoming a Brother in fact as well as in profession. He boasts of his adaptability (1 Cor 9.19–22), and a willingness to take on even "slavish" tasks was one way of disarming new acquaintances.

With the Gatherings

HOW DID HE BEGIN in any town? Since every urban center in the Empire had a sizable Jewish quarter, that was the first place where he would have had some ties and recommendations. Luke says that he normally began by arguing in the synagogue, and only when driven out did he turn to the non-Jews (Ac 9.20). Some think that beginning in synagogues would compromise Paul's vocation to the uncircumcised. Both positions are no doubt too schematic. Paul preaches the Messiah as a reconciler of all Brothers. And both positions ignore the great middle area that was Paul's obvious hunting ground—the "Reverent People" (Sebomenoi), also called "God-Revering" (Theosebeis). These are normally referred to in English as "Godfearers" because of the form Luke uses at Acts 10.2 and 13.26, Phoboumenoi ton Theon.

The people thus variously referred to were inquiring and sympathetic non-Jews welcomed in synagogues, where they could study, pray, and contribute money or advice, without

being (yet) circumcised. They might go on to full member-
ship in the faith, or they might just help create goodwill for
the Jews in their dealings with the "pagan" world. The Romans of the first century were out on quest for spiritual
knowledge, and they welcomed many Eastern sects or
cults—principally that of Mithras. But among the exotic be-
liefs being entertained, the Jews had, for some, a special ap-
peal, based on their monotheism (in a polytheistic world),
their purity of life, and their ancient learning. They were
feared by some Romans precisely because they could attract
curious and searching spirits, drawing people away from the
imperial cult. Juvenal the satirist (14.96–106) attacked a father who observed the Sabbath and let his son be circumcised. For the poet, such men undermined the ancient Roman
ways.

There were more Reverent People than used to be supposed. A synagogue inscription from the Roman city of
Aphrodisias in Asia Minor shows that 43 percent of the
donors, along with nine members of the governing board,
were *Theosebeis*. Admittedly, the inscription comes from
c 200 CE, but it reflects a long-standing trend in the culture.
There was anti-Semitism in the Roman world, as Juvenal's
poem shows, but Louis Feldman collected an astonishing
number of favorable or admiring references to Jews in the ancient literature.[2] They give force to a comment by Robert Tan-
nenbaum, a historian studying Aphrodisias:

Judaism, by the early third century, may well have been a more popular religion among the pagans, and therefore a more powerful rival to Christianity in the race for the soul of the Roman world, than we have had any reason to think until now. This helps us to understand the tension between the Church and the Synagogue in the first few centuries A.D.[3]

If Paul based his own mission on appeals to this body of Gentiles, his constant use of Jewish scripture in addressing them makes sense. They were interested in Moses before he offered them Jesus. This also helps explain Jewish hostility to Paul—he was drawing away people important to their own position in the Empire. Gerd Theissen, an expert on the sociology of Paul's world, is emphatic on this point:

God-fearers had already demonstrated an independence with reference to their native traditions and religion. They stood between differing cultural realms and were thus particularly receptive to the Christian faith, which crossed ethnic and cultural boundaries and offered an identity independent of inherited traditions. Judaism could not do this; within it these people would not be fully entitled. Christianity, however, especially in its Pauline form, offered them the possibility of acknowledging monotheism and high moral principles and at the same time attaining full religious equality without cir-

cumcision, without ritual demands, without restraints
which could negatively affect their social status. Seen in
this light, the conflict between Christianity and Judaism
is easier to understand: the Christian mission was luring
away the very Gentiles who were Judaism's patrons. . . .
Not only did their contributions now benefit the Christian community, but the Jews, as a minority, had come to
depend on the recognition and advocacy of such people in
a foreign Gentile world full of anti-Jewish prejudices.[4]

There is no reason to think Paul worked exclusively with
Theosebeis. But they would have given him a base originating
in the synagogue, from which he could move out into their
own broader network of relatives, friends, and associates.
When he said he made himself all things to all people—a Jew
with Jews, a Gentile with Gentiles—he was speaking of this
intermediate area where he could move about bringing religion to those who were already drawn to it.

How did Paul address these people in their intimate gatherings (and not by long-range emergency missives)? It is clear
that he brought them the revelation—that is, the fulfillment
of the Messianic hopes in the death and Resurrection of Jesus.
For expounding the Messianic tradition he was well equipped
by his Pharisaic training. When he needs a clinching passage
from scripture, he has it at hand, no matter where he is, on the
road or away from libraries. Which raises the question of his

education. Did he study with Gamaliel after all? Not unless he was lying when he said he was unknown in Judaea. There was learning in the Diaspora. But how had Paul afforded it? Was his father a rich tent maker? We simply do not know. However he managed it, he clearly got a good education—though he quotes Jewish scripture in the Septuagint Greek, not the Hebrew. That could, of course, be because he is addressing Greek speakers. But scholars find even his interpretation of passages relying more on the Septuagint than the Hebrew— another point against his having studied with Gamaliel.

What of Paul's broader education in the Greek culture of the Diaspora? Here scholars have swung from one extreme to the other over the years. When it was thought that Paul was jettisoning Jewish wisdom for Greek philosophy, many credited him with more Hellenic influence than can be sustained by careful study of his works. He never quotes a Greek or Roman philosopher. The pendulum swung decisively against the Hellenistic thesis in the influential work of E. P. Sanders, who renewed the thesis of Albert Schweitzer that Paul was a Jewish apocalyptic teacher. But this view has been tempered recently by intense work on the rhetoric of Paul, which shows a familiarity with Greek arguing styles, epistolary, didactic, and celebratory ("epideictic"). He is especially good at the competitive didactics of the Stoic "diatribe" (literally, "a wearing down"). Cynics like Epictetus taught in short bursts of simulated debate, with imagined interrogators challenging the master. This can produce a kind of instructive self-heckling. Here is Paul on the defensive:

> Has circumcision any use at all?
> Yes, in every respect . . .

> If Jews broke trust with God, does that make God abandon trust?
> Far from it . . .

> Is it wrong of God to be angry (to put it in human terms)?
> Far from it . . .

> Are we Jews then superior?
> Not in all ways . . .

> Do we cancel the Law with faith?
> Far from it. We give the Law a firm basis . . .

> Is the Law itself sin?
> Far from it . . .

> Was the Law, good in itself, deadly to me?
> Far from it . . .
> (Rom 3.1–5, 8, 31, 7.7, 13)

How he filled in the answers to this staccato drumbeat of questions shows the dialectical skills of Paul. The questions he here fires at himself are the kind he would have encouraged his interlocutors to direct at him in person. This method is the opposite of Socratic questioning. It is *being* questioned, an oral strategy echoed in his writing. It is easy to imagine members of his team supplying the questions if others were slow to raise them. Paul and his comrades proselytized together, as he reminds us in letters that say, "*We* brought you the revelation."

Paul's rhetorical skills are never clearer than when he abjures them. When the Corinthians decided that he was not as wise or eloquent as other "high-flying emissaries" who had come among them, he uses a kind of verbal judo, prevailing with a show of weakness. His critics boast of a superior wisdom and strength. He will boast of folly and feebleness:

Messiah did not make it my task to baptize you but to bring you the revelation, not in any learned words, lest the cross of the Messiah be a thing superfluous. What the cross says is to the abandoned sheer ignorance, but to those rescued it is God's miracle. For scripture says, "The learning of the learned I will obliterate, and the intelligence of the intelligent I will sweep aside." Where does that leave the learned of this age, where the scholar, where the quibbler? Has not God made the world's learning an ignorance? By the learning of God, the world's learning was useless for finding God. He chose to rescue those who trusted the ignorant revelation. So while Jews ask for miracles and Greeks seek learning, we reveal nothing but Messiah crucified—to Jews an affront, to Greeks ignorance, yet to us, the summoned, whether Jew or Greek, Messiah as God's miracle and God's learning. For God's ignorance surpasses human learning, and the trivial things of God surpass human importance.

Just think how you were summoned, Brothers—not many of you learned in human terms, not many important, not many highborn. But the ignorant things of this world God singled out to baffle the learned, and the trivial things of this world God singled out to baffle the important. The low and contemptible things God singled out, mere nothings, to baffle the somethings, so that what is human could show no pride before God. You, however, are now by his favor in Messiah-Jesus—who is our learning by God's favor, our vindication and hallowing and release, in accord with scripture: "Would you take pride, in the Lord take your pride."

For these reasons, Brothers, when I came to you I came with no pretentious speeches or teachings to announce what is established by God. I made up my mind not to display any learning to you, only Messiah, and him as crucified. For myself, I was weak and fearful and trembling before you, and my message for you, my preaching, was not persuasive by any eloquence, but in the mere presence of Spirit and miracle, so your faith would not rest on any human wisdom but only on God's miracle.

There is a kind of learning in our words, but only for

those who can take it in—not a learning of this age, or of those important in this age, who are perishing. We speak of the learning God kept as a secret hidden away, as he arranged ahead of time for our glory, a secret this time's important ones never penetrated—if they had, they would not have crucified the Lord of splendor. According to scripture: "What no eye saw, what no ear heard, what was never in the human heart—all that has God laid up for those who love him." This is what God has revealed to us by the Spirit. (1 Cor 1.17–2.10)

We should all have so little eloquence!

NOTES

1. Scholars have found traces of baptismal formulas or hymns at Rom 6.3–4, 1 Cor 6.11, 10.1–3, 12.13, Gal 3.27, Phil 2.6–11.

2. Louis Feldman, *Jew and Gentile in the Ancient World: Attitudes and Interaction from Alexander to Justinian* (Princeton University Press, 1993), p. 124.

3. Quoted in John Dominic Crossan and Jonathan L. Reed, *In Search of Paul: How Jesus' Apostle Opposed Rome's Empire with God's Kingdom* (HarperSanFrancisco, 2004), p. 27.

4. Gerd Theissen, *The Social Setting of Pauline Christianity: Essays on Corinth*, edited and translated by John H. Schultz (Fortress Press, 1982), pp. 103–4.

4. Paul and Peter

☩

PAUL REPEATEDLY makes it clear that he had the prickliest of relationships with the Brothers in Jerusalem. He went to that city only three times, each time with reluctance or trepidation. Luke, in the Acts of the Apostles, tries to obfuscate this matter. He has Paul making six trips there, counting an early one to study with Gamaliel. He takes him to the scene of Stephen's stoning, and gives him commissions from high priest and Sanhedrin to drag people from their homes and execute them. Then, after sending him with instructions from Jerusalem to Damascus, he presents his call from Jesus as occurring on the trip there. After this, he brings him back five times to what he takes to be the center of Christian life. The maps of Paul's travels—those polychrome spaghetti tangles in old Bibles—are based on Luke's exaggerated backings-and-forthings. No wonder the impression formed in some minds was of a man who never had time to stay with any gathering, so constantly was he on the move. Luke wants to present Paul as constantly "checking back with headquarters," as it were—though Paul emphatically denies that he ever did such a thing.

Luke is writing after the leader of the Brothers in

Jerusalem, James the brother of the Lord, has been killed—an event cited in Josephus's *Jewish Antiquities* (20.200). This took place after the break between James and the Jewish authorities in Jerusalem and before the destruction of the Temple by the Romans (in 70 CE). In Luke's time, therefore, the Jesus movement had been almost totally deracinated from its Jerusalem origins, and was being tugged in many directions. Luke tried to re-create a Jerusalem hub in his memory of the past, at a time when developments were shaking believers apart. He especially wanted to contain the Pauline mission within a central Jerusalem focus. He presents Paul's dealings with the founding generation in that city as an anachronistic Apostolic Council, in which Paul was given his mandate to the uncircumcised. He must reconcile that claim with Paul's own assertion that he was given his assignment directly from Jesus. One way Luke circumvents the difficulty is to let Peter pre-empt Paul's mission to the nations.

Peter's Vocation

THOUGH LUKE DEVOTES more of his narrative to Paul, since the Diaspora gatherings were the more successful ones, he gives Peter the leading role in almost every respect. The founding of the Christian church takes place, for Luke, in Jerusalem on the occasion of Pentecost, when Peter preaches the long first statement of the revelation to the nations.

Though the event takes place in Jerusalem, Peter is given a world audience, and his words go out in every possible language.

> We each hear it in our native tongue—Parthians and Medes and Elamites, and those who dwell in Mesopotamia, Judaea and Cappadocia, Pontus and Asia, Phrygia and Pamphylia, Egypt and the regions of Libya near Cyrene, Romans stationed here, Jews and proselytes, Cretans and Arabs, all of us hear them speaking in our own dialects of God's greatness. (Ac 2.8–11)

Paul says that at his confrontation with Peter and James in Jerusalem, he was given a mission to the nations and Peter to the circumcised; but Luke says that Peter was the first to be sent by God to the Gentiles. Peter leaves Jerusalem (where James the brother of the Lord is left as leader) to be an emissary to Lydda, Joppa, and Caesarea. As he came near Caesarea (the way Luke made Paul come near Damascus), Peter is given a vision that solved ahead of time Paul's problem of Gentiles forced to observe kosher laws.

> He was hungry and would eat. As others prepared a meal, he was rapt in a vision—he sees heaven open and some preparation like a great sheet lowered toward the earth by its four corners, and in it were all earth's quadrupeds and serpents, and air's flitting things. And a voice

sounded: "On your feet, Peter, to slaughter these and eat them." But Peter answered: "That is impossible, Lord, since I have never eaten profane and unclean things." And the voice came back: "Whatever God makes is clean, do not profane it." Three times this was repeated, then the preparation was snatched up to the sky. (Ac 10.10–16)

As it turns out, God has prepared a Reverent Person *(Theosebēs)* for Peter's arrival in Caesarea, and when Peter reaches his house he tells him: "You realize that the Law forbids a Jew's mixing with or entering the house of a Gentile. But God has shown me to call no one profane or unclean" (10.28). Luke has solved beforehand all the problems Paul later describes in his mission to the nations. Only then can Luke allow Paul to be called to that mission. Thus, after Peter has prepared the way, Paul can receive his (secondary) vocation to the nations.

Paul's Vocation

I HAVE ALREADY PRINTED the first of Luke's three accounts of Paul's call. The third one makes clear that this is a vocation story, based on the calls to ancient prophets, not a conversion story. Luke presents Paul as giving his own account—to King Agrippa during a hearing in Caesarea (exactly where Peter opened the mission to the Gentiles):

"At one time I considered it incumbent on me to do everything I could against the name of Jesus from Nazareth. I undertook this in Jerusalem, where I clapped many of the Holy into prison by mandate of the chief priests; and when their executions were decided, I voted for that. In every synagogue I tried to force them under torture to recant. My frenzy against them was so extreme that I hunted them down in foreign cities. One such was Damascus, where I was traveling with authority and warrants from the chief priests when at noon, Your Majesty, I saw a flash brighter than the sun lightning all about me and those journeying with me. As we all fell to the ground I heard a voice speaking to me in Aramaic: 'Saul, Saul, why are you persecuting me? It only hurts you to kick back when goaded.' But I said, 'Who are you, Lord?' And the Lord answered, 'I am Jesus, whom you are persecuting. But rise up and stand firm on your feet. This is why I have appeared to you, to single you out as my worker, as a witness to what you have seen of me and what further things I shall reveal to you, as I rescue you from your people and from the nations to which I am sending you, that you may open their eyes and turn from darkness to light, from Satan's thrall to God, so they may by faith in me gain forgiveness of sins and a share with the Holy.' " (Ac 26.9–18)

After the preliminary nonsense about Paul torturing people in every synagogue of Judaea and putting Brothers to death, Luke fashions Paul's vocation on that of Ezekiel—just as, in his Gospel, he took Jewish canticles and created the songs of Mary, Zachariah, and Simeon for his nativity stories. Ezekiel too is stunned by a bright light:

> When I saw that, I threw myself on my face and heard a voice speaking to me. "Man," he said, "stand up and let me talk with you." As he spoke a spirit came into me and stood me on my feet, and I listened to him speaking. He said to me, "Man, I am sending you to the Israelites, a nation of rebels who have rebelled against me. Past generations of them have been in revolt against me to this very day, and this generation to which I am sending you is stubborn and obstinate. When you say to them, 'These are the words of the Lord God,' they will know that they have a prophet among them, whether they listen or whether they refuse to listen because they are rebels. But you, man, must not be afraid of them or of what they say, though they are rebels against you and renegades, and you find yourself sitting on scorpions. There is nothing to fear in what they say, and nothing in their looks to horrify you, rebels though they are. You must speak my words to them, whether they listen or whether they refuse to listen, rebels that they are. But you, man, must listen to what I say and not be rebellious like them." (Ezek 1.28–2.8)

Luke's model, with assurances against the threats of the people among whom Ezekiel is being sent, explains the words he gives Paul about being "rescued from your people and from the nations." This fits Luke's scheme, in which Paul is threatened mainly by "his people"—namely the Jews. It does not fit so well with the threat Paul himself feels, as coming from his fellow Brothers. That problem comes to a head in Paul's description of his encounter with the Brothers in Jerusalem, seventeen years after his call to take the revelation to the nations. Luke's account of this meeting has been called, anachronistically, the Apostolic Council, even the First General Council of the church.

The Jerusalem Encounter

IN LUKE'S VERSION of this meeting, delegates from the Jerusalem gathering went to Antioch to demand that all Gentile Brothers be circumcised. After much debate over this, the Antiochenes commissioned Paul, Barnabas, "and some others" to defend their practice of noncircumcision before "the emissaries and elders" in Jerusalem (Ac 15.1–3). When this party presented its case to the gathering there, some Pharisaic Brothers repeated the demand for circumcision. Then the "emissaries and elders" went into formal session to decide the matter. "After an intense examination," Peter rose to speak. He referred people back to the vision in which he was ordered by heaven to eat "unclean" food, and said that this proved the old Law was no longer mandatory. One wonders why, given that preceding event, there was any doubt to be cleared up by the "council." As if to clinch the matter, James, the real authority in Jerusalem, then says: "Hear me, Brothers, Simeon gave an account of how God took steps to form from the nations a people in his name." Many commentators think James uses "Simeon" as a variant of Simon (Peter)—that is, he is telling them again what Peter just told them. It seems more likely that Luke is referring to his own poetic creation, the canticle of Simeon in his Gospel's nativity narrative. When Mary and Joseph take the child Jesus to the Temple, Simeon predicts that their baby is "a light to be unveiled to the nations" (Lk 2.32). The objection to this is that James's audience would not, presumably, have known what happened in Jesus' infancy. But neither, for that matter, would Luke have known. And if he can proclaim the event in his Gospel, why can he not refer to it in his Acts? It is not the least plausible of his inventions.

James then goes on to quote the prophet Amos as saying that God will gather in "all the nations among whom my name is invoked" (Ac 15.17). This says that Gentiles will be called, but it does not settle whether circumcision will be demanded of them. Nonetheless, James says that, given God's call to the Gentiles, the Brothers should not "heap up hindrances" to their responding. They should confine the rules for them to a few essentials—namely, that they refrain from pollution by idols, from sexual license, from animals that have been strangled, and from blood (Ac 15.19–20). Luke does not notice that these restrictions conflict with the vision of Peter, which said that *no* foods are unclean—including, presumably, blood and food from strangled animals. Nonetheless, the "emissaries and elders, along with the entire gathering," decided that these four demands should be promulgated.

This has been called "the Apostolic Decree," and Luke makes its enactment as formal as he can. After being written out, it is sent by way of two delegates from the Jerusalem gathering for delivery to Antioch. The delegates read it out before the assembled Antiochenes, who formally accept it and acclaim the delegates as prophets, and Luke seals the entire proceeding with an outpouring of the Spirit (Ac 15.22–33). This account is formal, hierarchical, legalistic, based on precedent. At every step of the process, forms are required and fulfilled. Luke is not only invoking the structures of his day but helping to advocate and create them.

Paul's account of the event—written, remember, three or more decades before Luke put down his version—could not be more different. There, Paul is neither summoned by Jerusalem nor sent by Antioch. He goes as a result of a vision urging him to go. He takes the uncircumcised Titus with him, to make him a test case. He does not submit his case to a formal meeting but to a private session with the so-called leaders. Peter's vision is not brought up—so the issue of kosher food (as opposed to circumcision) is not discussed. There is no formal decree sent by Jerusalem and accepted at Antioch, making four demands—there is a simple handshake extended by Peter and James. Paul is describing the charismatic conditions of the early gatherings, not the nascent church Luke would like to will into being.

Fourteen years passed before I went again to Jerusalem, this time with Barnabas, and taking along Titus as well. I went in response to a vision. I explained to them the revelation I reveal to the nations, but in private, with the apparent leaders, lest the course I was pursuing, or had pursued, should be discounted. But far from that: Titus, the Greek I brought with me, was not circumcised under compulsion, despite some interloping pseudo-Brothers, who slyly entered [Antioch] to spy on the freedom we were exercising in Messiah-Jesus, to return us to slavery—but to their dictates we gave not an instant's submission; rather, the real meaning of the revelation was maintained for you [Galatian Gentiles]. As for the apparent leaders, how important they were I care not (God does not play favorites), but they were the apparent ones, and they had no suggestions for me, but rather recognized that the revelation for the uncircumcised was entrusted to me, and that for the circumcised to Peter, since the same one who inspired Peter as an emissary to the circumcised had inspired me to go to the nations. Recognizing the divine favor granted me, James and Peter and John, the apparent pillars there, sealed things with a handshake, so we should serve the nations and they the circumcised, the only other point being that we keep in mind their needy ones, which I was eager to do. (Gal 2.1–10)

The Blowup at Antioch

PAUL AND LUKE agree that the question at Jerusalem was cir- cumcision. Luke also says that modified kosher rules were up- held. But Paul's account of another event, his clash with Peter in Antioch, treats this as a matter far from settled. Luke has to omit this event entirely, since it contradicts two of his stories—that of Peter's vision and that of the Jerusalem con- ference where that vision was cited as a guide for others to fol- low. When Peter and Paul were both in Antioch, a warning came to Peter from James in Jerusalem, telling him he should not be eating nonkosher meals with the Gentile Brothers. Peter complied with this directive from James—which infuriated Paul, for whom the Lord's Meal was the symbol of unity for all the Brothers, Jew or Gentile. His anger is not disguised as he reports the disagreement with Peter. He is so mad that he makes up a bran-new contemptuous word—*ioudaïzein*, which seems to mean not *being* a Jew but *playing at* being a Jew.

When Kephas came to Antioch, I rebuked him face-to- face, since he had no leg to stand on. Before the arrival of some men dispatched by James, he ate with those from the nations. But after they came, he withdrew from them into an isolation, intimidated as he was by the circumcisionists. The other Jews [Jewish Brothers] were just as hypocritical, and Barnabas was caught up in their hypocrisy. When I saw that they were not hewing to the clearly marked meaning of the revelation, I told Kephas before everyone, "If you, a Jew by birth, do not follow Jewish ways, how dare you make pretend-Jews of those from the nations?" (Gal 2.11–14)

It is easy to see why Luke could not tell this story. Some in later times would wish that Paul had not told it. Saint Jerome was so shocked by the idea that Peter and Paul could squabble that he claimed they did not really disagree but were putting on a kind of didactic charade. They had cooked up a way of dramatizing the truth that external rites are unimportant. Some people are still unable to face the fact that the great men could differ—Walther Schmithals, for instance, says that Paul just excoriates Peter as a cover for his own more important disagreement with Barnabas.[1] Even those who admit that Paul had reason to resent Peter's backpedaling on Jewish observance think he overreacted to mere eating arrangements. But for Paul it was not simply the unity of the Lord's Meal that was at stake. The risen Jesus was alive and present in Antioch in all those baptized into his mystical body. For Peter to withdraw from the presence of the risen Jesus was to repeat the rejection of Jesus. It was to throw up a barrier—pretend Jewishness—related to the barrier that had refused to extend the divine rescue to all nations. We learn from his reaction to faction in Corinth what he thought of dismembering the body of Christ.

Paul's Chronology

PAUL PUTS the blowup in Antioch after his account of the conference in Jerusalem, and most people treat the two events in that order, as I just have. But there is something suspect about this order. Why, if the handshake of peace had settled in principle the matter of enforcing the Law with Gentile Brothers, was it so quickly reopened? And why, if Barnabas was on Paul's side in Jerusalem, did he desert him on a similar issue in Antioch? And why does Paul later refer to Barnabas as if there had been no split between them (1 Cor 9.6)? Those who follow the account in Galatians seem to think that a parting of the ways took place between them after the Antioch dispute; but Luke says they argued over continuing to work with John Mark, who had left them in Pamphylia (Ac 15.36–39). That still does not explain Paul's later reference to Barnabas.

But there is reason to think Paul was not narrating chronologically in Galatians but arguing climactically—that he saved the conflict with Peter to show that he took a very firm stand on application of the Law, since that was the issue he was addressing among the Galatians. Since his argument there is over the kosher laws, it flows naturally out of the stand he took in Antioch. In fact, the argument comes so seamlessly out of the Antioch narrative that an editor of the letter says it is hard to say where the one ends and the other begins.

> Attempts to locate the end of the episode present a famous puzzle, sensed even by the earliest interpreters of the letter. In v. 14 Paul reports an incisive comment he made to Peter in front of the Antioch church, doing so with a clarity that enables one confidently to place the first of the quotation marks—"You, a Jew by birth, are living . . ." But he gives no clear indication as to where his remark to Peter ends, although by the time the reader comes to the final verses of chapter 2, he knows that he is no longer hearing the speech that Paul made to Peter in Antioch. Indeed, as regards literary form, the concluding verses of the chapter are unlike anything the reader of Galatians has encountered earlier. In fact, Paul's failure formally to close the quotation begun in v. 14 is no accident. It reflects his determination to connect his account of the Antioch incident to the situation in Galatia.[2]

In other words, the Antioch story *had* to come after the Jerusalem one to make possible this meld with the following argument.

Gerd Lüdemann argued for this order, noting that Paul does not introduce the Antioch event with his normal word for chronological sequence, *epeita*, "then . . ." (with the sense of "next"). Instead he says "but when . . ." *(hote de)*.[3] If we follow this sequence, then the clash over the food laws in Antioch caused a division that Paul, acting on a "revelation," took before the Brothers in Jerusalem. He and Barnabas go there, not as delegates from the Antioch gathering, as Luke would have it, but as people with a disagreement they meant to thrash out. It should be noted that Paul says he went there with Barnabas, but "*I* explained to them the revelation *I* reveal to the nations." Paul and Barnabas are not speaking together, as in Luke's picture of them as members of a delegation.

When the dispute is settled and the handshake of peace seals the agreement, then Paul's relations with Barnabas can continue amicably—and, for that matter, with Peter. Paul brings up the prior conflict only because the Galatians are acting as if the matter of food laws were *not* settled. This order makes better sense, as well as uncovering the sequence which Luke has re-created in his eirenic fashion. He talks of a problem in Antioch that is followed by a submission of the matter to Jerusalem for adjudication. The Antioch clash is thus referred to in the proper sequence, but in a disguised and ameliorative way.

If this is the sequence, then Paul's last reported dealings with Peter were not at the blowup in Antioch but after the handshake of peace in Jerusalem. This would accord with the tradition, well founded as I shall argue, that Peter continued to be an emissary in the Diaspora and ended with Paul in Rome, where they died together as victims of Nero's mad reaction to the fire that destroyed the city. The treatment of them as ultimately partners, seen in the early letters of Clement of Rome and Ignatius of Antioch, would thus be justified. The two great leaders ended up on the same side.

NOTES

1. Walther Schmithals, *Paul and James* (Alec R. Allenson, 1965), pp. 63–78.

2. J. Louis Martyn, *Galatians* (Doubleday, 1998), pp. 229–30.

3. Gerd Lüdemann, *Paul, Apostle to the Gentiles: Studies in Chronology,* translated by F. Stanley Jones (Fortress Press, 1984), pp. 75–77. With some hesitation, Rainer Riesner accepts Lüdemann's Antioch-Jerusalem sequence, in *Paul's Early Period: Chronology, Mission Strategy, Theology,* translated by Doug Stott (Eerdmans, 1998), pp. 232, 322.

5. Paul and Women

✝

PAUL BELIEVED in women's basic equality with men. He does not deserve the primary credit for this attitude. It was given to him in the practice of the Diaspora gatherings he first joined, as in the baptismal formula whose hymn form he records:

> Baptized into Messiah
> you are clothed in Messiah,
> so that there is no more
> Jew or Greek,
> slave or free,
> "man and woman,"
> but all are one,
> are the same in Messiah-Jesus.
> (Gal 3.26–28)

The hymn does not keep perfect symmetry by saying "man *or* woman," since this is a quotation from Genesis ("man *and* woman he created them," 1.27). There is no more "man and woman" as originally divided, since they are now united in Messiah—a concept Paul would expound when he said that the reborn Brother and Sister are "a new order of being" (*ktisis*, 2 Cor. 5.17).

The early gatherings of the Brothers were the most egalitarian groups of their day. Paul worked with, paid tribute to, and received protection from his Sisters in Messiah. There would be a concerted effort, over entire centuries, to hide or diminish this fact. There is no more spectacular instance of this than what was done to Junia, his fellow by background, his prison mate, his fellow emissary, and one who joined the Brotherhood before he did (Rom 16.7).

Junia

IN THE LONG list of people Paul greets at the end of his letter to the Romans, he gives special notice to the husband and wife evangelical team of Andronicus and Junia (Rom 16.6–7), whom he calls "my kindred" (*suggeneis mou*). That could mean his fellow Jews—he used the term in that sense earlier in this letter (Rom 9.3)—though Wayne Meeks thinks it meant Paul's countrymen, from Cilicia or even from his hometown of Tarsus.[1] By stressing that he knows of their baptism before his—they were "reborn before me in Messiah"— Paul may be referring to the early days when he was meeting those already in the Diaspora gatherings where he was inducted, in Syria and Cilicia. At any rate, he feels a special bond with these two, since they have been his fellow prisoners *(synaichmalōtoi).* That word could mean that they were actually incarcerated with him (at Ephesus or Philippi) or simply that they too had been prisoners at some time. The former seems more likely here, since he is stressing their kindred closeness. The supreme accolade comes when he calls them "outstanding among the emissaries."

Though there are no offices in the early gatherings, only functions, and though Paul stresses the equal dignity of all gifts of the Spirit, he does list emissaries *(apostoloi)* first in the "big three" charisms—emissaries, prophets, and teachers (1 Cor 12.28). For Junia to be included not only among the emissaries but among the outstanding *(episēmoi)* ones was a high honor, as John Chrysostom recognized in his commentary on Romans: "How great this woman's love of wisdom *(philosophia)* must have been, to merit her inclusion among the apostles." She and her husband had a liturgy devoted to them as married saints and apostles in the Byzantine church. Most early commentators and fathers of the church, including Origen and Rufinus, celebrated her extraordinary eminence.

But sometime in the Middle Ages, apparently before the ninth century, it was decided that a woman apostle was unthinkable. This offended the male monopoly of church offices and honors that had grown up by that time, so Junia had to be erased from history. It took only a little smudging to do this. Paul uses her Greek name, *Iounia,* in the accusative case, *Iounian.* A mere change in accent markings (a circumflex over

the last vowel) would make it the accusative form of a hypothetical male name, *Iounias*. But there is one problem here.
"Junias" is *only* a hypothetical name—it never occurs in all
the ancient literature and inscriptions—whereas Iounia is a
common name, occurring hundreds of times. Besides, the
other teams Paul mentions in Romans 16 are male-female
ones—Aquila and Prisca, Philologus and Julia, Nereus and
Olympas—with the exception of a female-female one
(Tryphaena and Tryphosa, probably sister Sisters). We know
from Paul's reference to Peter and the Lord's brothers, who
traveled with their wives, that male-female evangelical teams
were common (1 Cor 9.5). Only the most Soviet-style rewrit-
ing of history could declare Junia a nonperson and invent a
new team, Andronicus and the philologically implausible Junias. Paul was generous to his female coworkers, a title he
proudly gave them.

Prisca

PAUL BEGINS his long list of those he greets in Rome with
Prisca and Aquila, another wife-husband team of Jews baptized before he was. He had met them after their earlier expulsion from Rome under Claudius (49 CE), evangelized with
them in Ephesus and Corinth, and worked in their tent-
making firm (Ac 18.3). While he was in Ephesus, he sent

greetings to Corinth from their house-gathering there (1 Cor
16.19). His present salute to them, at the top of his long list in
Romans 16, suggests that he had sent them back to Rome to
prepare for his visit there—though they have been there long
enough to have a gathering in their home (16.5). Paul's knowledge that other acquaintances of his had reached Rome probably came from Prisca and Aquila, his primary correspondents,
who also informed him of the local problems addressed in this
letter, to a place he had not visited himself.

Prisca is usually listed first, before her husband, in Paul's
letters and in the Acts of Luke (who seems to have had good
sources on Prisca and Aquila). In the status-conscious Roman
world, this prior listing meant higher dignity, on some ground
or other. Meeks says that a freeborn woman would be listed
before a freedman husband, or a noble one before a com-
moner.[2] Prisca might have been the wealthier holder in their
tent-making firm—her dowry, for instance, could have included slaves to work the business. Some opine that she pre-
ceded her husband in baptism and helped instruct him, or took
the lead in their evangelizing activities; Luke puts Barnabas
before Paul in the early days of their evangelizing, which may
indicate that Paul was the junior partner at that point (Ac
11.30, 12.25, 13.2). It has even been claimed that Prisca had a
hand in the Pauline pseudepigrapha or in composing the Letter
to the Hebrews. But the egalitarianism of the Brothers counts

against thinking that she "outranked" her husband in theological terms. Probably it was a social convention of their past—in Pontus, according to Luke (Ac 18.2)—that gave her a priority.

Phoebe

PAUL SENDS his letter to the Romans by way of the woman he introduces in it, emphasizing her importance both to him and to the Brothers in general, so that she may get any cooperation she asks for in Rome. He has had an important history with her, as with Prisca and her husband.

> I commend to you our Sister, Phoebe, an attendant *(diakonos)* of the gathering in Cenchraeae, for welcome in the Lord as one of the Holy. Please support her in anything she may require, since she has been the protectress *(prostatēs)* of many others besides myself. (Rom 16.1–2)

Cenchraeae is the port of Corinth, so Phoebe had stood with Paul in his very troubled dealings with Corinth. Her importance in the busy port city, where she was clearly efficient (as *diakonos*) and able to champion Paul and "many" (as *prostatēs*) indicates that she would not be leaving that sphere unless she could perform important services in Rome. Was she going there on some errand of her own, while Paul just used this chance occurrence to send a letter along with her?

That idea does not fit in with the convergence of so many other important associates of Paul upon Rome. It has always puzzled people that Paul could send greetings to so many people with whom he had ties in a city he had not seen yet himself—twenty-five Brothers or Sisters already in Rome are named in the conclusion to his letter. These are not casual acquaintances. Two of them are, like Paul, emissaries. Three are "fellow workers in Messiah" with Paul. Four (all women) have been "hard workers" for the Lord. Two have been imprisoned with him. One is his protectress. One he calls "my mother too." Two are dearly loved friends (and one of these was "the first harvest for Messiah in Asia"). One (Apelles) is "tested in Messiah." Another (Rufus) is "the Lord's chosen one." This is a crack team, in effect the best possible muster of Paul's operatives who are free and able to join him when he gets to Rome.

Scholars are right to think that this assembly cannot be a mere chance gathering. But some of them draw the wrong conclusion. They believe that the list actually contains greetings Paul sent to other places as well as Rome (Ephesus is the top contender). The names became affixed to this letter by some accident. But there is good reason to think that Paul has assembled these people for a grand project, whose scale is suggested by the length and ambition of the letter that announces the project—his plan to take the revelation to Spain (Rom 15.20–24). Paul's operation has now reached a stage where he can coordinate the resources, skill, and dedication of many helpers to take on a vast new region, one that was very important in the Roman empire but where "Messiah's very name is unknown" (Rom 15.20).

Rome was to be the staging area for this vast endeavor. He means to raise support there while he mends his fences with Jerusalem, to anticipate and prevent any opposition or interference to the whole new front he is opening. As we shall see, he uses a dispute in Rome to recast the harsh rhetoric against Jerusalem employed by him during the earlier clash at Antioch. He no doubt hopes that the Romans will support him when they send their delegates with the collection for the needy. He will also circulate copies of this very letter in Judaea, through intermediaries and finally in person. Rome is the fulcrum on which he will balance what is, in effect, a "worldwide" reach, toward Jerusalem in the East and toward Spain in the West. Phoebe, Prisca, and her husband, along with the other members of Paul's assembled team, are to organize the elements for this campaign while Paul goes to solidify support in Jerusalem. It is all to be the climax of Paul's mission—one that is tragically cut short by the dark outcome of his eastward trip.

Women Prophets

PHOEBE WAS NOT the only woman of some resources giving support to Paul in Corinth. He heard reports of trouble there

from traveling members of "Chloe's establishment"—
literally, "they of Chloe" (1 Cor 1.11). Since Chloe herself did
not send the report, it is supposed that she had some business
or family at Corinth, and slaves or workers were traveling either to her or to her other holdings. Chloe was probably a
well-to-do widow, like another businesswoman Luke
mentions—Lydia, the dealer in precious dyes (Ac 16.14), who
had a gathering at her house in Philippi (16.40).

The troubles reported by Chloe's establishment were deep
and complex, as we shall see, and they afforded plenty of occasions for prophecy, the gift of the Spirit Paul lists just after
that of emissaries. Prophecy is now popularly thought to
mean prediction of the future. But the Jewish prophets were
inspired denouncers of those who lapsed from the Lord's
ways, reformers and purifiers. The faults of Corinth had their
excoriaters, and *some of the prophets were women.* Paul
writes that in the gatherings there a woman "should not pray
or prophesy with her head uncovered" (1 Cor 11.5). He is addressing a squabble that had arisen about clothing in the gathering, but the important point for us to notice is that Paul
takes it for granted that, bareheaded or not, women are
prophets in the gathering. He is just as strict in saying that
men should *not* have their heads covered when they pray or
prophesy. Since we do not have the grounds for the departure
from custom that was causing bitterness, we cannot say how
serious they were, or what they were supposed to signify—

apparently the arrogantly spiritualist party was introducing a daring innovation. At any rate, Paul obviously thinks of them as deliberately offensive, and the cause of needless ridicule from outsiders. He says that the head covering is a "sign of authority for a woman in respect of the angels" (1 Cor 11.10)—who veil their faces before God (Is 6.2).

Though Paul is adjudicating a situation that is merely a matter of social practice, he backs up his argument on theological grounds that are sexist. Man can go uncovered because he is the direct image of God, while woman is the image of God's image—man—created after him and meant to be his helpmate (1 Cor 11.7–9). It was impossible for a man in that culture, patriarchal in both its Jewish and Roman societies, to shed every remnant of sexism. But the important thing is to notice that Paul gives every kind of honor to the women he works with—as emissaries, as prophets, as attendants *(diakonoi)*. They are not second-class citizens in the gatherings he knows or in the ideals he holds up for them.

If that is the case, how did Paul get a reputation for misogyny? He owes that principally to his impersonators and interpolaters. The supposedly Pauline letters, written late in the first century, reflect a church that is cutting back on the radical egalitarianism of its early days. Male church officers are emerging—married overseers *(episkopoi)* and deacons *(diakonoi)*—and patriarchy is being reimposed (1 Tim 3.1–7). The First Letter to Timothy is especially blunt in telling women to shut up: "A woman must be an entirely submissive learner. I forbid a woman to teach, or to take the lead over her husband—she should hold her peace" (1 Tim 2.11–12). But here there is a great objection to be made. In a letter universally admitted to be authentic, Paul also tells women to shut up:

> As in all gatherings of the Holy, women must be silent in the gatherings. They are not to speak up *(lalein)* but to be submissive, as custom dictates. If they would learn, let them seek knowledge from their husbands at home. It is a disgrace for a woman to speak up in the gathering. (1 Cor 14.34–35)

Earlier in this very letter, Paul had told women to cover their heads when speaking up and prophesying. Paul can be accused of contradicting himself, but not so blatantly in the confines of a single document. This fact has led a great many scholars to condemn this passage as an interpolation, added to the letter when the policy of the letter to Timothy had been adopted. The pseudo-Paul has intruded upon real Paul.

"As I Am"

SOME MAY SUSPECT Paul of misogyny since he is opposed to marriage. He writes that he would prefer that the unmarried remain that way, "as I am," saying that married people are busied with concern for each other, which can drain away concern for the Lord (1 Cor 7.32–34). Did Paul never marry? Even Catholic Bible scholars, like Jerome Murphy-O'Connor and Joseph Fitzmyer, think that highly unlikely. In the second century, Clement of Alexandria thought that Paul had been married but was separated from his wife, and other early authors held that view.[3] Apparently Paul was a mature man by the time the risen Lord appeared to him, and a Pharisee was usually obliged to marry. Paul was probably married in his twenties, though he is no longer by the time he writes. His wife could have died, left him, or been sent away under Jewish Law. Even in the new gatherings, he says that a nonbelieving spouse can be let go if that spouse is opposed to the religion of a believer (1 Cor 7.15).

Of course, Paul cannot make his opposition to marriage a requirement, since Peter and the brothers of the Lord traveled about with their wives (1 Cor 9.5). In the Brotherhood, marriage is the normal way of life, even for emissaries. In the later letters to Timothy and Titus, marriage is usual for "bishops" and "elders" (1 Tim 3.2, Tit 1.6). Thus Paul can only recommend his preference. He repeatedly emphasizes that this is not a teaching he has from the Lord.

> I give this as a recommendation, not a direction: I prefer
> that all men be as I am. But each has his own spiritual

gift *(charisma)* from God, so one will act this way, another that. (1 Cor 7.6–7)

This is I speaking, not the Lord. (1 Cor 7.12)

I have received from the Lord no requirement concerning virgins, but I offer my opinion as one in a position of trust by the mercy of the Lord. (1 Cor 7.25)

I suppose *(nomizo)*, then, that it is a good thing in this imminent crisis, that it is good for a man to remain in the same condition [neither to dissolve a marriage nor to undertake one]. (1 Cor 7.26)

I say this for your benefit, not to tie you up. (1 Cor 7.35)

This is just my opinion, though even I have the Spirit of God, too. (1 Cor 7.40)

In saying that he has no instruction from the Lord on celibacy, Paul either does not know the saying of Jesus about those "castrated for heaven's reign" or does not take it as an instruction. All that Jesus says in the Gospel is "Let one who can yield to *(chorein)* this, yield to it" (Mt 19.12). Paul's only reference to castration is a sardonic comment on enthusiasts for circumcision. If they are so intent on it, he says, they should cut off not only the foreskin but the whole member (Gal 5.12).

Paul's own opposition to marriage is not misogynist but eschatological. He is against women marrying as well as men, and that does not make him a misanthrope. His stand is part of his general social passivity. He says that slaves, though they may welcome freedom if it is given them, should not agitate for it (1 Cor 7.20–21). "As a person was when called by God, so let him continue" (7.24). In the same way, he is against political agitation or reform (Rom 13.1–7). The spread of the revelation is so pressing a duty, as history reaches its conclusion, that all else is to be considered a distraction from that single concern. Paul has enough trouble with the Roman authorities just in carrying out his mission. He does not want to get entangled in any other concerns.

> I tell you this, Brothers: the crisis impends. During what time is left, let those with wives be as if they had none, let those who mourn be as not [having time for] mourning, let those celebrating be as if not celebrating, let those who buy be as if not possessing, and those using this world be as if not using it. For the whole frame of this present order is about to go. (1 Cor 7.29–31)

In this eschatological context, Paul can imagine only one condition where he thinks marriage preferable—if one is so enflamed by passion that this in itself is a distraction from the

work of the revelation: "Better to marry than to stay enflamed" (1 Cor 7.9). Neither here nor elsewhere does Paul
connect marriage with having children, the later Christian ra-
tionale. Since history is ending, the raising of children is no
longer a concern in Paul's eyes. The only reference he makes
to children is to say that the child of one Holy parent can be
considered Holy, even if the other parent is a nonbeliever (1
Cor 7.14). Paul's frame of thought is far from what would be
ascribed to him in the supposedly Pauline letters to Timothy
and Titus, where the disciplining of bishops' children is addressed (1 Tim 3.4–5, Tit 1.6).

Despite Paul's preference, he himself gives evidence that
married people were able to be intensely devoted to the Lord.
Prisca even went to prison with him. In his Letter to the Romans, he names four married people who "worked hard" for
the Lord. In Philippians, he adds another two, Euodia and
Syntyche, who were his "fellows in the struggle" (Phil 4.3).
Phoebe is his protectress. Another Sister is like his mother.
Chloe's establishment keeps him informed. His crack team assembled in Rome for the Spanish campaign includes ten
women, at least three of them married. He knows a woman
emissary *(apostolos)*, a woman attendant *(diakonos)*, and
women prophets. He knows two women leaders in Philippi,
Euodia and Syntyche, who have become rivals, and he begs for
their reconciliation (not their condemnation) at Philippians

4.2–3. The later misogyny of the Christian churches would never have occurred if the spirit of Paul had continued in them.

NOTES

1. Wayne Meeks, *The First Urban Christians: The Social World of the Apostle Paul,* second edition (Yale University Press, 2003), p. 132.

2. Ibid., pp. 20, 59.

3. Eusebius, *History of the Church* 3.30.1.

6. Paul and the Troubled Gatherings

✝

Six of Paul's seven recognizably authentic documents were addressed to gatherings with specific troubles. As John Gager puts it: "The circumstances under which Paul wrote all of his surviving letters, in modern terms we would call them attempts at damage control."[1] Some think that the last extant letter, to the Romans, is an exception to this statement, and others that the earliest letter, to the Thessalonians, is an at least partial exception. But there is good reason to think that they, too, fit under the same rule. I shall take them in the presumed chronological order.

Thessalonians

This is addressed to Thessalonica, the capital of northern Greece (Macedonia). I have already noticed that Luke in the Acts implies that Paul was run out of this community in a matter of weeks, and that Paul admits he was forced to leave by Jewish enmity. He says in the letter that the gathering there suffers from "straits" (*thlipsis*, 1 Thess 1.6). There is disagreement whether this means severe persecution or merely the difficulties that people who have left their own family and friends to take up a new discipline are bound to undergo. If Paul was expelled, why should the community he left behind be in peace? Besides, they are upset over those who have died since Paul was there, who may miss out on the Lord's Arrival *(Parousia)*. Can that many have died so soon without a persecution?

But if such a persecution had occurred, would Paul refer to it so vaguely as a generalized "pressure" *(thlipsis)*? The community seems to have been flourishing, since it has extended its influence over both parts of Greece, Macedonia and Achaea (1 Thess 1.7–8). Also, he says he has expected to return, and been prevented by things other than fear of further disturbance; and he sends Timothy without any expression of concern for his safety. His reference to reports on the Thessalonians' influence shows that he has been in communication with the place, not cut off or worrying about its fate.

Still, he does feel a need to send Timothy back, depriving himself of Timothy's important help. The mission he sends him on must be more than a way of sending his greetings. This letter is written as a response to Timothy's return, bringing reports that cheer Paul. But certain emphases in the letter indicate that there are sensitive matters to be dealt with. Why does Paul so pointedly stress how he and his fellows did hard manual work when they were in Thessalonica (1 Thess 2.9)?

We know that he also got help from Philippi while he was there. In Corinth and Rome, economic divisions in the gatherings caused tensions. Paul here seems to hint at a fear that the leaders of the community are now setting themselves apart from the working class or the poorer Brothers. He is probably admonishing those leaders, tactfully, when he urges the community to respect them: "We beg you, Brothers, to recognize those who *work so hard* for you and represent you in the Lord and advise you—give them generous esteem in your love for their *work*" (1 Thess 5.12–13). If the influence of Thessalonica has extended itself, it must be through the efforts of these leaders, but he is reminding them that they must earn their respect as he did by "night and day" labor for others.

The other notable thing about this letter has been noticed earlier, its first treatment of the end time in New Testament literature. The surface concern is that people worry about the fate of those who have died. This does not mean, necessarily, that a great number have actually perished since Paul's departure. The issue has obviously been debated in prospect. What concerns Paul is that different opinions are being offered (again diminishing the credibility of the leaders). That is why he brings his biggest weapon to bear—the Lord's own word (1 Thess 4.15). He is addressing not only an existential fear but a matter of doctrinal clarity. This is enough to show that even this "pastoral" letter had real controversial prompting.

Galatians

THERE IS NO DOUBT about the troubles prompting Paul to write his most polemical letter. It is the conflict between circumcised and uncircumcised Brothers, and it leads Paul to his most vitriolic comments, not only about the present antagonists, but about Peter and James in his earlier clash with them at Antioch. This is the letter that disconcerted Saint Jerome, and it became the model or excuse for reciprocal vilifications in the Reformation. The veracity of the early records of the faith is established by the fact that this letter was not suppressed. Paul later indicates that he came to regret the bitterness expressed here. He certainly did not follow his own counsel to others, that they correct each other with kindness. He takes an entirely different approach in his irenic Letter to the Romans.

Of course, we do not have the other side, which may have been just as intemperate. He could be trading taunt for taunt, fighting fire with fire. This is the only letter that is sent to a region, not to a single city. The circumcisionists (literally, "they of the circumcision") must have waged an aggressive campaign against Paul in several towns at once, and Paul sends a copy of his letter to each one. He says the Galatians are being bewitched by the agitators (3.1); they are tearing themselves apart (5.15). After dictating this tirade, he takes the pen himself to write the last paragraph: "Look at this large

scrawl put down with my own hand" (6.11). The whole letter
is a cri de coeur: "I wish I were already by your side, to modu-
late my tone, so frustrated am I" (4.20). He writhes with anx-
iety, as if in renewed birth pangs for his children (4.19). He is
wounded and he means to wound others—even telling them
to castrate themselves (5.12)—Raymond Brown wonders if
the scribe hesitated to put those words down as Paul dictated
them.

Philippians

PHILIPPI, in Northern Greece, was the first European town
Paul reached. He must have approached this new arena with
some apprehension, and he recalls with pride and pleasure the
warm response he was given there by people who are "my joy,
my crown" (4.1). Now he writes from prison (probably in
Ephesus), wishing he were back among his early supporters.
They have sent a representative, Epaphroditus, to cheer him
up; but they were upset when they heard that Epaphroditus
fell ill, so he is sending him back to them in recovered
strength (2.25–30). He is also about to send Timothy, to add to
their comfort (2.19–24). Paul is happy that the revelation is
still being spread despite his imprisonment, though he regrets
that some use that fact to cause division—presumably with
the Jews, who are blamed for turning him over to the Romans
(1.15–18). But he is concerned that the circumcisionists are at

work among them, too—the "dogs," as he calls them (3.2). There are divisions in the community, even dividing his old "fellow strugglers," Euodia and Syntyche (4.2). To heal these troubles he quotes the great hymn he had shared with them, on Jesus' "emptying himself" (2.6–11).

Philemon

PAUL HAD the services of a scribe, even in prison. He needed this because he no doubt wrote more letters to gatherings than the ones that have been preserved. He must also have written many letters to individuals, though this is the only one that has been preserved, perhaps because it helped a man who became well known to the Brothers for the help he gave to Paul. The occasion for this letter is not trouble in a whole gathering but the trouble of one man who held a gathering of Brothers at his home (Phlm 2). One of Philemon's slaves has done something wrong, and he has gone to Paul to act as an intercessor with his owner (a common procedure in Roman law). While dealing with Paul, the slave, Onesimus, has performed some service for him, perhaps as a scribe writing this very letter, which he carries back to his owner. Roman slaves were often well-educated Greeks who acted as scribes, tutors, or bureaucrats, and Onesimus is a common Greek slave name, meaning "Useful." Paul puns on the meaning of the name when he tells Philemon that his slave was once unbeneficial (akhrēstos) to him but has now become beneficial (khrēstos) to both of them (Phlm 11).

Paul asks for special favors for this slave. He is not setting a general policy on slaves, or asking Philemon to free others of his household. It has been estimated that slaves made up as much as a quarter to a third of urban populations in Paul's time—he was not ready to work for the great social disruption of manumissions on that scale. We know that there were slaves in the gatherings of the Brothers, from Paul's advice that they accept their condition (1 Cor 7.20–21). He brought whole households (oikoi) into the faith together (1 Cor 1.16), and oikos usually meant the extended "family" of all dependents, including slaves. The term "Chloe's establishment" was probably meant to include slaves (1 Cor 1.11), as could the tent-making operations of Prisca and Aquila. Onesimus, however, was not brought to the faith as part of Philemon's household—Paul tells us that he became a Brother only in his own company (Phlm 16). The fact that he was not baptized with Philemon's oikos might seem surprising, since that was a family center active for the revelation. Paul greets Philemon himself as a "coworker" in the faith; his wife, Apphia, as a Sister; and another member of the household, Archippus, as having "soldiered with me" (Phlm 2).

The explanation that suggests itself is that Onesimus, as an educated slave, operated away from his master's oikos, perhaps taking care of his financial interests in another city, which took him close to Paul. Paul hints that the slave's crime was financial when he writes to Philemon:

> If you and I are one, then think of him as me. If he has wronged you, or owes you, put that on my account. See, here I sign myself PAUL, that I will repay you—I will not mention that you owe your very self to me. Or, rather, Brother, put me in your debt and ease my anguish in Messiah. (Phlm 17–20)

Another puzzling thing about the letter is that Onesimus has had time to perform many and valuable services for Paul, which brought him so close to the prisoner that Paul now calls him "part of my very being" (literally, his "innards," *splagkhna*, Phlm 12), so that he is in "anguish" over the slave's fate (again, in his "innards," Phlm 20). If Onesimus went to Paul only to intercede with his master, why did Paul not send him back at once? I imagine that Onesimus, working for Philemon in Ephesus (if that is where Paul's prison was), had been told to perform services for Paul while continuing to do his master's business in that town. But in the course of dealing with Paul he came in time to accept the revelation, and only then confessed that he had been defrauding Philemon. Paul now sends him back to be reconciled with Philemon, hoping that he will be released into continued service with himself. If that was the outcome, as seems most likely, then the continued joint action of Paul and Onesimus would have made this event, and the letter accomplishing it, famous throughout the gatherings, insuring the preservation of the letter. It would hardly have been kept if all that eloquence had failed.

Corinthians

OF ALL THE GATHERINGS Paul addressed, those in Corinth were the most refractory. His dealings with them were sticky, thorny, and cantankerous. He stayed with them on three or more occasions (2 Cor 12.14, 13.1), sent personal assistants to them in his absence, received their delegations, and wrote them at least five letters, probably more, three or four or five of which are layered together in what have come down to us as two agglutinated letters. Factions spawned in Corinth. There were problems of doctrine, discipline, and vision, problems of class, of gender, of personalities. Paul was ridiculed there and he responded wrathfully, once in a wounding letter, once in a tearful one (these probably lost but leaving traces in what remains).

The community was divided over a marriage that was considered incestuous under Jewish Law—one of the Brothers had wed his father's widowed second wife (a woman who was no blood relative and may have been the new husband's own age or younger). Paul claims that this would not be allowed "even among the nations"—the Gentiles (1 Cor 5.1). He demands that the whole gathering, by its joint authority, with him present in spirit, drive the man out of the gathering. He is as solemn as can be about this: "All of you coming together in the name of the Lord Jesus, myself present in spirit, with the power of our Lord, turn such a man over to Satan for the destruction of his flesh, that his spirit may be rescued on the day of the Lord" (1 Cor 5.4–5). The baptized Brothers are one "in Messiah." To be outside Messiah is to be back in the realm of Satan, exposed to his ravages. Subject again to the law of the dying flesh (Paul seems to be saying), the man will strive back toward being in Messiah by the time Messiah comes. Some might well have thought Paul rather arbitrary in this proceeding, and we have difficulty understanding it until we look at the other clusters of misunderstanding in the place.

The main trouble in Corinth seems to have been a form of superspirituality. Like New Age types seeking fashionable preachers, some people became puffed up and "airy," saying their newest gurus (claiming to represent Apollos, for instance, or Peter) are higher minded than Paul (1 Cor 1.12, 3.22), that their own gifts of prophecy and speaking in tongues bring them closer to the Spirit than more ordinary folk, that they know of a better form of baptism (1 Cor 1.13–17). Paul calls the preachers of such attitudes high-flying emissaries—literally, the "super-too-much *(hyperlian)* emissaries" (2 Cor 11.5, 12.11), and repeatedly says that their followers are "inflated" *(physioi)* or self-inflated (1 Cor 4.18, 5.2, 8.1, 13.4). Krister Stendahl describes the high-flying emissaries as "slick operators."[2] Their women's newfangled way of prophesying (without headdress) is modishly "daring." Without disparaging spiritual gifts, and while saying he has experienced them himself, Paul reminds them that these are given for the good of the whole gathering, and that without love the spiritualists become as a resonating gong (prophecy?) or a jangling cymbal (speaking in tongues?).

While ironically calling high-minded people the "stronger" element in the gathering, Paul boasts of his own weakness (1 Cor 2.1–5, 2 Cor 12.7–10). He will admit that the stronger may have superior insight—for instance, since they realize that idols are a mere nothing, they can eat meat sacrificed to idols (1 Cor 8.4–6, 10.25–27). But Paul tells these high flyers to defer to "the weak," who still see some taint in that kind of food (1 Cor 8.7–13, 10.19–21, 28–33). Above all, he tells the strong not to draw themselves together to eat better things at the Lord's Meal, since that destroys the whole point of the union of Messiah being realized in their eating together (1 Cor 11.20–22). The lofty-souled seem to have done what later superspiritualists would, putting themselves above the observance of laws binding ordinary mortals. That is why Paul criticizes what seems to have been one of their mantras:

"Everything is permitted" (to the higher spirits; 1 Cor 6.12, 10.23). This may have been the point of the "strong" in saying that the marriage of a man to his stepmother, who lacked any blood tie, was permissible, though vulgar opinion held it to be incest. It is clearly why the high-flying emissaries said they were following the Lord's command in taking pay for their spiritual activities (1 Cor 9.14–18). The high flyers also seem to have thought they had already entered into the spiritual state of the glorified body. That is why Paul makes the odd point that they have to die first before they can live so exempt from earthly morals, and then their bodies will be so entirely different as to be unimaginable now (1 Cor 15.35–43).

By the time of the collection of texts cobbled together in what we call Second Corinthians, Paul must have realized that simple denunciation was not working. He was now looking for ways to compromise. When his very integrity was questioned, with regard to the Jerusalem fund's collection and security, he brought in neutral supervisors appointed by "the gatherings" (2 Cor 8.18–22). His account of his own spiritual gifts was a way of granting the validity of those in other people. He became autobiographical in order to forge ties with those making new claims for the Spirit. Grappling with the Corinthians was for him a harrowing struggle, one that makes for heady reading, even in the jumbled record it left behind.

Romans

THE LETTER to the Romans is the only one, extant and authentic, in which Paul does not mention cosenders (though he delivers it by way of Phoebe). It is the only one addressed to a place he had never seen, to gatherings that were formed before he even became a Brother. But it is also his longest and most theologically ambitious letter. Some think that the lack of a troubled community within his own experience freed him to a more leisurely exposition of basic themes. But that plays down the fact that he had received reports of a way in which the Roman gatherings *were* troubled. He may have exaggerated the trouble for his own purposes, since it gave him a chance to rework an earlier stand he had come to regret. But more important, it gave him the opportunity to address the *Jerusalem* Brothers without direct confrontation or solicitation of a good opinion.

He clearly wanted copies of this letter to be seen in Jerusalem—and probably elsewhere. Some copies he would take with him, others he hoped his team in Rome would circulate there before his arrival and encourage Roman Brothers to send on to their friends and allies in Jerusalem. One of the reasons Paul needed scribes was to produce multiple copies of his letters, for his own records and to verify the copies others would make of them. Before the age of printing, an author "published" only by having the same text laboriously copied out over and over. The letter to Rome was a production Paul took great pains over. Its rhetoric is highly wrought, its argument dense and ingenious. It is not a calm summary of his thinking, but an intense engagement with his Jewish past and his offended brethren. It is peppered with those heckling rhetorical questions characteristic of diatribe. It is a careful beginning to his last and largest campaign.

The trouble in Rome, however unfortunate for those experiencing it, was perfect for Paul's needs. It was the same conflict that had made him erupt in Antioch, a division in the gathering over Jewish food laws. But the dynamics had shifted. In Antioch, the "Judaizers" had the upper hand, while the Gentile Brothers were the innovators, suspect and easily intimidated by pressures emanating from Jerusalem. Paul became absolutist in that situation, telling Peter that he was nullifying the freedom of Christ as he insisted on kosher discipline. Paul called any compromise at that point a form of "hypocrisy," and his stand made him temporarily lose his partner Barnabas and break off his efforts to raise the Jerusalem fund in Antioch. Now, however, writing to the Romans, Paul argues for tolerance and reconciliation. Partly this reflects the shift in dynamics just mentioned. In Rome, it is the Gentile Brothers who have the upper hand and are intimidating the Jewish Brothers. What makes this possible is a break in the social continuity of Jewish life not experienced elsewhere, one caused by the emperor Claudius.

In his *Life of Claudius* (25.4), the Roman historian Suetonius records that the emperor "expelled from Rome the Jews because of continual disturbances provoked by Chrestus." It is universally held that Suetonius misunderstood the title *Christus*, an odd term for a Roman, as a proper name, and assimilated it to a name that was common at the time, Chrestus (from Greek *Khrēstos*. "Worthy" or "Beneficial"). By 49 CE, in other words, there was a sizable enough community of the Brothers in Rome to create dissension in the Jewish community over something connected with "Chrestus," and the emperor, without getting into the causes or sorting out who was really involved, solved the problem by throwing out the whole lot. Jews, whether Brothers or not, were expelled from the city.

It is easy to reconstruct what happened, since it had parallels throughout the Empire, ones that brought Paul and others before Roman tribunals. Jews had good reason to fear and resent the Brothers. They had worked out a cautious and precarious modus vivendi with the Roman authorities, one in which they were tolerated and even protected, despite resentment of their separatist ways, their different holidays, their abstention from pagan feasts, their private food supplies and preparations. The Brothers disturbed this delicate situation, dividing

Jewish family members by their departures from the Law, and luring the Reverent (the *Theosebeis*) away from them. These important Gentile friends and patrons were a source of protection, of political and financial support, for the endangered Jewish minorities. It was necessary for Jews to represent the Brothers as not authentic participants in the allowed space earned and confirmed by Jews over the years. The Brothers, they would say, were more like the odd and menacing "new" religions from the East that Romans considered disruptive and a menace to Rome's cults. Jews therefore appealed to the Roman authorities they had cultivated, asking them to prevent disruption in the Jewish community caused by the Brothers. The "disturbances" that Claudius punished need have been no more than the nuisance of repeated attempts to involve Roman courts in religious squabbles.

When the Jews were cast out of Rome, Jewish Brothers would not have been distinguished from those not involved in "Chrestus." According to Luke, Prisca and Aquila were among the Jewish Brothers who had to leave Rome, and who ended up in Corinth, where they met Paul (Ac 18.2). But most of the Jews from Rome were likely to stay near the networks they had formed in Italy, holding together their communities in exile, maintaining synagogue organizations and economic relations with the surrounding country. When, in 55 CE, Claudius died, they were able to return with social structures intact, to reclaim properties they had leased or committed to friendly Romans, resuming the pattern of their lives within the old guarantees.

The Jewish Brothers would have returned as well, but to a new situation. The Gentile Brothers, who were not covered by the decree, had for six years been able to expand their own community without any harassment from the synagogues—a unique occurrence in the early history of the Brotherhood.[3] Returning Jewish Brothers would now be the outsiders in their own surroundings. Those who had maintained their ties to the Jewish Law would find little sympathy for their ways in gatherings that had lived with only minimal connections to the Jewish origins of Jesus.

Paul's letter is an impassioned assertion that those connections can never be severed. It used to be thought that the recipients of the letter were made up mainly of Jewish Brothers, since Paul argues at length and learnedly from intimate acquaintance with Jewish scripture. But the reason for this is just the opposite of what was then supposed. He stresses the Jewish foundations because they are so *little* familiar to the one community of Brothers who had been isolated for a time from that past. It will be seen how useful this argument was for approaching the Brothers he was about to see again in Jerusalem. He was making it clear that his mission to the nations was not a separate endeavor, unrelated to the lives and history of Jewish Brothers, or unrelated to the calling of the whole Jewish people in their uncanceled covenant with God.

Paul's main task is to tell the Gentile Brothers that God's promise to the Jewish people is not broken—it cannot be broken. He devotes most of the first thirteen chapters (as we now know them) to this thesis. Only in chapters fourteen and fifteen does he get around to the observation of food codes in Rome. It is not surprising, then, that commentators have seen these late chapters as a mere addendum to the large-scale argument preceding them. But that long discussion was a careful way of sorting out the problem of the community he was addressing. Admittedly, he went beyond the immediate issue, which was the relation of Gentile to Jewish Brothers, and addressed the relation of all Brothers to all the Jews. But this added an a fortiori power to his argument in the immediate situation. If the Brothers must recognize God's unbreakable commitment to the whole Jewish people, *how much more* must they see the reason for Brothers to honor their ties to the people God first chose.

When it comes to the actual situation in Rome, Paul does not go back to the clash in Antioch, where he was for an absolute break with certain provisions of the Mosaic Law, but to Corinth, where he talked of a strong party and a weak one. Here, too, he says that the strong party may have the more defensible reason for its "freedom," but a regard for the united body of the Lord must make it defer to the fears of the "weak" members. In Corinth, the strong party saw no problem in eating meat killed for idols. In Rome, the strong party sees no problem in eating meat not killed to the kosher requirements. The case might seem less urgent in Rome, but Paul makes it more symbolically important. Admittedly, a higher principle is involved—that *nothing* is unclean in itself, not merely things directly connected with idolatry—but a more urgent priority is at stake on the actual scene: regard for the Jewish roots of the Brotherhood. Where once he had excoriated Peter for insisting on the food code, now he tells Romans to accept it out of regard for tender consciences:

> If your Brother takes offense with you over the food being eaten, it is because you are not observing the love you should walk in with him. Do not put his soul at stake over your food observance—Christ died for him. What you see as good should not be another's reproach. God's reign is not a matter of food or drink, but of God's vindication, of peace, of joy in the Holy Spirit. Messiah's slave in these matters is the one loved of God and favored of men. Let us then seek peace and the mutual upbuilding of each other. Why use food to block God's own project? Nothing is unclean of itself. But the individual may wince at one form of eating. Some find it best not to eat meat, or drink wine, or to do anything that a Brother finds offensive. If you, however, are assured in doing these things, keep it a matter of confidence with God. Happy the person who can act out of assurance, and one who acts against his own principles in eating is

self-convicting, not keeping his integrity, for anyone who is not in accord with himself is in the wrong. Still, we who are confident should favor the weakness of those who are not confident, not trying to coerce them. Each should defer to the other, to strengthen the structure of the whole gathering, since Messiah himself gave way to others. (Rom 14.15–15.3)

Paul would have been far better off if he had taken this stand in Antioch. But he should be credited with the fact that he reached it in time. One of the ways he teaches us is by learning himself. We find out what Paul meant by seeing how he eventually came closer to what Jesus meant.

NOTES

1. John G. Gager, *Reinventing Paul* (Oxford University Press, 2000), p. 77.

2. Krister Stendahl, *Paul Among Jews and Gentiles* (Fortress Press, 1976), p. 47.

3. James C. Walters, *Ethnic Issues in Paul's Letter to the Romans* (Trinity Press International, 1993).

7. Paul and Jews

✝

IT HAS LONG and often been alleged that Paul is a father of Christian anti-Semitism. Where does he stand on the staples of that vile record? Take two of these. First, did he call the Jews Jesus-killers? Second, did he say that Jews are cursed by God?

On the killing of Jews, he first denies that the Jews did it. "Not a single one of the rulers of the world knew this [the revelation]. Had they known, they would not have crucified the Lord of splendor" (1 Cor 2.8). The Jews were not the rulers of the world when Jesus was killed. They were themselves ruled by the rulers of the world, the Romans, who killed Jesus. On the other hand, Paul does say that the same Jews who killed earlier prophets also killed Jesus. Writing to the Thessalonians, he says:

> You, Brothers, have repeated what happened to God's Judaean gatherings that were in Messiah-Jesus, since you have suffered from your own kinsmen what they did from the Jews, who killed the Lord and the prophets—the same who drove us away from you, displeasing God and opposing all men by preventing us from telling the

nations how they are rescued, which completes their account of guilt over all time, anticipating the last anger against them. (1 Thess 2.14–16)

This is the greatest proof text in the authentic letters for Paul's anti-Semitism. Some argue that it, like the passage telling Corinthian women to shut up, is an interpolation by later people with later attitudes, and there are some oddities about the text that might help them in their claim. But the effort to get rid of the passage is too clearly a matter of wishful thinking. The matter must be considered later.

On the second point, did Paul say that God cursed the Jews? Definitely not: "I tell you: Has God repudiated his own people? Far from it!" (Rom 11.1). How could they be his own people if he repudiated them? On the other hand, Paul wrote: "Those who act under the Law are under a curse" (Gal 3.10).

How is one to reconcile such divergent statements? A first reaction may be to say that this was one crazy mixed-up Jew—and that may, in fact, be the beginning of wisdom. It may free us from the false starting point so many take with Paul—one assuming that that he left Judaism to join and promote a different religion, the Christian church, pitting the latter against the former. But there was no such entity in his time as a Christian church. There were only Jews who saw Jesus as the promised Messiah of the Jews and, supplementarily, Gentiles who saw Jesus as the promised Messiah of the Jews, who were the people Paul was sent to call in. He teaches his followers from nothing but the Jewish scriptures, and presents the Messiah as the fulfillment of the Jewish covenant. We thus have a continuum between three groups:

1. Jews not accepting Jesus as the Messiah of the Jews
2. Jews accepting Jesus as the Messiah of the Jews
3. Non-Jews accepting Jesus as the Messiah of the Jews

There is no one here outside a Jewish context, no group to be opposed to the Jews as a whole. There are only divisions within the Jewish understanding of Yahweh. What we have is a family quarrel.

Paul never presents Jesus as the God of the Greeks, as the Wisdom of Plato, as the Unmoved Mover of Aristotle. He never quotes a passage or an argument about God from pagan philosophers or non-Jewish authors. (Luke makes him do that once—but Paul never does it in his own writings.) Paul's Gentile Brothers are instructed over and over in the intricacies of Jewish history and prophecy. They are told that *they* are the seed of Abraham, and told in detail why this is so (Rom 4.1–17). The prophets foretold their rescue—Paul calls the roll of them (Rom 15.9–12). For Paul there was no such thing as "the Old Testament." If he had known that his writings would be incorporated into something called the New Testament, he would have repudiated that if it was meant in any way to repudiate, or subordinate, the only scripture he knew, the only word of God he recognized, his Bible.

One of the most basic problems in reading Paul is knowing what he means when he refers to "Jews." People repeatedly mistake him as referring to the Jews of the number 1 group (page 127) when he is talking about those listed as number 2. The latter are the ones he has continuing contact and conflict with, as they try to impose Jewish Law on their Gentile brothers. Thus, when he says that Jews are "preventing us from telling the nations how they are rescued," he is referring to people like the "circumcisionists," or those imposing the Jewish food code *on Brothers*. Those are the adversaries that "dog" him from Antioch to Philippi (Phil 3.2). They precede him into Rome. In fact, as we shall see, it will be the Jewish Brothers who betray Paul to Nero for execution. Paul's harshest words about his fellow Jews are about his fellow *Brother Jews*, the ones who would later be called Christians. These are the ones he calls hypocrites (including Peter and James and Barnabas) and dogs (Gal 2.13, Phil 3.2). These are the ones he calls "damned" *(anathema)* in his anger against them (Gal 1.8–9).

That is enough to make us go back and look at the proof text for his anti-Semitism (1 Thess 2.14–16). Clearly in that passage the ones who are preventing the spread of the revelation to Gentiles are the *Brother* Jews. Are they the ones killing Jesus and the prophets? Not in the sense that the "rulers of the world" did at the crucifixion, but Paul sees the

life of Jesus as his continuing presence in the body of the believers. Those who oppose him there are trying to kill him, as
they did the prophets who proclaim the risen Lord (Paul
among them). They are the ones who are "completing an account of guilt." If anyone thinks this is too strong a thing to
say about Paul's fellow believers in Jesus, what do they make
of his calling his fellow believers hypocrites and dogs and
damned? These are ones who will turn Paul—and Peter as
well—over for execution.

It would, in fact, make more sense to call Paul an anti-
Jewish-Christian polemicist than an anti-Semite. But in any
case there is no more Semitic a Semite than Paul. "If one re-
lies on lineage, I can do so more than others—circumcised on
the eighth day, by race a man of Israel, by tribe of Benjamin,
Hebrew from Hebrews, in Law a Pharisee, in dedication a per-
secutor of the gathering, in vindication under the Law a man
faultless" (1 Phil 3.4–6). "For Jewishness I outstripped many
contemporaries of my own lineage, extreme in my jealous
preservation of the patriarchs' traditions" (Gal 1.14). Paul is
just as Jewish as Jewish can be. "I, after all, am an Israelite, of
Abraham's seed, of Benjamin's tribe. God has not repudiated
our people, recognized as his from the outset" (Rom 11.1–2).
He cannot say it often enough or emphatically enough. "I
could prefer to be outcast from Messiah myself if it would
help my brothers, the forebears of my flesh, who are the Israelites. Theirs is the sonship, and the splendor, and the

covenants, and the gift of Law, and the rites, and the promises. From them are the patriarchs, and from them, by fleshly descent, is the Messiah, the God above all, may he ever be praised. Amen" (Rome 9.3–5). Paul never boasts, as Luke makes him boast, of being a Roman citizen. He never boasts of coming from "a city of some note" (Ac 21.39). He boasts only of his Jewish roots and observance.

Then how, it is asked, can he attack the Jewish Law?

To be brief, he doesn't.

The Letter to the Romans, often taken to be Paul's central statement of doctrine, is usually misread because of the confusion of the three meanings of "Jews" already listed. It is thought to contrast the number 1 group of Jews with a fictive entity, Christianity. Actually, as I argued in the last chapter, Paul was addressing the number 3 group of Jews (Gentile believers in the Jewish Messiah), saying that they should defer to the scruples of the number 2 group in Rome, a minority of the Brothers in Rome. But this meant that he was speaking over the heads of number 3 Jews to number 2 ones (the Jewish Brothers who are to be accepted). And he is speaking over *their* heads to the Brothers in Jerusalem, whom he expects to read this letter, assuring them that he has not lost touch with their concerns. He is even speaking over the latter heads to the number 1 group, of Jews not yet accepting Jesus as the Messiah, saying that to do so is not to show disrespect for the Mosaic Law.

All this interplay of audiences is made possible, but also complicated, by the diatribe technique in this letter, the voicing of various views by various assumed personae. The complex relations thus set up are trampled into indistinguishable muddle by those who say Paul was attacking "Jewish Law" from the standpoint of "Christianity." And that simplism is further simplified by those who think he is attacking "law" or "works" in general from the standpoint of "faith" as a means of "justification" (the Lutheran reading at the very heart of Protestantism). All such approaches misread the first and obvious intent of the letter, which was to reconcile all groups of Jews, telling them not to judge one another (Rom 2.1), since God, who plays no favorites (2.11), is on the side of them all: "There is no distinction between Jew and Gentile, since there is only one Lord over all, profuse toward all who call on him, and all who call on the Lord's name will be rescued" (10.12).

The important first thing to notice about the letter is that when Paul speaks of moving beyond God's Law he is speaking of two laws laid down by God—not only the Jewish Law given to Moses, but the natural law given to Gentiles. He contrasts both *laws* with a single *promise* given to *both* Jews and Gentiles, the promise to Abraham that he would be the father of many nations (4.13). Jesus moves beyond both *laws* by being the fulfillment of the single *promise*.

The law given to the Gentiles is graven not on stone tablets but in their hearts: "From the universe's framing, men have perceived his unseen attributes, knowable from what he has done—his boundless power and divinity. This left them no excuse, when, despite knowing there is a God, they did not acknowledge his splendor and give thanks for it" (1.20–21). "Even when not expressly given law, the nations acknowledge the law, finding, even without law, a kind of law in themselves—those at any rate who show the effects of law written in their hearts, calling conscience as their witness when they argue with each other over whether this party is wrong, that party right—against the day when God will sift the secret things of man, according to the revelation I bring, in Messiah-Jesus" (2.14–16). But simply knowing natural law does not make men follow nature. The Gentiles are, as a whole, sinners. Proud of their philosophy, they proved fools (1.22).

Nor does having God's express Law make Jews follow it. On the contrary, as prophet after prophet assured them, the Jews are a rebellious people (10.21)—and their rebellion brings dishonor on God's name among the Gentiles (2.24). God punishes the offenders against both laws, natural law and covenant Law, the Jews in the first place, since the Law was their special possession to honor, but also the Gentiles (2.10)—just as he chose in the first place the Jews, but also the Gentiles (1.16). "Are we Jews ahead? Not entirely. We have seen the single sentence against all of us, Jew and Gentile, for the reign of sin, just as scripture tells us, 'None, not one, is vindicated.' " (3.9–10). To shame the Jews, God has called in the Gentiles to share the blessings promised to Jews. He is using the Gentiles, as he used Pharaoh (9.17), to correct the Jews. For they will be corrected. Their defection is only temporary.

> I say they have been tripped up. Does that mean they have fallen? Far from it. Their tripping means rescue for the Gentiles, to stimulate the Jews to compete. If their tripping up enriches the rest of the universe, if their loss is the Gentiles' gain, how much greater will be their own restored gain. If their lapse has meant the winning over of the universe, what can their restoration mean but life rising up from death? (11.11, 15)

As Krister Stendahl puts it, the Letter to the Romans is about God's cosmic "traffic plan." The Jews have been put "on hold," to bring the Gentiles up to speed. "The Jews in God's plan had to step aside for a little while so that the Gentiles had time to come in."[1] This is God's surprise way of completing the promise issued in the first place:

> All Israel will be rescued, as scripture says: "Out of Zion comes the Rescuer, to rip away iniquities from Jacob, so my covenant abides with them, to remedy their sinfulness." (11.26–27)

Paul says that it is necessary to honor the Jewish Law, even though Gentiles are not required to observe all its ceremonial requirements. He even says that "Jesus is an attendant *(diakonos)* on circumcision" (Rom 15.8). Why is Paul making these points to the Romans? Remember the situation he is addressing, where the Gentile Brothers are receiving back the Jewish Brothers, after the Claudian expulsion ended. Some Gentile Brothers were not honoring the Jewish Brothers' wish to keep up their observance of the Law. Paul has to remind the Gentile Brothers that the promises fulfilled by Jesus are *Jewish* promises, and the memory of the promise was passed down under the protection of the Law. "Has circumcision any use at all? It matters a great deal, chiefly because they were the custodians of the pronouncements of God" (3.1–2). Gentiles must acknowledge that the Mosaic Law was the custodian ("pedagogue" he calls it at Galatians 3.24) of the revelation that Jesus fulfills. Gentiles are grafted on to the Jewish trunk. But for that trunk, they would be floating in air, unconnected with God's design for the world and its rescue. This reminder to the Gentile Brothers is rightly called by Stendahl the first and best warning against what would become Christian anti-Semitism:

> Some branches have been stripped away, and you, an alien olive branch, have been grafted on in their place and have taken on the life of the olive tree's original root—

which is no reason to crow over the replaced branches. However you may crow, you do not support the root—it supports you. Do you boast that those branches were stripped away to graft you in? Exactly. They were stripped away because they betrayed their trust. That is no reason for your elation, but for apprehension. If God did not spare those natural growths, why should he spare you? Consider God's beneficence, but also his rigor. His rigor was exercised against those who failed, and his beneficence toward you, provided you retain his beneficence, lest you too be cut away. And they will be grafted on again if they do not continue betraying their trust—it is easy for God to graft them on again, since you were unnaturally grafted when torn from an alien stock, but he can far more naturally graft them back on to their native tree.

I would impress this secret providence on you, Brothers, to keep you from confidence in your own conceit—that part of Israel has lost its vision, but only until the full number of Gentiles is brought in. Then all Israel will be rescued, as scripture says: "Out of Zion comes the Rescuer, to rip away iniquities from Jacob, so my covenant abides with them, to remedy their sinfulness." They are now foes to the revelation for your sake, but by their singling out they are the patriarchs' favored sons. God does not go back on what he gave them, they are his chosen ones. As you were outside the trust in God but are now spared, their betrayal of trust leads to your being spared—

but they will be spared in their turn. God provides for the betrayal of all to bring about the sparing of all. (11.17–32)

This optimism about God's inclusive plan hardly reflects the dark views of election, justification, and predestination that have been wrested out of the letter to the Romans. This is a letter of consolation and reconciliation: Paul did not think in terms of individual souls damned but of the rescue of whole peoples—indeed of the whole cosmos.

I would not count the suffering of this present order as at all comparable with the splendor that is to be unveiled for the offspring of God. The very frame of things is giddy with apprehension at what will be unveiled for the sons of God. The frame of things has been baffled, despite itself, by the one constraining it—yet with hope, since the whole frame will be liberated from its imprisoning decay, freed into the splendor of God's offspring. All this frame of things, we realize, has been moaning in the throes of some birth—and we, moreover, though we have the first harvest of the Spirit, moan along with it, yearning for full adoption as heirs and for the release of our bodies, saved by our trust. (8.18–24)

Even after some people admit the inclusiveness of Paul's hopeful vision for all peoples, they misunderstand him in any number of ways. To list just three:

1. Some think that he says the conversion of the Jews must precede the end of the world. But that would be grafting the trunk onto the branches. Paul speaks of the Brothers as joined to the Jewish promise, history, and fate, not vice versa. As Krister Stendahl says, Paul always thought of Gentiles as "honorary Jews."[2] How the original Jews and the honorary ones will be united at the climax of time is a mystery Paul leaves to God for accomplishment. He talks always of God's initiative, not man's. He does not know how the promise will be fulfilled, only that it will be, since God is the promiser. God's word must and will be kept. He never goes back on a promise (Rom 11.29). It is his responsibility. Our job is to trust in that word. "Does their betrayal of trust legitimate God's betraying his trust? Far from it. God will prove true though all men lie. As scripture has it: 'Whatever charge is brought against you, you are vindicated, in every judicial proceeding you prevail'" (3.4). "Has God rejected his own people? Far from it" (11.1).

2. Others have argued that Paul, since he does not see God canceling the Jewish Law, believes in a "two-track" rescue of mankind. Gentiles will believe in Jesus and Jews will stay with their Law, and only Gentiles will be rescued by Jesus. But Paul does not ever see Jesus as separate from the Jewish covenant and its fulfillment. Later generations would talk of conversion to Jesus as to a

separate religion, that of "the New Testament." It cannot
be repeated often enough that Paul knew of no New Testament, and no rescue but that of the promise given to
the Jewish people. He did not believe in a substitution of
a new way to be rescued. He did believe, with Jesus, that
the claims of the prophets had to be fulfilled, making a
religion of the heart replace that of external observances.
But he retained the core value of the Jewish Law, as both
Jesus and he affirmed it. "The entire Law is fulfilled in
this one saying, Love your neighbor as yourself" (Gal
5.14). "This is the Law and the prophets" (Mt 7.12).
Modern Jews no longer believe in the observance of animal sacrifice. Paul said that circumcision was a great
advantage, since it was the seal on the promise to Abraham. Though the promise was given before the seal was
affixed to it (4.12), Jewish Brothers are right to observe
the seal as a symbol of the promise. In the same way,
Paul tells the Romans to defer to the Jewish Brothers
who observe the food code, since that reaffirms the historic tie to God's covenant with his people. Nonetheless,
Jesus is the fulfillment of the Jewish scripture, not of
some separate revelation. Jesus believed in a religion of
the heart that would oppose later Christian religious observance as much as any Jewish ceremonies. Jesus
founded no new religion, and Paul preached none.

3. A deeper misunderstanding of Paul's inclusiveness

would move off entirely from the Jewish-Gentile issue. It turns the contrasts between a religion of the heart and that of the external purity code into Luther's contrast between faith and works. Luther said that faith in God alone "justifies" a person, apart from any virtuous acts. Paul was saying that observing external acts—like circumcision, prescribed holy days, and kosher law—is not a substitute for the internal acts of the Law, for love of God and one's neighbor. He calls this interior observance a "circumcision of the heart" (Rom 2.29). Paul criticized as sinners those Jews who departed from this internal law, just as he criticized Gentiles who departed from the natural law given them by God.

Luther was thinking in terms of the internal struggle of the individual sinner, not of the rescue of whole peoples, as Paul did—and as a prominent Lutheran bishop like Krister Stendahl does. Paul saw God's plan as dealing "wholesale," not retail. He was in a race with history, on his way to Spain, recruiting Romans in his effort to cover the whole Gentile world while he went back to bring the Jewish Brothers "on board" this mission. He was counting on the Jewish Brothers to bring their countrymen to a realization that Jesus is the one they had been promised and were still hoping for. His message was always of and for his—and Jesus'— blood kin.

NOTES

1. Krister Stendahl, *Final Account: Paul's Letter to the Romans* (Fortress Press, 1995), pp. 6–7.

2. Krister Stendahl, *Paul Among Jews and Gentiles* (Fortress Press, 1976), p. 37.

8. Paul and Jerusalem

✝

PAUL'S CONTINUING STRUGGLE with the Jerusalem church is made clear in his concern to fulfill what he agreed to in his first clash with it—that he should "keep in mind the needy" of Jerusalem. Much of the extant letters is devoted to making up the great fund for Jerusalem, a matter that became an obsession with him. He saw the collection as a bridge to the Jewish Brothers in Judaea, and even perhaps to the whole body of Jews. He was organizing the collection on a grand scale, one to rival the immense Temple tax payments that poured into Jerusalem annually from the millions of Diaspora Jews. He told the Corinthians how they could accumulate a considerable sum.

> With regard to the collection for the Holy, you should follow the procedures I arranged in the Galatian gathering. Every Sabbath you should lay aside for saving some portion of your income, so it need not all be raised when I come. Once I am with you, I shall send representatives chosen by you with letters to carry your spontaneous favor *(charis)* to Jerusalem, myself going with them if that seems best. (1 Cor 16.1–4)

It became a massive operation. Each Diaspora gathering of the Brothers was to send a number of representatives with its offering. Paul was waiting to see whether his presence among them would be helpful or not—he had reason to worry about that. The result could be seen as a visible knitting together of the whole body of Jesus, in reciprocal care of each member for all others. Or might it be seen, and possibly resented, as a demonstration of the great superiority of numbers in the Diaspora Brotherhood over the Jerusalem gathering? With such a large-scale activity, might his foes suspect that Paul was trying to equal, perhaps to surpass, even to ridicule, the Temple tax that observant Jews sent? Paul will worry at such issues as he devotes increasing energy to his great scheme.

In his troubled later correspondence with the Corinthians, the collection has become hostage to the multiple misunderstandings in that city's gatherings. In an atmosphere of spreading distrust, questions have arisen about the safe and honest collecting of such a large sum. To deal with the controversy, Paul has asked the gatherings to choose neutral overseers of the collection, who will collaborate with Titus, the man the Corinthians accepted as Paul's spokesperson. Titus has been collecting sums in Macedonia, which—though the region is not as wealthy as Corinth—has proved spectacularly generous. Now Paul tries to coax the Corinthians, who are resisting, into at least matching the Macedonian contributions:

We have asked Titus, who set in motion this spontaneous favor from you, to bring it to fulfillment.
Abounding as you do in faith, profession, love, and in
every great effort—as well as in the love we share—
abound as well in this spontaneous favor. I issue no order here. By mentioning the effort of others, I would
impress them with the soundness of your love. You are
aware how our Lord, Jesus-Messiah, has favored you,
how from being rich he became poor for you, that his
poverty might enrich you. My opinion on this is all I can
give you, which is for your advantage. You yourselves
led the way last year, not only by your actions but in
your eagerness to act. Now you should complete what
you began, matching your desire to give with actual giving, according to your means. The desire is approved if
one gives within one's means, not beyond them. Relief
of the Holy should not come from your deprivation, but
a balance should be struck between your present having
and their want, so that one day their having may supply
your want, balancing things out, according to scripture:
"The one taking much [of manna in the desert] did not
have too much, nor did the one taking little have too little." (2 Cor 8.6–15)

For Paul, this interplay of giving and receiving among the
gatherings was just the material expression of members' reci-
procity in the body of Jesus:

For God has tempered all parts of the body, giving special attention to the lesser parts, to prevent internal division of the body with itself, all taking a common care of one another, so that if one part grieves they all grieve, and if one part thrives, they all take pride in it. You are Messiah's body, each part having its role. (1 Cor 12.24–26)

After Paul has decided to lead the delegations with their offerings toward Jerusalem, he informs the Romans (whom he has not yet visited) of his plan. Before, he had talked of balancing present giving with future receiving, as if Jerusalem might one day have a material surplus to render back to the Diaspora gatherings. Now he talks of a *simultaneous* balance to be struck between material giving and spiritual receiving. Jerusalem has already given the riches of its Jewish legacy to Diaspora gatherings, the promise of the covenant and the heritage of the prophets fulfilled in the life of Messiah. This is the most direct tribute he has ever paid to the Jerusalem Brothers. (As we have said, he means for the Jerusalem gathering to read these words.)

At this moment I am off for Jerusalem, in service to the Holy there, since Macedonia and Achaia have decided to express their oneness with the needs of the Holy in Jerusalem. They decided this out of a feeling of indebtedness to them. Since the nations were at one with the spiritual gifts of the Holy there, they thought it right to minister to their material needs. When I have finished with this, and sealed my part in their endeavor, I will stop by with you on my way to Spain. (Rom 15.25–28)

Despite his confidence about a mission to Spain, he betrays his uneasiness over the Jerusalem trip:

> But I entreat you by our Lord, Jesus-Messiah, and by the love of the Spirit, take part in my ordeal by praying to God for me, that I may escape the rejectionists in Judaea, and that my service to Jerusalem may be taken in good part by the Holy there, that I may reach you in good spirits by the will of God, and be tranquil in your company. (Rom 15.30–33)

He has two concerns, his physical safety among the rejectionists (*apeithountes*, literally the "unpersuaded") and his spiritual acceptance by the Jerusalem Brothers.

Paul's relations with the Jerusalem Brothers, for all Luke's efforts to disguise the fact, were always strained when not downright hostile. But if this was the case, why did Paul risk a dangerous trip there? He had earlier said that the delegates from the various cities might go without him. With the misgivings he expressed to the Romans, why did he change his mind? We have to remember that he was planning to take the revelation to a whole new level of expansion, using Rome as a base to go into Spain. The roving emissaries of Jerusalem and the other gatherings posed a threat to unity he would not want to leave behind him. His long Letter to the Romans sets up a kind of fulcrum on which he wants to unite the new areas with the old. His long efforts in different cities to raise the collection were a continuing assurance to the old center that he was not forgetting them, cutting himself off, launching into the unknown with no umbilical cord back to the center— not only to Jerusalem, but to cities in close contact with it, and to groups within all the gatherings that circulated Brothers back to the city of the Temple and of Jesus' death and resurrection. Paul no doubt hoped that he was doing repair work on relations with Jerusalem, not only in the climax of his effort, the actual journey there, but in the well-publicized activity he and his team members were engaged in throughout the Diaspora to "keep in mind the needy" of Jerusalem.

After this dramatic buildup for the delivery of the great collection, we topple over into an abyss of silence about the collection's ultimate fate. Paul can tell us no more (Romans is counted his last extant letter) and Luke, if he knew what happened to the great sum, is not going to let us in on it. He brings Paul to an audience with James, where the collection is not mentioned (Ac 21.18–25). James warns Paul against enmity in the circumcised Brotherhood, and tells him he can defuse this by paying the Temple expenses of four members of the Nazarite (oath-taking) community. But in Luke's version of things the advice of James backfires. Some Jews seize on

Paul's presence in the Temple to claim that he contaminated it with Gentile associates. They arrest him and prepare to execute him (raising that old Luke problem of Jewish jurisdiction over capital punishment) when Roman soldiers intervene. The Romans are about to flog Paul when he claims that they are not allowed to beat a Roman citizen (Ac 22.25). Where, in this flurry of activity, has the collection gone? We do not know. But scholars are probably right in thinking that Paul's misgivings about his reception from James and his fellow Brothers were confirmed. That is the kind of information Luke would not want to memorialize—remember how he omitted any mention of Paul's conflict with Peter at Antioch.

Why would the Jerusalem Brothers resent a sizable collection taken up for their benefit? Walther Schmithals argues that James and his fellows were having trouble maintaining their identity against Jews who did not accept Jesus—a hostility that would soon claim the life of James himself. To have Paul's perhaps largely Gentile contingent of uncircumcised Brothers bringing material resources to James could make his position ever more difficult, even untenable. "The Jerusalem church was already then struggling for the last chance of missionary work in Israel. If it accepted Paul's contributions, then it was declaring in the eyes of the Jews its solidarity with him. This threatened to destroy the possibility of its own mission."[1]

Dieter Georgi even suggests that it was Paul's intent to

force the hand of James by an act of deliberate provocation, making James give up his hypocrisy as Peter was challenged to do in Antioch. "The great number of uncircumcised Gentile believers [bringing the collection] was bound to exacerbate the difficulties, tensions, and risks [for James]. The unconditional acceptance of the collection would have constituted a highly compromising step in the eyes of the local Jewish congregation."[2] Georgi suspects that Paul was trying to bring on an eschatological showdown, in which the Jews would be forced to accept the Messiah. This gives the collection for the needy an immense load of possibly catastrophic meaning:

> A program of this kind was bound to become a provocation. To judge by Romans 11.11–24, more than being simply aware of this, Paul had made it his declared intent. He hoped that his mission among the Gentiles and their conversion to the Christ faith right in front of the Jews would have the effect of a permanent "irritation" to the Jews, and that the salvation of the latter would eventually result from that irritation. The salvation he had in mind, however, was not one of individual Jews, but one involving the whole world in one universal eschatological miracle (Rom 11.25–36), corresponding in its nature to the collective conversion of the peoples at large, an expectation already present in certain parts of Jewish Scriptures and in certain branches of Judaism. Paul's mission had, therefore, become a symbolic act like the symbolic

acts of the biblical prophets. They, too, had often intended to disturb the security Israel derived from the traditonal ideology of salvation. And as was the case with the prophets, so now Paul's provocative thoughts and actions were based heavily on Israelite and Jewish traditions, which would provide the necessary symbolic frame of reference.[3]

But if Paul were going to Jerusalem to trigger the great showdown and end of history, why would he be laying plans to visit Rome and take the revelation to Spain? Besides, he seemed less worried about provoking Jews than about offending James and the Brothers.

It must be admitted, however, that Schmithals and Georgi are right in seeing some deep theological meaning that Paul had invested in the collection for Jerusalem. The nature of that meaning is hard to recover. Paul took his mystery with him into the darkness that descends on his last years. What does seem clear is that his view of things generally was not that of James and the Brothers in Jerusalem, try as he did to effect a reconciliation in his spectacular last journey there. He had been prickly in showing that James had not summoned him earlier, that he went because of "a vision." By contrast, in his last trip, he said he was meeting the obligation incurred in his earlier trip, the agreement to keep in mind the needy. Beyond that, he was repaying the great spiritual debt he and all the Diaspora Jews owed to the original scene of Jesus' re-demptive acts.

If we admit some clash between the Jerusalem gatherings and those of the Diaspora, are we not endorsing the view that Paul departed from the original revelation ("gospel") as well as the original scene of Jesus' revelation? We must not fall into some fallacy of firstness here. The easy assumption would be that the Jerusalem gatherings were closer to Jesus' life, death, and meaning than were Brothers in the Diaspora. But remember that our first reports on the gatherings' faith are from Paul. Presence in Jerusalem was no guarantee of fidelity. In fact, the ascendancy of James and the other brothers of the Lord—he had four brothers, including Joseph, Judas, and Simon (Mk 6.3)—after the death of Jesus is a matter for surprise. They had been at odds with Jesus during his lifetime, when "not even his brothers gave him credence" (Jn 7.5). His family, in fact, "tried to take him into custody" (Mk 3.21). Their townspeople tried to throw Jesus over a cliff (Lk 4.29). Jesus was notably cool toward his family members, including his mother (Mk 3.33–35, Lk 11.27–28, Jn 2.4).

If there is any split between Jerusalem and the Pauline gatherings, the real firstness we should look to is Paul's temporal precedence over the Jerusalem reports of Luke. Remember that in the clash with Peter and Barnabas, Barnabas and Paul ended up on the same side (1 Cor 9.6)—as Peter and Paul probably did in their continued Diaspora activity (away from

James), concluding with their deaths in Rome. The genuine meaning of Jesus is to be sought in Paul's revelation, not that of James, in the Diaspora and not in Jerusalem. The Gospels, we should note, were also written in the Diaspora. Few claim, anymore, that they were written in Jerusalem, or even in Judaea.

Luke's Chronology

MUCH OF THE DISPUTE over Luke's account of Paul has to do with his placement of the Jerusalem conference in the chronology of Paul's mission, over which Luke has been the principal (for some the sole) guide. There was for a long time a tendency to save as much as possible of Luke's account, since he was thought to provide the only fixed (nonrelative) date in the whole story. He says that during Paul's first trip to Corinth he was tried in front of the proconsul Gallio (Ac 18.12). An inscription found at Delphi dates Gallio's proconsulship to 51–52 CE. This has been seized on as the pivot on which all other dates could be surmised, as preceding or following the one sure point.

But John Knox noted the ideological usefulness of this point to Luke. By dating the trip to Corinth *after* the Jerusalem encounter, as late as 52 CE, Luke was able to suggest that Paul's preceding work was a kind of apprenticeship under Barnabas, and that Paul's launch out into the fully Gentile world of Europe was done under the aegis of the Jerusalem decree. If this was true, then there was a strange bunching of Paul's extant work and letters *after* 52 CE, a mere decade before his death during which much of his time was (according to Luke himself) spent in prison, while the seventeen years *before* the Jerusalem encounter were comparatively barren of results. And if, on the one hand, Paul's actions and writing were compressed in the last ten years, his collection for Jerusalem must be squeezed into the early part of that time, before his final imprisonments. Knox argues, instead, that when Paul finally went to the Jerusalem "Council," "he had reached the zenith of his career. He had labored in Galatia and Asia, *in Macedonia and Greece*" (emphasis added).[4]

Some try to reduce the problem by trimming the time before the Jerusalem encounter from seventeen to fourteen years. They argue that when Paul said he went first to Jerusalem three years after his calling by Jesus, and then stayed away for fourteen years, he was dating the second period from his calling, not from his first trip to Jerusalem. But if you say that you have gone to a place after three years and then went back after another fourteen, the category remains the same—the time of the visits, not of some preceding event.

Once Knox broke the spell that Luke cast over chronological charts, people began to see many things wrong with the account in Acts. This has led even to skepticism about the one fixed date that everyone relied on, the appearance before Gallio in 51–52 CE. Donald Harman Akenson writes:

> The date is treasured because all the relative chronology of Saul's life suddenly can be hung on a real-world "absolute" date. It is usually cited as the sole absolute dating point in the entire mass of material related to the great Apostle. We want it to be accurate, very, very much. But remember the rule: because of the demonstrable inaccuracy of Acts on many issues on which it can be checked, the grounds of presumption have to be that this event did not take place. Of those events unconfirmed in Saul's letters, it is no different from any other of the events reported in Acts, so no matter how desperately we desire the convenience of an absolute date, it has to be set aside as untrustworthy (again, not necessarily as untrue, but as not commanding trust).[5]

Others see Luke's theological program at work in the Gallio story:

> All of that is much more likely Lukan parable than Pauline history. It is, indeed, Luke's first and most paradigmatic combination of Jewish accusation, Pauline innocence, and Roman dismissal. Look, therefore, at our picture of Corinth's *bema* [tribunal] and see it as a Lukan metaphor for the proper attitude of Rome toward Christianity in

general and as a Lukan symbol of the appropriate response of Rome to Paul in particular. Nothing, however,
in this book presumes the historical actuality of that encounter with Gallio at Corinth or builds the chronological biography of Paul upon its information.[6]

Of course, one need not conclude that Paul was never tried
by Gallio in order to alter Luke's chronology. Paul surely appeared twice in Corinth, probably an intended third time, and
perhaps more (it was a troubled spot much in need of care).
He could have had some judicial moment with Gallio in a later
visit. That would fit with the view of increasing numbers of
scholars who follow Knox's skepticism in questioning Luke's
timetables. They believe Paul took his revelation to Europe
before the Jerusalem encounter that, in Luke's view, validated
it. He no longer has to be seen as receiving his mission to the
nations and then delaying it for seventeen (or fourteen or
whatever) years in order to be blessed by the "apparent leaders" in Jerusalem. These revisions of the old chronology allow
us to recover the original Paul from Luke's sanitized—
"Jerusalemized"—version of his career.

NOTES

1. Walther Schmithals, *Paul and James* (Alec R. Allenson, 1965),
p. 82.

2. Dieter Georgi, *Remembering the Poor: The History of Paul's Collection for Jerusalem* (Abingdon Press, 1992), p. 125.

3. Ibid., p. 118.

4. John Knox, *Chapters in a Life of Paul,* revised edition (Peeters, 1987), p. 40.

5. Donald Harman Akenson, *Saint Saul: A Skeleton Key to the Historical Jesus* (Oxford University Press, 2000), p. 142.

6. John Dominic Crossan and Jonathan L. Reed, *In Search of Paul: How Jesus' Apostle Opposed Rome's Empire with God's Kingdom* (HarperSanFrancisco, 2004), p. 34.

9. Paul and Rome

✝

AFTER PAUL WRITES his Letter to the Romans, we have no more words from him. We must rely on Luke's Acts for his travel to Jerusalem, his treatment there, and his putative final journey toward execution in Rome. The key to the Jerusalem events as presented by Luke is Paul's Roman citizenship. The Jews try to kill him, but he asserts his right as a Roman citizen to be tried in Rome—a dubious right, but just one of many dubious things in Luke's account, including Paul's citizenship. Paul never calls himself a Roman citizen. In fact, he never names a Roman magistrate before whom he appeared. The closest he comes is a reference to one of Rome's client kings, Aretas, whose agent tried to capture him in Damascus (2 Cor 11.32)—Luke's version of that event omits the Roman connection and says simply that the Jews attempted his murder (Ac 9.23–25). The only actual Roman official Paul refers to is a Brother in Rome who had held a provincial office as fund manager *(oikonomos)* in Corinth (Rom 16.23). Paul was not singling the man out for his rank in this list of those to be greeted in Rome. Since Erastus was a common name, he probably called him "Erastus the fund manager" to distinguish him from other Erastuses.

There are several reasons to doubt Luke's claim that Paul was a Roman citizen. Paul says that he was three times flogged by Roman officials, apart from the five times he was whipped by Jews (2 Cor 11.25)—but flogging Roman citizens was against the law. As Cicero put it in the second trial of Verres (5.66), "It is forbidden to chain a Roman citizen, it is criminal to flog him, it is practically an act of parricide to execute him." Some exceptions to this immunity have been unearthed, but are we to suppose that exceptional circumstances were found for Paul on eight different occasions (presumably in eight different locales)? This would make us conclude not only that the Romans were regularly willing to break their own law, but that the Jews repeatedly risked official anger by flogging a Roman citizen in their synagogues.

The lengths people will go to support Luke's dubious account (in this and many other areas) is shown by Rainer Riesner, who says that Paul might have waived his immunity from flogging in order to be more like Jesus: "Should one not suppose that the apostle, from the perspective of his understanding of the suffering Christ, consciously took such mistreatment upon himself? We should be cautious about precipitately classifying as psychopathological a phenomenon alien to modern secularized Christianity."[1] That Paul, already struggling with epilepsy (or whatever his debilitating "thorn in the flesh" was), would gladly risk his health further when he had missionary work to do is simply unthinkable.

As it turns out, Paul's citizenship backfires on him according to Luke's account. Paul invokes it when Festus, the governor of Caesarea, threatens to send him back to Jerusalem, where the Jews are threatening his life (Ac 25.9). But after Festus refers the matter to Rome, he invites King Agrippa, ruler of the Judaean tetrarchy, to attend a hearing on Paul's presumed offenses. The king is so impressed by Paul that he says, "With a little more persuading you make me a Christian" (26.28). Agrippa then tells Festus privately (how would Luke know this?): "The man could have been freed had he not appealed to the emperor" (26.32). Paul ends up a captive of his own legal "protection."

All Luke's handling of Roman officials is suspect. He artificially arranges for Paul to appear before *four* different tribunals in Jerusalem-Caesarea, where Paul shines and wins sympathy. In one case, the governor's wife is won over by Paul (Ac 24.24). Luke seems to know the story of Pilate's wife sympathizing with Jesus (Mt 27.19), though he did not use it in his own Gospel. At any rate, he draws many parallels between Paul's hearings—before high priests, Sanhedrin, Roman magistrates, and a Herodian king—and Jesus' shuttling back and forth between similar tribunals. It is the same technique Luke had used in creating similarities between Jesus' death and that of Stephen.

Luke, it has been noticed, is as easy on Roman authorities as he is harsh on Jewish ones. He has an almost snobbish interest in officials and wealthy people who are kind to those of the Path, reflecting the need of Luke's churches to cultivate good relations with the Empire. We have also seen that he tries to suppress or soften any clashes between Paul and the Jerusalem Brothers. He not only omitted the blowup between Paul and Peter in Antioch, but offers a strange tale of Paul's reception on his last trip to Jerusalem. Paul had come, remember, to deliver the fund he had collected for the Jewish Brothers. He had feared that James would not receive the offering with grace or favor—and clearly he did not, since Luke has them meet and not even discuss the matter. This was clearly impossible, so whatever happened was so embarrassing to Luke's purpose that he had to excise it from the record. Instead, James is shown warning Paul against Jewish enmities. To disarm that animus, he suggests that Paul should go to the Temple to purify himself (a normal enough procedure after travel in "unclean" countries)—and instead of delivering a fund, proposes that Paul should donate money to some Nazirites (vow takers) for their own purification expenses. This advice, too, backfires, since it is while in the Temple that Paul is seized by Jews who claim he is defiling it. These Jews try Paul and turn him over to the Romans for execution.

This whole matter is fishy. Luke has earlier (Ac 18.18) made Paul himself, during his travels, take a Nazirite vow, letting his hair grow until he had discharged the period of his vow (Hebrew *nazir* means "vow"). Luke does not say why Paul should have done such a thing, and it goes against his whole campaign to make Gentile practice acceptable. Both these vow episodes are totally out of character for Paul, since the Nazirite vow involved the most extreme shunning of "unclean" things (Num 6.2–21), and Paul had written: "I know, relying on the Lord Jesus, that nothing is unclean of itself. Only if a man supposes it unclean does it become unclean for him" (Rom 14.14).

Luke sends Paul off toward Rome, after two years in prison in Caesarea, and has him spend another three months on the island of Malta after a shipwreck. When Paul finally reaches Rome, he is put under house arrest, treated leniently while awaiting trial—and then what? Then nothing. Tradition will say that Paul and Peter, along with a large crowd of Brothers, were killed by Nero as scapegoats for the Roman fire of 64 CE, which destroyed ten of the city's fourteen districts. The tradition has Paul beheaded and Peter crucified, since Paul as a Roman citizen could not be crucified. Actually, the reference to crucifixion in Tacitus's account shows manuscript corruption, and it may have been added by a Christian copyist to accommodate the legend of Peter's death. Tacitus says that Nero's victims were given most "original" *(quaesitissimae)* forms of execution. Tacitus specifies sewing them up in animal skins and letting dogs rend them, or smearing them with pitch and lighting them up at night as garden lamps. Crucifixion was not an "original" form of punishment but a common one. Mention of it does not belong in Tacitus's passage.

It is not surprising the Luke does not want to tell this story. Nero, in effect, destroyed one of Luke's principal theses, that Christians were a peace-loving people who won the respect of Roman authorities. Nero could not have expected to shift blame to the Brothers if they were a respected minority. Tacitus says that Nero made torturing the Brothers a "popular amusement" because the victims were such "foes of human society." But he says something even more damaging to the story of the church's growth that Luke wants to tell. He says that the vast majority of the victims were identified *by informants in their own number.* Apparently the factions that Paul wrote to reconcile—that is, the Jewish Brothers and the Gentile Brothers—had become even more hostile to each other, a development we shall find confirmed in a letter from Clement of Rome. Here is what Tacitus says in his *Annals* (15.44):

> Nero, in order to quash the rumor [that he caused the fire himself], found substitute perpetrators and subjected them to the most original forms of execution. These were the ones popularly called Christians, a group hated for its abominations *(flagitia).* They take their name from a

Christ who was executed by the procurator Pontius Pilate when Tiberius was emperor.

This vile superstition was thus checked for a time but then it broke out again, not only in Judaea, the source of the malady, but in our city, where all that is outlandish or detestable drains in and gets a following. At first the open practitioners were arrested, and by their informing *(indicio eorum)* a vast multitude was taken, not only for setting the fire as for being the foes of human society. Their executions were made a form of public amusement *(ludibria)*, since dogs tore them apart after they were sewn up in animal skins [or they were crucified or flames . . .] or, after nightfall, they were set on fire to serve as lamps. Nero turned over his gardens to these exhibitions and made games of them in the Circus, where he joined the crowd costumed as a charioteer or simply sitting in his chariot—so that, despite the victims' guilt, which merited extreme punishment, there was a reaction of pity, since they seemed to be served up not for the safety of all but for the sadism of one.

That passage could be interpreted to mean that Nero's agents first arrested some Jews who were not Brothers, and that these turned in the Jews who were Brothers. But the best (if indirect) evidence for what happened comes from the aforementioned letter from Clement of Rome. He writes as a scribe for the whole Roman community of Brothers, and the

letter is dated to the nineties CE—that is, about three decades
after Nero's response to the fire in the city. In Clement's time,
the Brothers in Corinth are still engaged in loud internal conflicts, and the Romans write counseling calm and referring to
enmities that had earlier rent their own community.

The letter is long and carefully argued, with many proof
texts from scripture denouncing strife *(eris)* and division *(stasis)* and calling for mutual forbearance and love. It quotes to
the Corinthians what Paul had written to them decades earlier, the praise of love as supreme. It is reasonably supposed
that all these arguments were not elaborated just for long-
distance advising to another community. They were probably
worked out in trying to solve Rome's own problems, including those that led to the deaths of Peter and Paul. They are
placed at the climax to a series of "case studies" of the effect of
"rivalrous grudges" (the hendiadys *zēlos kai phthonos*). Each
of these cases involves betrayal *by one's own*, either one's
own family or one's own people, so the deaths of Peter and
Paul must involve that too, or there would be no point in the
selection of these parallels for them. The carefully wrought
passage uses anaphora (repeating *zēlos* at the beginning) to
structure the cases:

A *rivalrous* grudge caused the fratricide of Abel by Cain.
From *rivalry* father Jacob fled the presence of his
brother, Esau. *Rivalry* caused Joseph to be threatened

with death and betrayed into slavery. *Rivalry* forced
Moses to flee Pharaoh's presence when those of his own
blood asked, "Who gave you rule over us—would you
kill us as you slew yesterday the Egyptian?" By *rivalry*
were Aaron and Miriam ostracized from the encamp-
ment. *Rivalry* carried Dathan and Abiram, while still
living, into Hades, since they sowed division *(stasis)*
among the followers of Moses, God's servant. From *rivalry* David suffered not only the foreigners' grudge
(phthonos) but was hounded by Saul, who was Israel's
own king. But enough of ancient cases. Turn we now to
the glorious prize winners *(athlētai)* of recent time; take
we up the model of our own age. From a *rivalrous
grudge* our most prominent and approved pillars were
hounded and they won the prize *(ethlēsan)* of death. Put
we before your gaze our own emissaries. From *rivalry*
Peter suffered not one or two but many ordeals and, offering his life as witness, achieved his merited rank of
honor. From *rivalrous strife* Paul won through to the
trophy for endurance. Though seven times in captivity,
though put to flight, though stoned, this herald of the
faith in both the East and West won a sterling reputation
for his belief, teaching all the world about the right rela-
tionship with God. After he had reached the farthest
term of the West, he offered the authorities the witness
of his life, escaped this world, and entered the sacred
precinct, the very prototype of endurance. (1 Clement,
paragraphs 4–5)

Though it is not said in Luke's Acts, or anywhere else in the New Testament, not even in the pseudo-Pauline letters written years later, that Paul died in Rome, this letter makes that clear—not so much because the gathering that wrote it shows intimate details of the two men's deaths as because it ascribes those deaths to Brothers' "rivalrous grudges"— which meshes perfectly with what Tacitus wrote about the Christian informers in Rome.

The letter gets further confirmation from one written only a few years later, by Ignatius of Antioch. Ignatius, traveling toward Rome, says that he wants to be martyred there and asks the Brothers not to prevent this. He adds to his request this note: "I cannot put you under obligation, as Peter and Paul did. They were emissaries, I am a mere prisoner. They were free, I a slave" (To the Romans, paragraph 4.3). It is interesting that neither Clement nor Ignatius describes Peter and Paul as anything but emissaries. Ignatius is the bishop of Antioch, where he too has been betrayed by Brothers, and he makes much of the bishop's office, addressing the bishop in every other locale he writes a letter to—but to no bishop in Rome. Peter was never the bishop of Rome. Of course, he was a latecomer there, even later than Paul, who did not include him in the Brothers he addressed in the letter to Rome.

It should be noticed that Clement saves Paul for the climactic example in his list of those betrayed, and describes his career far more fully than he does that of Peter. This is not surprising. Paul had a large group of fellow missionaries assembled in Rome by the time he wrote his letter there. If, as Luke indicates, the trip to Jerusalem misfired for Paul, if the fund was not well received, if the Jews (whether Brothers or not) caused him trouble and delayed his arriving in Rome for years, then the Pauline team would have had time to organize and proselytize, gaining new recruits for their project. This probably had something to do with the fact that Tacitus can refer to a vast multitude *(multitudo ingens)* of believers caught in his dragnet of victims. It should be remembered, too, that a minority informed on this majority. That would fit with the idea that the returning Jewish Brothers found a thriving Gentile Brothers community in place after the six years of exile under Claudius—not to mention that a devoted group of Paul's followers had entered the situation and extended its influence while he was gone. Paul and Peter were both members of the betrayed party—themselves Jewish Brothers, they would have stood with the Gentile Brothers, as befits their status as emissaries in the Diaspora.

Clement seems to tell us something more about Paul. Luke says he went to Rome and was under house arrest, presumably to stand trial for some charge Festus sent ahead with him—Luke suggests no charge more specific than causing trouble among Jerusalem's Jews. Clement does not indicate

that Paul was killed because of any legal proceeding that orig-
inated in Jerusalem. He tells us something far more
interesting—that Paul taught "all the world" after "he had
reached the farthest term of the West." This indicates that he
did in fact lead his mission team to Spain, after the Jerusalem
case against him failed.

Legend says that James, one of the Twelve, was the emissary who took the faith to Spain, but it is far more likely, and
more fitting, to think that Paul did it, that his careful plan to
go there with a team of missionaries was finally carried out,
despite many intervening obstacles. But if that is the case,
why do no further letters tell us of this mission? The troubles
in Rome may have called Paul back, and anything he wrote
about those troubles was too sad or disheartening to be preserved. *Nothing* direct is preserved on the believers' side of
the final disgrace of internal division in Rome and the death
of the two greatest emissaries there. The only direct evidence
is that of the pagan Tacitus. Clement and Ignatius give us only
indirect (discreet) evidence. The most plausible guess about
what happened is that Paul came back to deal with the conflicts between the Brothers, and fell as one of the victims of
the informers' dirty work with Nero. If this is the case, then
he followed his divine master in one final respect. They were
both killed by religion.

Clement chimes with Tacitus, as well, in saying that Peter
underwent "not one or two but many ordeals" and that Paul

"won through to the trophy of endurance." This may be the Roman community's uneasy way of remembering the "original forms of execution" Nero invented as a public amusement. If the two great emissaries died under Nero, then Peter was not crucified, either upside down or right side up, and the citizen status Luke foisted on Paul had nothing to do with his death. They probably died in one of the obscene ways Tacitus describes, torn apart in animal costumes or serving as ornamental torches in Nero's garden. This was not an end Luke could bring himself to set down. One comfort is to realize that Peter and Paul, who had clashed bitterly in Antioch, died as comrades.

We have no description of their bearing at the end. But it is safe to think that Paul, who had not been cowed or deterred by endless sufferings, from the thorn in his flesh, from shipwrecks, from floggings, from imprisonments, was not one to flinch from the last blow. He had earlier said that he wanted to die and be with the risen Jesus, the God he had seen directly. With that as a stay, he would not waver: "I have learned self-reliance in any situation. I know how to get along with little or with a lot. Experience has given me an edge over any or all turns, to cope with fullness or hunger, with surplus or deprivation. I am up to any test so long as he gives me strength for it" (Phil 4.11–13).

We do not know what his last words were. But his last words for us, the ones we may well turn to as we face our own final test, are these:

God with us, who is to oppose? If he spared not his own Son, but gave him up for us all, how can every other favor not be given with that one? Who can reject the ones he chooses? Where God vindicates, who can incriminate? The dead man is Messiah—say rather the risen man, now at God's right hand, and taking our cause. What, then, can sunder us from the Messiah's love? Will dire straits, impasse, persecution, starvation, nakedness, peril, or the sword? Scripture says, "We are dying for you all day, nothing but sheep to be cut down," yet in every way we win the victory because of the one who loves us. I am firmly convinced that neither death nor life, neither angels nor supremacies, neither present nor future force, not what is already or what will be, not any powers, no high thing, no low thing, not some other frame of things, can keep us away from the love of God that is in Messiah-Jesus, our Lord. (Rom 8.31–39)

NOTE

1. Rainer Riesner, *Paul's Early Period,* translated by Doug Stott (Eerdmans, 1998), p. 150.

Afterword: Misreading Paul

✝

IT IS NOT HARD to see why Bernard Shaw thought the world would have been better off had Paul never lived. Consider, out of many cases illustrating this, one typically bleak Pauline moment in history, from the history of the Massachusetts Bay Colony. Anne Hutchinson crossed the Atlantic to follow a vision hatched from Paul's Letter to the Romans. She was seeking a "justification" that would free her from her own dark and baffled quest for virtue. She knew only one pastor who could assuage her longing, John Cotton, and he had left England for Boston. She, with her husband and children, followed Cotton in 1633. She championed Cotton against all the other ministers of New England.

He had taught her an extreme version of what Luther took from Paul (Rom 3.20), that observing "the works of the law" avails not at all toward "justification." She took this to mean that any pastors urging people to do virtuous deeds were preaching "a covenant of works" that undermined the real Gospel (the covenant of grace). She engaged in competitive helplessnesses so far as all human effort was concerned. To do this, she gathered a group of women in her home to correct what they were hearing in church. These women were gradually joined by some of their husbands or male relatives. When Cotton became leery of where she was taking his teaching, she came to believe that only she was true to the real covenant of grace. Her flaunted helplessness became a self-confidence that she could lay down the law for everyone else, because it was not she but the Spirit within her that was speaking—an arrogance that often issues from Pauline "humility."

The male authorities of church and state in Boston fought genuine Pauline teaching (however misunderstood) with pseudo-Pauline strictures (understood all too domineeringly well). They invoked against her the letter of "Paul" saying, "I forbid a woman to teach" (1 Tim 2.12). She countered from another pseudo-Pauline letter, to Titus (Tit 2.4), saying the older women should teach the younger. But her accusers caught her up on what the elders were to teach their young sisters—"to be submissive to their husbands" (Tit 2.5). She was teaching men, not women, and teaching them contempt for their pastors. She could not win any game where "Paul" could trump Paul. It is hard to tell which was the more blighting influence, real Paul or fake Paul, in this exchange—or in any of thousands of transactions where the ability to use Paul for dark purposes has been evident.

The heart of the problem is this. Paul entered the bloodstream of Western civilization mainly through one artery, the vein carrying a consciousness of sin, of guilt, of the tortured conscience. This is the Paul we came to know through the brilliant self-examinations of Augustine and Luther, of Calvin and Pascal and Kierkegaard. The profound writings of these men and their followers, with all their vast influence, amount to a massive misreading of Paul, to a historic misleading of the minds of the minds of people down through the centuries—or so goes the argument of Bishop Krister Stendahl. In 1961 Stendahl gave a short but incisive lecture to the American Psychological Association, a work he called "The Apostle Paul and the Introspective Conscience of the West."[1] He argues that Luther and his followers took Paul's argument for freedom from the externals of the Mosaic code as a confession of his own inability to follow moral law in general. They read as autobiography Paul's exclamation at Romans 7.22–24: "In my inner self, I am pleased with God's Law. But I observe another law in my limbs doing battle with the law in my mind, holding me prisoner to the law of sin in my limbs. Miserable person that I am, who is to set me free from this body doomed to death?" These words have echoed thunderously in the depths of generations for whom they are an autobiographical outcry.

But Stendahl notices an odd thing. In all of Paul's undoubtedly autobiographical references, there is no expression of guilt. Far from finding it hard to observe the Mosaic Law, he says that he observed it perfectly in his days as a Pharisee (Phil 3.6), and in his days among the Brothers he says repeatedly that he has done nothing for which his conscience could reproach him (1 Cor 4.4, 2 Cor 1.12, Rom 9.1). In fact, says Stendahl, Paul manifests a "robust conscience," not a guilty one. What sets him so at odds with his dark interpreters, and what does their favorite passage mean? How could this one place be so at odds with what he tells us about himself in other places?

Stendahl gives us the obvious answer. In this one place *he is not telling us about himself*. The Romans passage is part of a complex interplay of "persons" in diatribe-exchanges, meant to show that Gentiles and Jews—not as individuals but as societies—have both failed to observe their covenant with God. Pagans, given the natural law, became unnatural. Jews, given covenant law, repeatedly rebelled against it. The Jewish diatribal figure is speaking in the passage at Romans 7.22–24. Paul is arguing that neither side can reproach the other, and that God is on neither side. Modern exegetes—for instance, Wayne Meeks—emphasize this as the whole point of the Letter to the Romans, where Paul was addressing the divisions between Gentile Brothers and Jewish Brothers.[2]

Paul was speaking of God as the savior of whole peoples. American black religion was closer to him than have been individualist members of intellectual elites. The blacks spoke of the whole people being delivered from Pharaoh, or reaching the Holy Land, or surviving the Ark's passage. Luther reflects a brilliant but hypertrophic blending of late medieval penitential disciplines and the Renaissance's subjective individualism.

This speaks to us at a very intimate level because we are a part of the world created by those trends. But Paul was entirely innocent of such cultures.

If we ask why Paul has come down to us as the Bad News Man, we have to remember the wisdom of Lucretius (1.101):

> *Tantum religio potuit suadere malorum.*
> How suasive is religion to our bane.

Religion took over the legacy of Paul as it did that of Jesus—because they both opposed it. They said that the worship of God is a matter of interior love, not based on external observances, on temples or churches, on hierarchies or priesthoods. Both were at odds with those who impose the burdens of "religion" and punish those who try to escape them. They were radical egalitarians, though in ways that delved below and soared above conventional politics. They were on the side of the poor, and saw through the rich. They saw only two basic moral duties, love of God and love of the neighbor. Both were liberators, not imprisoners—so they were imprisoned. So they were killed. Paul meant what Jesus meant, that love is the only law. Paul's message to us is not one of guilt and dark constraint. It is this:

> Finally, Brothers, whatever things are true, whatever honorable, whatever making for the right, whatever

lovable, whatever admirable—if there is any virtue, anything of high esteem—think on these. All you have
learned, have taken from tradition, have listened to, have
observed in me, act on these, and the God who brings
peace will be yours. (Phil 4.8–9)

NOTES

1. Stendahl's lecture is reprinted in *Paul Among Jews and Gentiles*
(Fortress Press, 1976).

2. Wayne Meeks, "Judgment and the Brother: Romans
14.1–15.13," in Gerald F. Hawthorne, editor, *Tradition and Interpretation in the New Testament* (Eerdmans 1987), pp. 290–300.

Appendix: Translating Paul

KRISTER STENDAHL AND JOHN GAGER both tell us that modern translations, even those that seem most "objective," distort what Paul was saying. Paul's writings are the first to reach us from a follower of Jesus. It is hard to avoid anachronism when we try to reenter Paul's world—to avoid terms that did not exist for Paul, terms like *Christian, church, priests, sacraments, conversion.* All such terms subtly, or not so subtly, pervert what was being said in its original situation. Even a direct transliteration like *apostle* can be misleading. These poor translations come with heavy suggestions of later developments, giving Paul an atmosphere of "religion," a thing he opposed. To scrub away linguistic accretions on Paul's text is as necessary as to cleanse away the buildup of foreign matter on old paintings. Only by doing this can we travel back into the Spirit-haunted, God-driven world of Paul in the heady first charismatic days of Jesus' revelation.

Below I list first the customary translation, then the Greek term, then a more adequate rendering. I use the last terms for translating Paul throughout this book.

"Christians" *(Adelphoi)*
Brothers

The term *Christian* was first used by pagan opponents of Christianity—by Pliny the Younger, for instance, or Tacitus, or Lucian. Religious groups often end up being called by names that were initially derisory—Jesuits, Lollards ("Mumblers"), Puritans, Quakers, Shakers, Ranters, Diggers, Mormons, and so on. Luke in the Acts of the Apostles (Ac 11.26) says that the followers of Jesus were first called Christians at Antioch, but neither he nor Paul uses it of their fellows in faith. King Agrippa is the only person quoted by Luke as referring to a Christian (Ac 26.2). People we now call Christians had a number of expressions for each other, stressing their affective bonds. There are so many terms precisely because *Christian* had not yet been accepted, to absorb them all.

1. Brothers *(Adelphoi):* This is the normal term, both in Paul and Luke, for the followers of Jesus. In the short First Letter to the Thessalonians, Paul uses it twelve times in direct address and three times in description. Though the masculine noun was used generically for the whole Brotherhood, Paul addressses specific women followers of Jesus as Sister *(Adelphē)*—the wives of Peter and the Lord's brothers, for instance (1 Cor 9.5), or Phoebe (Rom 16.1) or Apphia (Phlm 2). And when he distinguishes between male and female duties, he refers

to what should be done by "the Brother or the Sister" (1 Cor 7.15).

2. The Holy *(Hagioi, or Hēgiasmenoi):* Paul also refers to "the Holy" in such-or-such a place, or to "the needs of the Holy" (Rom 12.13). They were the Holy because they had been incorporated into Jesus by baptism: "For just as one body has many members, and all the members make up that single body, so, in Christ we became one body by baptism, through the action of a single Spirit, whether we be Jews or Greeks, slaves or free, all were given to drink of the one Spirit" (1 Cor 12.12–13).

3. Those in Messiah *(Hoi en Christō[i]):* Because they are baptized into Jesus, the Holy can be said to be "in Jesus"—or in Messiah-Jesus or in Jesus-Messiah. Thus Paul can say, "I was not known by my features to the Judaean gatherings in Messiah" (Gal 1.22). Or similarly: "Anyone in Messiah is a new order of being" (*ktisis,* 2 Cor 5.17).

4. The Called *(Klētoi):* Paul thinks of the Brothers as summoned to holiness (Rom 1.6, 8.28, 1 Cor 1.24).

5. Housefellows *(Oikeioi):* Since the followers met mainly in each other's homes *(oikoi),* Paul calls them, in general, housefellows of our trust (Gal 6.10, Eph 2.19).

6. Those of the Path *(Hoi tēs Hodou):* This term has become common by the time of the Acts of the Apostles. Luke therefore can speak of detractors or persecutors of

the Path (Ac 22.4), of debating or understanding the Path (19.23, 24.22).

"Christ" *(Khristos)*
Messiah

One reason Paul did not use the term *Christian* is that *Christ* was not a proper name for him. "Jesus Christ" was not praenomen-cognomen, any more than was "Jesus Lord." *Khristos* is, like *Kyrios* (Lord), a title. It is simply the Greek word for *Messiah*. They both mean "Anointed," with the same theological sense. It is essential to keep in mind that the full Jewish force of the title was always important for Paul, since he always thinks of Jesus as fulfilling Jewish Law and prophecy. Paul sometimes uses the word with the article—*the* Messiah—sometimes without (not on any regular plan). He uses it with the name of Jesus, either as Messiah-Jesus or Jesus-Messiah, but in all cases it is the title that is at issue, as N. T. Wright has properly emphasized.[1]

"Church" *(Ekklēsia)*
Gathering

The Greek *ekklēsia* simply means "gathering." The meeting place of the Brothers was almost always in Paul's time the house of a Brother or a Sister, or both—as in "the gathering at Prisca's and Aquila's house" (1 Cor 16.19, Rom 16.5) or "the gathering at your [Philemon's] house" (Phlm 2). So basic is this cell of the Brothers' assembly that Paul could refer, as we have seen, to all the Brotherhood as "the housefellows *(oikeioi)* of our trust" (Gal 6.10). Some towns or regions had two or more such gathering spots—like "the gatherings in Macedonia" (2 Cor 8.1) or "the gatherings in Galatia" (Gal 1.2)—with no hierarchy among them. All those in one city could be called, for instance, "God's gathering at Corinth" (1 Cor 1.2, 2 Cor 1.1). What would later be called "the church" is, for Paul, "all the gatherings" (1 Cor 4.17, 7.17, 14.33), "God's gatherings" (1 Cor 11.16), or simply "God's gathering" (1 Cor 10.32, 11.22, 15.9), or "the gathering" (1 Cor 12.28).

"Gospel" *(Euaggelion)*
Revelation

The gospel is what Paul is told to take to the nations. It is so central to his vocation that he uses it as a verb—he must be "gospeling." He talks indeed of "the gospel I gospeled to you . . . in the sense in which I gospeled it to you" (1 Cor 15.1–2). What precisely does that mean? We are somewhat confused by the fact that later compositions, the four Gospels, are now equated with "the gospel." Yet giving the etymology ("favorable announcement") is not translating, either. That would make Paul speak of "the favorable announcement I favorably announced to you." For Paul as an emissary carrying a message, the gospel is the *revelation* that Jesus died for our sins and rose again, and this is the entire meaning of history, it is what God wants to reveal about himself.

So "the gospel I gospeled to you" is "the revelation I revealed to you," and Paul warns against those who would "gospel against what I gospeled"—that is, who reveal something at odds with what he revealed (Gal 1.8). Such people "were not hewing to the clearly marked meaning of the revelation" (Gal 2.14). The revelation is not only something that Paul and his coworkers carry to others, but what they "serve" (Phlm 13). It has its own power: "The revelation was not brought to you in words only but in miracle and the Holy Spirit" (1 Thess 1.5).

"Preach" *(Euaggelizein)*
Bring the Revelation

Other New Testament authors use *kērysso* ("proclaim") for preaching, but Paul uses that verb only six times, and two of them are for dubious proclamations (Gal 5.11, Rom 2.21). Overwhelmingly the word usually translated as "preach" is the verb from *euaggelizo*. This has the meaning of God's still actively revealing his plans. Paul even "does priestly service" *(hierourgōn)* to this revelation (Rom 15.16). Paul never uses the word for priest *(hiereus)*, since no such office existed among the Brothers. Priesthood in the Jewish tradition had to do with the offering of animal sacrifice, and later Christians would import that meaning into their use of the term. In the New Testament, Jesus is the only individual called a priest, in the late anonymous Letter to the Hebrews. Paul in Romans uses "priestly service to the revelation" to suggest coming out from behind the Temple veils: "The revelation *(euaggelion)* I brought you proclaiming Jesus-Messiah unveils the secret kept hidden through the ages, but now brought forth as confirmed by the prophets in the order appointed by the ageless God for all nations to recognize with an acknowledging trust" (Rom 16.25). "Scripture made a prior revelation [literally pregospeled, *pro-eueggelisato*] of this to Abraham" (Gal 3.8). The revelation in Paul has its own divine power, so he speaks of "when the revelation first began to work" (Phil 4.15). As usual, God is acting directly through Paul.

"Faith" *(Pistis)*
Trust

We normally think of our faith as having faith *(pistis)* in God. But Paul talks of God having faith *(pistis)*. What is God's faith in? In himself? In his own words? In us? The last might seem the least plausible. How can he believe in us? But this problem reveals the inadequacy of our sense of trust. God takes us into his trust. There is no longer an estrangement. He promotes us into a partnership with him because we are members of his Son's mystical body. We trust him as sons. He trusts us as a father trusts his beloved children. This explains the difficult passage at Romans 1.17, "from *pistis* to *pistis*." If we already have trust, how do we move to get it? But if one of these is God's *pistis*, the passage makes sense: "God's vindication is unveiled, from [his] trust to [our] trust, it is written: 'The vindicated will live from trust.'" Too often faith now means belief in a proposition, a dogma, the stand taken by a church. It is, instead, an active response to a *Person*, a trust in him.

"Justification" *(Dikiaosynē)*
Vindication

The verb *dikaoiun* means "to set things right." In means to uphold the law. When God is *dikaios* he is upholding his law. When we are *dikaioi* we are upheld by law. Does that mean that we are innocent, or acquitted, or both? In any case we are vindicated, our title is made clear. Paul says that God is our vindicator. That is why we trust him. The initiative is his. When Paul says, "Abraham was vindicated by trusting God" (Rom 4.2–3), he is not saying that he won vindication but that he accepted what God told him with trust. When God is said to have been "vindicated in what you said, and proved innocent in what you did" (Rom 3.4), it is not because he can be put on trial, but because he can vindicate his claims by his power, by manifesting it. In the same way, when we pray in the Our Father "Your name be made holy" (Mt 6.9), *we* cannot make it holy. No human being can. We are praying that

God vindicate his title (name) by manifesting it. In the same way, he vindicates *our* title when he makes us holy, out of his munificence uniting us with his Son, making "Messiah-Jesus our vindication" (*dikaiosyne*, 1 Cor 1.30). In fact, Jesus makes us "God's vindication" (2 Cor 5.21).

Luther tried to separate "justification" from "works," in a sterile way. When we trust God, we gladly keep our part of the covenant with him. Luther wanted to excise from the New Testament canon the Letter of James 2.20, "Trust without action is feckless," but he would have to pare away many authentic parts of the Pauline corpus to deny the same basic point—for instance: "All you have learned, have taken from tradition, have listened to, have observed in me, *act* on these" (Phil 4.9). Speaking to the Corinthians on their good works for the Jerusalem fund, he says, "God will make fertile the effects of your vindication" (2 Cor 9.10). "Good works" were hardly scorned by Paul.

"Be Converted" *(Klēthēnai)*
Be Summoned

When it is said that Paul became a Christian, or was converted to Christianity, this offers a polar expression that implies that he converted from Judaism to Christianity. Paul did not think of himself as being converted from Judaism, and there was no such thing as Christianity, or a Christian church, for him to join. He converted others to the Jewish God,

Yahweh, but he did not need to be converted to Yahweh himself. He taught non-Jews from the Jewish scripture (the only "Bible" that existed in his time), saying they must become part of the "seed of Abraham," inheritors of the Jewish covenant that had been extended to them *without having been canceled for the Jews.* He always spoke of himself as a Jew, spoke of "my people," of the people of Abraham.

If Paul was not converted, neither did he convert others. The normal words for conversion, *metanoein* ("repent" or "rethink") and *epistrephein* ("turn back"), were used, in the Septuagint, for prophets recalling Jews to the covenant that they were neglecting. John the Baptist issues a call for *metanoia* in the Gospels (Mk 1.15, for instance). But when Paul uses such language, it is usually in a negative sense, when he tells Gentiles *not* to "turn back" *(epistrephein)* to idols (Gal 4.9) after they had once turned from idols (1 Thess 1.9); when he rebukes the Corinthians for *not* rethinking *(metanoesantes)* their return to sinful ways (2 Cor 12.21); or when he quotes the Septuagint (2 Cor 3.16). What people call Paul's "conversion" was his reception of a vocation, of a call—to carry the revelation (gospel) to the nations. He did not ask the Gentiles to be "converted" but to receive *their* call. For him God always takes the initiative toward humankind. Paul asks not that people know God but that they be known by him (Gal 4.9), that they be his chosen ones *(eklektoi),* his called ones *(klētoi),* his summoned ones *(klēthentes),* the ones he made holy *(hagioi)*. God is always the dynamic principle for Paul.

"Salvation" *(Sotēria)*
Rescue

The revelation is that all the nations, not merely the Jews, are to be "saved" *(sōzesthai)*. "Salvation" has become something we think of as a condition of the individual, something he or she gains, loses, or feels sure of ("Brother, are you saved?"). This reflects the introspective individualism Krister Stendahl calls a deflection of Paul's message. Paul did not think of the person's own sense of himself, but of God's activity as the rescuer. Rescue was for him a divine initiative, God's raid on enemy territory, bringing the people out from captivity. As black Americans think of the whole people as escaping Pharaoh or reaching the Promised Land, so the whole of creation is to be rescued and restored to God.

> The very frame of things is giddy with apprehension at what will be unveiled for the sons of God. The frame of things has been baffled, despite itself, by the one constraining it—yet with hope for it, since the whole frame will be liberated from its imprisoning decay, freed into the splendor of God's offspring. All the frame of things, we realize, has been moaning in the throes of some birth—and we, moreover, though we have the first

harvest of the Spirit, moan along with it, yearning for full adoption as heirs and for the release of our bodies. (Rom 8.19–23)

We might wonder how Paul, who expected the consummation of the world to be completed soon, thought he could, in effect, convert persons one by one throughout the world. But he did not see God working retail. He was moving a great cosmic plan forward.

God initiates it all by rejoining us to himself through Messiah and by making us active in this rejoining—as we profess that God is rejoining the world to himself through Messiah, not counting their lapses against them, entrusting to us the message of this rejoining. This makes us Messiah's ambassadors, as God issues his call to you through us. We implore you, then, to be rejoined to Messiah. The one who was innocent of sin he treated as sin for our sakes, to make us in him the vindication of God. (2 Cor 5.18–21)

"Redemption" *(Apolytrōsis)*
Release

Apolytrōsis means, literally, "ransom." But its translation into Latin *redemptio*, "buying back," has been caught up into Anselm's notions of paying off God the Father by sacrifice of his Son, a concept foreign to Paul. Paul means by the ransoming of the whole world a release of it from thralldom to the evil order he personified as Satan. It is a massive liberation act, like the breaking open of every prison, and only God's energy can accomplish this.

"Grace" (Charis)
Favor

"Grace," too, has acquired foreign associations through the history of the churches. It is often thought of as a quantum acquired by an individual, as something one gains or loses. To be "in grace," or deprived of grace, is like having or losing gas in one's spiritual tank. Once again, the introspective individual has got in the way of Paul's thinking. Grace is God's gratuitous activity, his favor, his bounty, in a continuing dynamic activity on his part.

"Apostle" (Apostolos)
Emissary

The Greek apo-stolos, from apo-stello, means one "sent off." It is used of an emissary, and in Paul's time it meant a messenger from or to the gatherings—or, in Paul's special vocation, "an emissary to the nations" (Gal 2.8, Rom 11.13). Paul gives, as a synonym for "emissary," "ambassador" (2 Cor 5.20). This was not an office but a function (like the other ministries of Paul's time). One became an emissary by being sent off from one body or mission to another—either by election (2 Cor 8.19, 23) or by appointment, as when Paul dispatches an assistant to one of the gatherings (1 Thess 3.2, 1 Cor 4.17, 2 Cor 8.18, 22, 9.13).

The misunderstanding of this term comes from trying to turn it from a function to an office, and a ruling office at that. Most often we hear of "the twelve apostles"—or thirteen if we add Paul. "The Twelve" do have an office in the Gospels, an eschatological one—they are symbolic judges of the end time, to sit on the seats of the Twelve Tribes (Mt 19.28, Lk 22.30). But they are usually just "the Twelve" in the Gospels, or the twelve followers *(mathētai)*. They are referred to as "twelve emissaries" *(apostoloi)* when they are "sent off" on a mission to Judaean villages (Mt 10.1–8)—that is, when they exercise the technical *function* of emissaries. They are never rulers of any gathering. The leader of the Jerusalem church was James the brother of the Lord, who was not a member of the Twelve. Peter is an emissary in the strict sense because he goes as an emissary into the Diaspora, to Lydda, Joppa, Caesarea, and Antioch (Ac 9.32, 10.18, Gal 2.7–10–11)—and eventually to Rome. The later tradition that restricts apostles to the Twelve is not something Paul knew. He says that the risen Jesus appeared to the Twelve and *afterward* to "all the emissaries" (1 Cor 15.5–7). Those are distinct groups. That is why he can refer to his fellow emissaries, like Andronicus and Junia (Rom 16.7), or to "emissaries" as a regular part of the gatherings (1 Cor 12.28).

"Bishop" *(Episkopos)*
Overseer

Paul uses the word *episkopoi* ("overseers") only once, when he greets the Holy in Philippi (Phil 1.1), "along with their overseers and attendants *(diakonoi)*." These are informal leaders who have nothing in common with the later *bishops* and *deacons* of the church. The plural and mixed "overseers" referred to are not the single-rule *(monarchoi)* bishops that arose half a century later in the time of Ignatius, and the "attendants" are not the seven supply managers elected in Jerusalem according to Luke (Ac 6.1–6). *Attendants* is such a general term with Paul that he can refer to Satan's attendants (2 Cor 11.15), to his foes in Corinth as so-called attendants on Messiah (2 Cor 11.23), to Jesus himself as an attendant on the circumcision (Rom 15.8), as well as to himself and his team as attendants on God (2 Cor 6.4) and on the new covenant (2 Cor 3.6). Those who try to make *diakonos* mean the later "deacon" are embarrassed by the fact that Phoebe is a *diakonos* (Rom 16.1). Paul is not referring to a ruling structure under any of these titles, since the gatherings are still charismatic groups where the Spirit singles out people for their function, not their office. These include a wide variety of gifts—emissaries, prophets, teachers, healers, readers, miracle workers, guides, speakers in tongues, interpreters of tongues, wise men, spirit testers, trainers, attendants, exhorters, distributors, patrons, almsgivers, shepherds (1 Cor 4.15, 12.8–10,

27–28, Rom 11.6–8). None of these are ruling roles, and "overseers" make only one fleeting reference among them. "Priests" make no appearance at all.

NOTE

1. N. T. Wright, *The Climax of the Covenant* (Fortress Press, 1993), pp. 41–55.

Acknowledgments

MY EDITOR at Viking, Carolyn Carlson, had the idea for my preceding book *What Jesus Meant,* so she must take the blame for this companion volume. Martin Marty read the whole manuscript and made valuable suggestions improving it. My agent, Andrew Wylie, undergirds it all. The final arbiter, as always, is my own special Italian tempest and solace, Natalie.

RUNAWAY
MAX

STRANGER THINGS

RUNAWAY MAX

Brenna Yovanoff

Random House  New York

Jacket and interior art used under license from Shutterstock.com

Jacket art copyright © 2019 by Netflix Inc.

Text copyright © 2019 Netflix Inc. All rights reserved. Published in the United States by Random House Children's Books, a division of Penguin Random House LLC, New York.

Random House and the colophon are registered trademarks of Penguin Random House LLC. Stranger Things and all related titles, characters, and logos are trademarks of Netflix Inc. Created by the Duffer Brothers.

Visit us on the Web! GetUnderlined.com
ReadStrangerThings.com

Educators and librarians, for a variety of teaching tools, visit us at RHTeachersLibrarians.com

Library of Congress Cataloging-in-Publication Data is available upon request.
ISBN 978-1-9848-9595-0 (trade) — ISBN 978-1-9848-9596-7 (ebook) —
ISBN 978-1-9848-9714-5 (lib. bdg.)

Printed in the United States of America

10 9 8 7 6 5 4 3

First Edition

For the daring girls and the hopeful boys

And for V., my strangest thing

PROLOGUE

The floor of the San Diego bus station was mostly cigarette butts. A million years ago, the building had probably been fancy, like Grand Central or those huge places you see in movies. But now it just looked gray all over, like a warehouse full of crumpled band flyers and winos.

It was almost midnight, but the lobby was crowded. Next to me, a wall of storage lockers ran all the way down to the end. One of the lockers was leaking a little, like something had spilled inside and was dripping out onto the floor. It was sticking to my shoes.

There were vending machines on the other side of the lobby, and there was a bar over in the corner, where a bunch

1

of skinny, stubbly men sat smoking into ashtrays, hunched over their beers like goblins. The smoke made the air look hazy and weird.

I hurried along, close to the lockers, keeping my chin down and trying not to look obvious. Back at my house, when I'd imagined this scene, I'd been pretty sure I'd be able to blend into the crowd, no problem. But now that I was here, it was harder than I'd pictured. I'd been counting on the chaos and the size to cover me. It was a *bus* station, after all. I didn't figure I'd be the only one here who was still too young to drive.

On my street or at school, I was easy to overlook— twelve years old and average height, average shape and face and clothes. Average everything except for my hair, which was long and red and the brightest thing about me. I yanked it into a ponytail and tried to walk like I knew where I was going. I should have brought a hat.

Over at the ticket windows, a couple of older girls in green eyeshadow and rubber miniskirts were arguing with the guy behind the glass. Their hair was teased up so high it looked like cotton candy.

"C'mon, man," said one of them. She was shaking her purse upside down on the window ledge, counting out quarters. "Can't you cut me a break? I'm barely short. Only a buck fifty."

The guy looked sarcastic and bored in his ratty Hawaiian shirt. "Does this look like a charity? No fare, no ticket."

I reached into the pocket of my warm-up jacket and ran my fingers over my own ticket. Economy from San Diego to LA. I'd paid for it with a twenty from my mom's jewelry box and the guy had barely looked at me.

I walked faster, sticking close to the wall with my skateboard under my arm. For a second, I thought how badass it would be to set it down and go zooming between the benches. But I didn't. One wrong move and even a bunch of late-night dirtbags were going to notice I wasn't supposed to be here.

I was almost to the end of the lobby when a nervous ripple went through the crowd behind me. I turned around. Two guys in tan uniforms were standing by the vending machines, looking out over the sea of faces. Even from across the station, I could catch the glint of their badges. Cops.

The tall one had fast, pale eyes and long, skinny arms like a spider. He was pacing up and down between the benches in that way cops always do. It's a slow, official walk that says *I might be a creepy string bean, but I'm the one with the badge and the gun.* It reminded me of my stepdad.

If I could get to the end of the lobby, I could slip out to the depot where the buses pulled up. I'd slide into the crowd and disappear.

The scuzzy guys at the bar hunched lower over their beers. One of them mashed out his cigarette, then gave the cops a long, nasty stare and spit on the floor between his feet. The girls at the ticket window had stopped arguing with the cashier. They were acting really interested in their press-on nails, but looked plenty nervous about Officer String Bean. Maybe they had the same kind of stepdads I did.

The cops waded out into the middle of the lobby and were squinting around the bus station like they were looking for something. A lost kid, maybe. A bunch of delinquents up to no good.

Or a runaway.

I ducked my head and got ready to blend in. I was just about to step out into the terminal when someone cleared his throat and a big, heavy hand closed around my arm. I turned and looked up into the looming face of a third cop.

He smiled a bored, flat smile, all teeth. "Maxine May-field? I'm going to need you to come with me." His face was hard and craggy, and he looked like he'd said the same thing to different kids about a hundred times. "You've got people at home worried sick about you."

CHAPTER ONE

The sky was so low it seemed to be sitting right on top of downtown Hawkins. The world whipped past me as I clattered along the sidewalk. I skated faster, listening to the wheels whispering on concrete, then thudding over the cracks. It was a chilly afternoon, and the cold made my ears hurt. It had been chilly every day since we'd rolled into town three days ago.

I kept looking up, expecting to see the bright sky of San Diego. But here, everything was pale and gray, and even when it wasn't overcast, the sky looked colorless. Hawkins, Indiana: home of low gray clouds and quilted jackets and winter.

Home of . . . me.

Main Street was all tricked out for Halloween, with storefronts full of grinning pumpkins. Fake spiderwebs and paper skeletons were taped in the windows of the supermarket. All down the block, lampposts were wrapped in black-and-orange streamers fluttering in the wind.

I'd spent the afternoon at the Palace Arcade, playing *Dig Dug* until I ran out of quarters. Because my mom didn't like me wasting money on video games, back home in California I'd mostly only gotten to play when I'd been with my dad. He'd take me to the bowling alley with him, or sometimes the laundry, which had *Pac-Man* and *Galaga*. And I sometimes hung out at the Joy Town Arcade at the mall, even though it was a total rip-off and full of metalheads in ratty jeans and leather jackets. They had *Pole Position,* though, which was better than any other racing game and had a steering wheel like you were actually driving.

The arcade in Hawkins was a big, low-roofed building with neon signs in the windows and a bright yellow awning (but under the colored lights and the paint, it was just aluminum siding). They had *Dragon's Lair* and *Donkey Kong,* and *Dig Dug,* which was my best game.

I'd been hanging out there all afternoon, running up the score on *Dig Dug,* but after I entered my name in the number-one spot and I didn't have any more quarters, I started to feel antsy, like I needed to move, so I left the arcade and skated downtown to take a tour of Hawkins.

I pushed myself faster, rattling past a diner and a hardware store, a Radio Shack, a movie theater. The theater was small, like it might only have one screen, but the front was glitzy and old-fashioned, with a big marquee that stuck out like a battleship covered in lights.

The only time I really liked to sit still was at the movies. The newest poster out front was for *The Terminator,* but I'd already seen it. The story was pretty good. This killer robot who looks like Arnold Schwarzenegger travels back in time from the future to kill this waitress named Sarah Connor. At first she just seems kind of normal, but she turns out to be a total badass. I liked it, even though it wasn't a real monster movie, but something about it also made me feel weirdly disappointed. None of the women I knew were anything like Sarah Connor.

I was zipping past the pawn shop now—past a furniture store, past a pizza place with a red-and-green-striped awning—when something small and dark darted across the sidewalk in front of me. In the gray afternoon light, it looked like a cat, and I just had time to think how weird that was, how you'd never see a cat in downtown San Diego, before my feet went out from under me.

I was used to wiping out, but still, that split second of a fall was always disorienting. When I lost my balance, it felt like the whole world had flipped over and skidded out from under me. I hit the ground so hard I felt the thump in my teeth.

I'd been skating since forever—since my best friend, Nate Walker, and his brother Silas took a trip to Venice Beach with their parents when we were in the third grade and came back all jazzed up on stories about the Z-Boys and the skate shops in Dogtown. I'd been skating since the day I found out about grip tape and Madrid boards and rode down Sunset Hill for the first time and learned what it felt like to go so fast your heart raced and your eyes watered.

The sidewalk was cold. For a second, I lay flat on my stomach, with a thudding hollow in my chest and pain zinging up my arms. My elbow had punched through the sleeve of my sweater and the palms of my hands felt raw and electric. The cat was long gone.

I had rolled over and was trying to sit up when a thin, dark-haired woman came hurrying out of one of the stores. It was almost as surprising as a cat in the business district. No one in California would have come running out just to see if I was okay, but this was Indiana. My mom had said that people would be nicer here.

The woman was already kneeling next to me on the concrete with big, nervous eyes. I was bleeding a little where my elbow had gone through my sleeve. My ears were ringing.

She leaned close, looking worried. "Oh, your arm, that must hurt." Then she looked up, staring into my face. "Do you scare easily?"

I just stared back. *No,* I wanted to say, and that was true in all kinds of ways. I wasn't scared of spiders or dogs. I could walk along the boardwalk alone in the dark or skateboard in the wash in flood season and never worry that a murderer was going to jump out at me or that a sudden deluge of water would come rushing down to drown me. And when my mom and my stepdad said we were moving to Indiana, I packed some socks and underwear and two pairs of jeans in my backpack and headed for the bus station alone to escape to LA. It was a total trip to ask a stranger if they got scared. Scared of *what*?

For a second I just sat in the middle of the sidewalk with my elbow stinging and my palms raw and gritty, squinting at her. "What?"

She reached out to brush gravel off my hands. Hers were thinner and tanner than mine, with dry, cracked knuckles and bitten fingernails. Next to them, mine looked pale, covered in freckles.

She was watching me in a quick, nervous way, like I was the one acting weird. "I just wondered if you scar easily. Sometimes fair skin does. You should put Bactine on that to keep it from getting infected."

"Oh." I shook my head. The palms of my hands still felt like they were full of tiny sparks. "No. I mean, I don't think so."

She leaned closer and was about to say something else when suddenly her eyes got even bigger and she froze. We both looked up as the air was split by the roar of an engine.

A swimming-pool-blue Camaro came bombing through the stoplight at Oak Street and snarled up to the curb. The woman whipped around to see what the trouble was, but I already knew.

My stepbrother, Billy, was leaning back in the driver's seat with his hand draped lazily on the wheel. I could hear the blare of his music through the closed windows.

Even from the sidewalk, I could see the light glinting off Billy's earring. He was watching me in the flat, empty way he always did—heavy-lidded, like I made him so bored he could barely stand it—but under that was a glittering edge of something dangerous. When he looked at me like that, my face wanted to flush bright red or crumple. I was used to how he looked at me, like I was something he wanted to scrape off him, but it always seemed worse when he did it in front of someone else—like this nice, nervous woman. She looked like someone's mom.

I scrubbed my stinging hands on the thighs of my jeans before bending down to get my board.

He let his head flop back, his mouth open. After a second, he leaned across the seat and rolled down the window.

The stereo thumped louder, Quiet Riot pounding out into the chilly air. "Get in."

• • •

Once, for two weeks back in April, I thought that Camaro was the coolest thing I'd ever seen. It had a long, hungry body like a shark, all sleek painted panels and sharp angles. It was the kind of car you could rob a bank in.

Billy Hargrove was fast and hard-edged, like the car. He had a faded denim jacket and a face like a movie star.

Back then, he wasn't Billy yet, just this hazy idea I had about what my life was going to be like. His dad, Neil, was going to marry my mom, and when we all moved in together, Billy was going to be my brother. I was excited to have a family again.

After the divorce, my dad had hightailed it to LA, so I mostly only saw him on second-rate holidays, or when he was down in San Diego for work and my mom couldn't think up a reason not to let me.

My mom was still around, of course, but in a thin, floaty way that was hard to get a hold on. She'd always been a little blurry around the edges, but once my dad was out of the picture, it got worse. It was kind of tragic how easily she disappeared into the personality of every guy she dated.

There was Donnie, who was on disability for his back and couldn't bend down to take out the trash. He made us Bisquick pancakes on the weekends and told terrible jokes, and then one day he ran off with a waitress from IHOP.

After Donnie, there was Vic from St. Louis, and Gus with one green eye and one blue one, and Ivan, who picked his teeth with a folding knife.

Neil was different. He drove a tan Ford pickup and his shirts were ironed and his mustache made him look like some kind of army sergeant or park ranger. And he wanted to marry my mom.

The other guys had been losers, but they were temporary losers, so I never really minded them. Some of them were goofy or friendly or funny, but after a while, the bad stuff always piled up. They were behind on their rent, or they'd total their cars, or they'd get drunk and wind up in county.

They always left, and if they didn't, my mom kicked them out. I wasn't heartbroken. Even the best ones were kind of embarrassing. None of them were cool like my dad, but mostly they were okay. Some of them were even nice.

Like I said, Neil was different.

She met him at the bank. She was a teller there, sitting behind a smudgy window, handing out deposit slips and giving lollipops to little kids. Neil was a guard, standing all day by the double doors. He said she looked like Sleeping Beauty sitting there behind the glass, or like an old-timey painting in a frame. The way he said it, the idea was supposed to sound romantic, but I couldn't see how. Sleeping Beauty was in a coma. Paintings in frames weren't interesting or exciting—they were just stuck there.

The first time she had him over for dinner, he brought flowers. None of the other ones had ever brought flowers. He told her the meat loaf was the best meat loaf he'd ever had, and she smiled and blushed and glanced sideways at him. I was glad she'd stopped crying over her last boyfriend—a carpet salesman with a comb-over and a wife he hadn't told her about.

A few weeks before school let out for the summer, Neil asked my mom to marry him. He bought her a ring and she gave him the extra key to the house. He showed up when he felt like it, bringing flowers or getting rid of throw pillows and pictures he didn't like, but he didn't come over after ten and he never spent the night. He was too much of a gentleman for that—*old-fashioned,* he said. He liked clean counters and family dinners. The little gold engagement ring made her happier than I'd seen her in a long time, and I tried to be happy for her.

Neil had told us he had a son in high school, but that was all he said about him. I figured he would be some preppie football type, or else maybe a younger copy of Neil. I wasn't picturing Billy.

The night we finally met him, Neil took us out to Fort Fun, which was a go-kart track near my house where the surf rats went with their girlfriends to eat funnel cakes and play air hockey and Skee-Ball. It was the kind of place that guys like Neil would never be caught dead in. Later, I figured out that he was trying to make us think he was fun.

Billy was late. Neil didn't say anything, but I could tell he was mad. He tried to act like everything was fine, but his fingers left dents in his foam Coke cup. My mom fidgeted with a paper napkin while we waited, wadding it up and then tearing it into little squares.

I pretended that maybe it was all a big scam and Neil didn't even have a son. It was the kind of thing that was always happening in horror movies—the guy made up a whole fake life and told everyone about his perfect house and his perfect family, but actually he lived in a basement, eating cats or something.

I didn't really think it was the truth, but I imagined it anyway, because it was better than watching him glare out at the parking lot every two minutes and then smile tightly at my mom.

The three of us were working our way through a game of mini golf when Billy finally showed up. We were on the tenth hole, standing in front of a painted windmill the size of a garden shed and trying to get the ball past the turning sails.

When the Camaro roared into the parking lot, the engine was so loud that everyone turned to look. He got out, letting the door slam shut behind him. He had on his jean jacket and engineer boots, and raddest of all, he had an earring. Some of the older boys at school wore boots and jean jackets, but none of them had an earring. With his mop of sprayed hair and his open shirt, he looked like the metalheads at the mall, or David Lee Roth or someone else famous.

He came over to us, cutting straight through the mini-golf course.

He stepped over a big plastic turtle and onto the fake green turf.

Neil watched with the tight, sour look he always did when something wasn't up to his standards. "You're late."

Billy just shrugged. He didn't look at his dad.

"Say hello to Maxine."

I wanted to tell Billy that wasn't my name—I hated when people called me Maxine—but I didn't. It wouldn't have mattered. Neil always called me that, no matter how many times I told him to stop.

Billy gave me this slow, cool nod, like we already knew each other, and I smiled, holding my putter by its sweaty rubber handle. I was thinking how much cooler this was going to make me. How jealous Nate and Silas would be. I was getting a brother, and it was going to change my life.

Later, the two of us hung out by the Skee-Ball stalls while Neil and my mom walked down along the boardwalk together. It was getting kind of annoying, how they were always all gooey at each other, but I fed quarters into the slot and tried to ignore it. She seemed really happy.

Skee-Ball was on a raised concrete deck above the go-kart track. From the railing, you could look down and watch the cars go zooming around in a figure eight.

Billy leaned his elbows on the railing with his hands hanging loose and casual in front of him and a cigarette balanced between his fingers. "Susan seems like a real buzzkill."

I shrugged. She was fussy and nervous and could be no fun sometimes, but she was my mom.

Billy looked out over the track. His eyelashes were long, like a girl's, and I saw for the first time how heavy his eyelids were. That was the thing that I would come to learn about Billy, though—he never really looked awake, except . . . sometimes. Sometimes his face went suddenly alert, and then you had no idea what he was going to do or what was going to happen next.

"So. Maxine." He said my name like some kind of joke. Like it wasn't really my name.

I tucked my hair behind my ears and tossed a ball into the corner cup for a hundred points. The machine under the coin slot whirred and spit out a paper chain of tickets. "Don't call me that. It's Max or nothing."

Billy glanced back at me. His face was slack. Then he smiled a sleepy smile. "Well. You've got a real mouth on you."

I shrugged. It wasn't the first time I'd heard that. "Only when people piss me off."

He laughed, and it was low and gravelly. "Mad Max. All right, then."

Out in the parking lot, the Camaro was sitting under a streetlight, so blue it looked like a creature from another world. Some kind of monster. I wanted to touch it.

Billy had turned away again. He was leaning on the rail with the cigarette in his hand, watching the go-karts as they zoomed along the tire-lined track.

I sent the last ball clunking into the one-hundred cup and took my tickets. "You want to race?"

Billy snorted and took a drag off the cigarette. "Why would I want to screw around with some little go-kart when I know how to drive?"

"I know how to drive too," I said, even though it wasn't exactly true. My dad had taught me how to use the clutch once in the parking lot at Jack in the Box.

Billy didn't even blink. He tipped his head back and blew out a plume of smoke. "Sure you do," he said. He looked blank and bored under the flashing neon lights, but he sounded almost friendly.

"I *do*. As soon as I'm sixteen, I'm going to get a Barracuda and drive all the way up the coast."

"A 'Cuda, huh? That's a lot of horsepower for a little kid."

"So? I can handle it. I bet I could even drive your car."

Billy stepped closer and leaned down so he was staring right into my face. He smelled sharp and dangerous, like hair stuff and cigarettes. He was still smiling.

"Max," he said in a sly, singsong voice. "If you think you're getting anywhere near my car, you are extremely mistaken." But he was smiling when he said it. He laughed again, pinching the end of his cigarette and tossing it away. His eyes were bright.

And I'd figured it was all a big goof, because it was just how guys like that talked. The slackers and the lowlifes my dad knew—all the ones who hung out at the Black Door Lounge down the street from his apartment in East

Hollywood. When they made jokes about Sam Mayfield's daredevil daughter or teased me about boys, they were only playing.

Billy was looming over me, studying my face. "You're just a kid," he said again. "But I guess even kids can tell a bitchin' ride when they see one, right?"

"Sure," I said.

And I'd actually been dumb enough to believe that this was the start of something good. That the Hargroves were here to make everything better—or at least okay. That this was family.

CHAPTER TWO

My first day at Hawkins Middle School was a Tuesday, more than a month after the school year had already started. My mom hadn't made us go the day before because they didn't have all our records yet. But that morning, she stuck her head into my room and told me to get up.

All my stuff was still in boxes, and I thought she was going to make me unpack, but instead, she just smiled thinly and said it was time for school. I had an idea that maybe having Billy around all the time was starting to make her a little crazy. Or maybe she finally just noticed that I'd spent three days at the arcade. I would have spent a fourth there, but I couldn't skip school forever, and I was out of money anyway.

After breakfast, I got my backpack and my board and followed Billy out the door.

The Camaro smelled the way it always did—like hairspray and cigarettes. Billy slid into the driver's seat and gunned the engine. The car roared awake with a ragged snarl, and then we were tearing down the two-lane farm road into town, past woods and fields and a whole lot of cows.

In the driver's seat, Billy stared straight ahead. "God, this place sucks. I bet you're already planning your next jailbreak, right?"

I looked out the passenger window with my chin in my hand. "No."

My mom'd nearly had an embolism when the cops had brought me home from the San Diego bus station. She kept going on and on about how bad I'd scared them, and how dangerous it was to just go running off to god knew where, but she was totally missing the point. I hadn't been running off to god knew where, I'd been going to LA to see my dad. To my mom, though, that was pretty much the same thing.

Ever since they split up, my dad had been living in this crappy little apartment in East Hollywood with matted carpet and windows so dirty they made everything look like it was underwater.

He sunburned even more easily than I did—Black Irish, with hair so dark it looked dyed and skin you could see the veins through. He knew science and math and all the answers to the Sunday crossword puzzle, and could pick a Master Lock padlock with just a paper clip and a piece of Coke can.

My mom hated it when I went to stay with him. She worried about everything—muggers and traffic accidents and whether or not I'd have a bedtime. Even back when they'd gotten along, he was always giving her fits just by letting me do things that she wouldn't. It wasn't hard to make my mom freak out, but the things she worried about with him weren't even major. It wasn't like he was taking me to dog fights—he was just letting me light off Black Cats or showing me how to use his drill to make a derby car out of roller skates and orange crates.

After the divorce, my mom got even more nervous, and my dad got more careless. When I came home with a torn jacket or a new scrape on my knee, she would practically go into hysterics. I didn't tell her about the parking lot at Jack in the Box and him teaching me to drive his ratty old Impala.

When I told her about weekends at my dad's, it was easy to leave out the parts she wouldn't like. How he was always late to meet me at the bus station, or how he sometimes passed out in front of the TV. On weekends, he liked to drive up to the racetrack, and I'd sit on a vinyl stool next to him and eat peanuts and watch the horses.

Moving in with him wouldn't have been the worst thing in the world. LA was cool. They had punk clubs and Oki Dog and all-girl skater gangs. I'd miss my friends, but things had gotten weird with them that summer. I wasn't even sure it mattered anymore.

I'd never really thought about San Diego one way or another until I found out we were leaving. Neil and my mom sat us down in the living room and told us they'd decided that we were moving to Indiana, but that was a lie. Neil had decided. My mom just nodded and smiled and went along with it.

Billy was the one who lost it. He blasted his music and slammed around the house and stopped showing up for dinner.

I just decided I wasn't going.

My escape was short-lived, though. The police brought me home, and I packed all my stuff in ten cardboard liquor boxes and watched the movers stack them in the back of a rental truck. And now we were here in Hawkins.

The whole place was smaller than I'd pictured, but kind of sweet, too. It might be okay. The little downtown was small and shabby, but at least they decorated for Halloween. And they had an arcade. How bad could a place be if it had an arcade?

Next to me, Billy was staring at the road ahead like it offended him.

• • •

Hawkins Middle was a long brick building across the parking lot from the high school. It was plain and sturdy, more

like a county jail than a school. My mom had told Billy to drop me off and then come in with me and make sure they had all my stuff, but he just blew past the front entrance and gunned it up to the high school parking lot.

"Hey!" I stared at him and banged my hand on the dashboard. "You're supposed to drop me off."

Billy rolled his head sideways to look at me. "But I don't want to, Max. They're not paying me to babysit you. If you don't like it, maybe tomorrow you can walk."

I didn't answer, just grabbed my board and my schoolbag. When I got out of the car, I didn't look back.

The main office was easy to find, down a little hall to one side of the front doors.

The woman behind the counter had a shiny old-fashioned blouse. When I told her why I was there, she looked at me like I was some kind of strange new creature.

Finally she turned and called back to another lady who was digging through a filing cabinet. "Doris, do we have a class schedule for Mayfield?"

The second lady put down her folders and came up to the counter. "What do you need a class schedule in the middle of the semester for?" she said, like I'd confused her.

I didn't answer, just sighed and made my eyes wide and impatient. It was a look my mom couldn't stand. She said it was because I was making things harder for myself, but I could tell it made her feel embarrassed, like she had to apologize for me. I wasn't being nice.

I was almost sure the office ladies would make me stow

my skateboard. In Cali, the rule had been that you had to keep it in your locker, but here no one said anything about it. Maybe they didn't even have a rule for skateboards. Maybe they'd never seen one.

My first class was science, and I got there after the bell.

Even though everyone was already seated, the room had a lot of empty desks, like the class was supposed to be bigger. I knew it was just because the classroom was big and Hawkins was small, but the empty places made it seem like the part in a story where everyone goes off to fight a monster and they don't all come back.

The teacher made me stand at the front of the room while he introduced me. It's so annoying how certain kinds of grown-ups always call you by your full name, like you've done something wrong. When I corrected him, some of the girls giggled or whispered, but the boys only stared.

The rest of the morning was even worse, like the school was trying to prove to me exactly how much I didn't belong there. In history, everyone else was working on their semester projects. The teacher, Mr. Rogan, had me do a photocopied worksheet while everyone else pushed their desks together in threes and fours, and then he didn't even remember to make me hand it in.

I hadn't had to actually make friends since I was a little kid. I'd never figured out how to talk to other girls. Back home, they always acted weirded out over how I didn't care about press-on nails and perms, or how when I watched

monster movies, I didn't do it just to squeal and scream. Every day during summer, they'd lie out by the pool and cover each other's shoulders with baby oil and talk about boys. I wasn't interested in burning myself up trying to get a tan, and I knew actual boys and pretty much none of them were worth swooning over.

This past weekend my mom had been on a homemaker kick, unpacking everything, then folding and ironing it. Finally, she ran out of her own clothes, and I caught her in my room, going through the boxes. That morning, she'd gotten out the floppy Esprit cardigan she bought me last year at Fashion Barn and put it on my bed. The cardigan was pastel striped, with big plastic buttons. I'd never worn it in my life. I stood looking at it, trying to figure out exactly what she wanted. I was already dressed in jeans and a pullover like I wore every day.

"What's that for?" I said. I knew I should want to make her happy, but I wasn't about to show up to my first day at a new school dressed as someone else.

She smiled weakly. "It's your first day. I thought you might like to wear something a little special."

"Why?"

Her smile faded and she looked away, fiddling with the sleeve of the cardigan. "Oh, I don't know. It just seems like a waste, you know? You're so pretty, but you never dress up or try to look nice."

The idea that I needed to dress up for Hawkins was so

idiotic I almost laughed. I didn't feel very pretty, and I definitely wasn't nice.

At lunch, I ate beef jerky and pretzels out of a paper bag and sat alone on the cracked concrete steps by the gym. We still hadn't unpacked the kitchen, and we needed to go grocery shopping. For the first time since leaving San Diego, I really let myself feel the hollow in my chest. It took a minute to recognize it. *Loneliness*.

At home I'd had Ben Voss, Eddie Harris, and Nate. We spent summers and afternoons after school skating, or else building forts in the dry creek behind my house.

And even after he moved to LA, I'd had my dad. He was full of ideas and knew how to make it feel like he was with me even when he wasn't. He'd always gotten really excited about puzzles—spy kits, secret codes, dead drops. It was the solving that he liked. When I was little, before he moved to LA, he used to hide notes for me in my homework. I'd be working on a history report or flipping through my language arts book, and there between the pages would be a little square of folded paper with a message in code, or a puzzle he'd made using circles and triangles, or words that sounded alike but were spelled different.

I thought it was cool, but it drove my mom nuts. She could never seem to get over how mad she was that he could be that smart and that good at things but still work nights at the bail bond place, or sometimes not work at all. He wasn't a nine-to-five person, though. The jobs he did were mostly under-the-table, and after the divorce, he kind of stopped pretending it had been any other way. He slept late and spent his nights hustling pool or making fake IDs. The ways he made money embarrassed my mom, but they made sense to me. I got how it was to know you were supposed to be following the rules but still feel so spun up you thought you were going to explode. The only thing was to hold still and wait it out and as soon as the bell rang, go tearing out the door and down the street in a whoosh of air.

Over by the four-square grid, a little pack of girls was standing in a circle, lazily bouncing the rubber four-square ball between them. They were all the kind of girl my mom probably wished I'd turn into, in corduroy jumpers and plaid skirts down to their shins. They didn't even wear wet n wild nail polish or tease their bangs. Two of them were wearing cardigans, and all I could think was how relieved my mom would be to know she'd been right after all.

For a second, I thought about going over to them, but what was I supposed to say? I could never figure out the right things to say to make some girl in a flannel skirt be my friend. How pathetic.

I spent the rest of the lunch period cruising back and forth over the sloping pavement behind the school. I was rattling down the hill for the third time when I got a weird, twitchy feeling, like being in a spotlight.

There was a group of boys over by the gate to the football field. They were all clustered together behind the chain-link fence. Watching me.

I wasn't sure, but I thought I recognized them from first period. They were half-hidden behind the fence, and I realized they were spying on me, but they weren't being very slick about it. One of them whispered something, and they all leaned closer, as if I couldn't see them standing there.

All day, I'd been feeling off balance, like time was moving much too slow. I needed to prove something, or maybe just make up for the fact that besides my teachers and the ladies in the office, no one had talked to me all day.

I took out the crumpled history assignment and scrawled a message on the back, not a puzzle, not in code. In plain English, telling them to stay away from me. I wrote fast and slanted, but I wasn't even sure that I meant it. If I really wanted to be left alone, maybe I wouldn't have written anything at all.

I threw the note in the trash and walked inside, the doors sighing shut behind me.

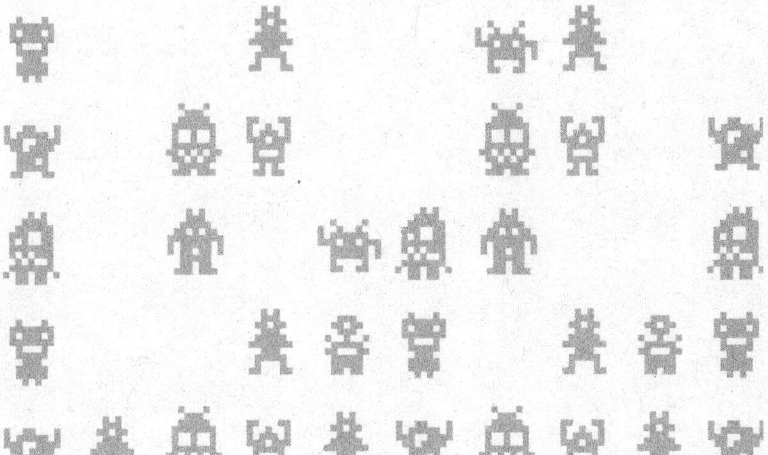

CHAPTER THREE

My mom had only been married to Neil for three weeks the first time I got a clear picture of him.

It was a Wednesday night, which used to just mean my mom would make rigatoni and meatballs and we'd sit on the couch to watch *Family Feud*. Since the wedding, though, Neil was always wanting to do things together. School had just let out for the year, and he decided that we were all going out to eat at Captain Spaulding's. As a family.

The restaurant was the loud, sticky kind where people go to sit around a table for an hour, eating onion rings and acting like they're having a good time.

Billy didn't even bother to pretend. He spent the whole meal leaning back in his chair and staring at the ceiling.

My mom picked at her salad for a while, then reached over and put her hand on mine. "You know, I was thinking that maybe this summer, we could sign you up for volleyball camp?"

"It's not really we, since you don't have to go."

My mom smiled a big, anxious smile, and I saw there was lipstick on her teeth. "It would be a good way to spend time with other girls for a change. Don't you want to make some new friends?" The waxy smear made her look like she'd been eating something bloody. I frowned and stopped looking at it.

Neil was eating his cheeseburger with a fork and knife. He stopped chewing and leaned close, staring into my face. "You answer your mother."

I twisted away. "Why? It doesn't matter what I want." His breath smelled like pickles.

"Maxine," he said. "I'm warning you."

"My name," I said, feeling a hot rush of fury in my cheeks, "is *Max*."

Neil breathed through his nose like he was trying to keep something locked inside. Then he set down his fork and reached for my arm. "If you don't get that mouth under control, you're going to be one sorry little girl."

And I knew I was supposed to apologize and act like the good, smiling daughter my mom and Neil wanted me to be, but I could feel everything inside me speeding up. It was like being stuck in class for the whole afternoon, and then the bell rings and all you want is to get outside and go and go and go. My dad always said that my brain was fast but my mouth was faster.

"I'd rather be sorry than be at volleyball camp."

Neil gave me a level stare that seemed to burrow its way under my skin. "You need to learn a thing or two about how you talk to your father."

"But you're not my father." I said it very quietly, just under my breath.

Not quietly enough.

Neil tightened his grip on my arm and pulled me out of my chair. "You're done here. Go wait in the car."

I stared at my plate, still heaped with fruit salad and french fries and the rest of my hamburger. We were supposed to get sundaes after. "I haven't even finished my fries!"

Neil gave me a long, freezing stare, like something inside him was turning to ice while I watched. "Wait. In the car."

I stared back until the weight of his gaze got too heavy to stand, and then I looked away.

I wasn't going to cry. I told myself he was just another temporary interruption to my life—I just had to wait him out. But I didn't really believe it. Things were changing too fast. My mom had never sent me away from the table. I wasn't crying. But almost.

I walked stiffly out of the restaurant, past the waitresses

and the hostess. I was mortified by the way they looked at me, like they knew I was in trouble and were sorry for me. I was almost thirteen and the whole restaurant was watching me get time-out like a little kid.

Out in the parking lot, I sat in the backseat of my mom's Skylark with the door open and thought about how much I hated Neil.

I'd found half a package of sunflower seeds in the pocket of my shorts and was eating them and dropping the shells on the ground when I realized that someone was standing over me.

Billy had come outside and was standing in the pale yellow circle of the streetlight, looking down at me.

After a long time, he sighed and lit a cigarette. He always smoked them in this insolent punk-rock way, clamping the butt between his teeth so it jutted from the center of his mouth. "You really did it this time, declaring war on Neil."

I didn't want him to see how stupid I felt for yelling at his dad and getting sent away from the table. I scowled and looked down at my shoes. They were green suede Vans. The color on the toes was scuffing, but the rubber was all right. "I just don't want him acting like he's my dad, and I'm not going to pretend that he is."

"Don't worry about it," Billy said, looking up at the neon CAPTAIN SPAULDING'S sign. The waving, smiling clown flashed over the parking lot. "It's not like he's my dad either."

I glanced at him, not sure I'd heard right. "What?"

Billy turned back to me, and I was sure he was going to tell me it would be okay. Maybe even hug me.

But his eyes were flat and heavy like always. "He's a horrible guy, Max. Haven't you figured that out? You really think a guy like that could be a father? Not to me, and not to you."

• • •

"You don't want to wear your costume?" my mom said when I came into the kitchen for breakfast on my second day of school. She was unwrapping dishes from a cardboard box full of newspapers and putting them in the cupboard.

Neil was at the table, eating scrambled eggs and reading the sports page. He shoved the last bite of toast into his mouth and answered her, even though she'd been talking to me. "You shouldn't encourage her. She's getting too old for that."

My mom gave me a shy, apologetic look, but she didn't argue with him. I just rolled my eyes and reached past her for the cereal. *Whatever.*

Anyway, it felt wrong to get ready for Halloween alone. Usually, I spent all of October hanging out in the garage with Nate, working on our costumes and thinking up cool ways to beg for candy when people came to their doors, and now I was two thousand miles away and it felt like an entire chunk of myself was missing.

I'd been a little bit of a fanatic about Halloween ever

since I was tiny. It was the perfect holiday. Maybe not my favorite—Christmas was still pretty rad, even though it was cheesy to admit that—but Halloween was the one night I got to feel like something bigger than just myself.

The year before, I'd gone as Nosferatu, and Nate was Dr. Van Helsing. He colored his hair gray with baby powder and had a canvas bag of wooden tent stakes, but no one could tell who he was supposed to be, even when he took out one of the stakes and pretended to stab me. His turned out pretty good, but my costume was scarier, with jagged plastic teeth and a rubber cap to make me look bald. My mom was practically distraught over how ugly it was, when that was the whole point.

Ever since I was little, I had loved monsters. I never missed an episode of *Darkroom,* and sometimes my dad would take me to the Bluebird Theater, where they showed old black-and-white movies full of mummies and wolfmen and Frankensteins.

Lately, though, I was more into movie slashers like Leatherface and Jason, or the guy in this new one they kept showing previews for, who had a ratty striped sweater and a face like Sloppy Joes. There were all kinds of monsters with superpowers and magical abilities, but slashers seemed scarier because they were less imaginary. Sure, a vampire was creepy, but psycho killers could actually happen. I mean, I saw the news. Creepy guys in dark alleys or white vans went after girls all the time.

After breakfast, I stood in the hall to my bedroom, trying to decide what to do. I hadn't really planned to wear the costume, but the way Neil had written it off without even looking at me and the way he'd talked to my mom made me want to, just to piss him off. I was pretty sure I knew where my mask was.

The moving boxes were all still piled in the corner of my bedroom, labeled with my mom's neat, fussy writing. When I opened the one marked *Max's Treasures,* the mask was there, lying on top of my Flash comics like a floppy rubber nightmare.

I'd picked Michael Myers from *Halloween* because he had no weaknesses. He never moved fast, but he still caught up to you every time. He was impossibly strong—you couldn't overpower him and you couldn't outrun him. He was unstoppable.

Nate had been planning to go as Shaggy from *Scooby-Doo* because his mom never let him see R-rated movies. Mine probably wouldn't either, but I didn't have to worry about that because there was always my dad. *Had* always been my dad.

Michael Myers was the kind of monster I was most afraid of, because he was real. Not real-life, but the kind you could believe in anyway. He never talked or took his mask off, but underneath he was still a man, and a man could be lurking anywhere. There are all kinds of dangerous things in the world. Maybe not exactly like him, but close enough. You can't avoid them, so sometimes you just have to learn how to live with them.

The mask was white rubber, with molded plastic eyebrows and a wig of thick black hair and blank everything else, and I stood looking down at it, trying to decide whether I was going to put it on.

"Ma-aaax," Billy called from out in the hall. I knew he was in a mood when he called to me in that singsong voice that sounded sweet on top and dangerous underneath. "Where the hell are you, Max?"

I threw the mask on the bed and started digging through the box for the rest of the costume—maybe not the coverall, but the machete at least. I picked up a House of Mystery anthology and dropped it on the floor, trying to find the machete, but it was buried somewhere at the bottom, and I was running out of time.

From out in the hall, Billy called to me again. His voice had changed. He was farther away now. "If you're not in the car in ten seconds, I'm leaving without you."

I hurried out to the living room, still holding my mask. He raised his eyebrows when he saw it, but didn't say anything.

I shrugged and gave the mask a shake. "It's Halloween."

He still didn't answer, just looked at me with bored, heavy eyes.

"What? Now I'm not even allowed to dress up?"

"Go ahead, but don't be shocked when you look like a

baby. No one in middle school dresses up for Halloween. It's for losers, okay?"

I shrugged, but it was small and empty. When I couldn't think of anything to say, I went back into my room and shoved the mask in my dresser. One more thing that had stopped being mine.

CHAPTER FOUR

Even though I'd caved to Billy about the costume, I'd still sort of thought I was going to show up to Hawkins Middle in my everyday clothes and find a sea of mummies and witches. But no one else was dressed up either. As much as I didn't want to admit it, I was a little grateful not to be the new girl and the only person wearing a costume.

I was getting used to the school, but compared with the one I'd gone to at home, it seemed sprawled out and plain. The way there were no skylights and no windows made it feel like everything had stalled and I was stuck in an alternate reality that was all fluorescent lights and linoleum. I needed to move.

When the slow, sticky feeling finally got so bad I couldn't take it anymore, I dropped my board and rode it lazily through the halls. I was pretty sure that wasn't actually allowed, but I needed to do something that made the floor stop feeling like quicksand.

I was at my locker, trading out my books, when someone cleared their throat behind me. When I turned around, two of the stalker boys who'd been watching me out by the football field yesterday at lunch were standing side by side. One had thick, curly hair that stood out around his head and a broad, sunny face. He was beaming like he'd never had a better day. The other was a wiry black kid with a short 'fro. His smile was steadier and less intense but nice.

They were dressed like Ray Stantz and Peter Venkman from *Ghostbusters*. When they'd showed up to science that morning, everyone had giggled and whispered, but the costumes were pretty good. I thought about the mask in my dresser. Even if my mom had told me I couldn't wear it and made me go as something else, I wouldn't have picked *Ghostbusters*. It was a good movie, but the whole point of Halloween was to be something scary.

The curly-headed one was talking before I could even work out what they were doing there. "Hi, Max, I'm Dustin, and this is—"

The other one was less frenetic. I'd noticed him yesterday, because he was watching me from behind a fence. But also because there were basically no black kids in Hawkins. "Lucas," he said.

The look I gave them was bored and scornful. "Yeah, I know. The stalkers."

They both started talking at once, bumbling over themselves. Dustin launched into a hectic monologue. I couldn't tell if he was just nervous or if he was trying to sell me on something. He sounded like he was pulling some kind of scam, like the scalpers who were always trying to get you to buy concert tickets outside the clubs in LA.

He and Lucas were rambling over each other, and it took me a minute to figure out what they were even saying. Finally, Dustin looked at me wide-eyed, like he'd just had a revelation. "You're new here, so you probably don't have any friends to take you trick-or-treating."

It was rude to say it, maybe, but he was obviously right.

He grinned, showing white, even front teeth. "We're all meeting at the Maple Street cul-de-sac. Seven on the dot."

I'd come to Hawkins with no plans to fit in or be popular or make friends or anything, but it was hard to remember that now. They were smiling, and I stared back, trying to understand whether this was all some kind of game. Whether they really wanted me to come with them. I'd spent so much time hanging around Billy it was getting harder and harder to tell when something was serious and when it was a joke.

I'd always thought I was good at being on my own. Independent, not afraid to take the bus downtown by myself or climb under the fence at the impound lot just to see what was in there.

But I'd never actually spent a lot of time without my friends. We were always doing projects together, or else making plans to. After school and in the summer, we spent pretty much every day building forts or skating in the park.

Nate Walker had been my very best friend since we were six. He was shorter and skinnier than me, with knobby elbows and the kind of mouse-brown hair that no one stared at or made fiery-redhead jokes about. We were field-trip buddies and science partners and we played street hockey and camped out in my backyard and it didn't even matter that I was a girl.

On the first day of first grade, I saw this skinny little boy in a red Spider-Man shirt crouched under the slide at lunch. Some of the other boys had been chasing him with a dead worm on a stick until he started crying and then ran away to hide. Even at six, I thought it seemed like a pretty pointless thing to cry over, but I liked his shirt, so I crawled under and sat with him.

"What's wrong?" I said. The air under the slide was hot. I can still remember the way the sand made my hands feel like chalk.

He ducked his head and didn't answer.

"Do you want to see my Man-Thing comic?" I said, and he nodded and wiped his nose on his arm.

The Man-Thing comic was a million years old, and the cover was falling off because I liked to take it everywhere. In it, the Man-Thing has to battle an evil biker gang that's been hanging around his swamp, along with a shady developer who wants to destroy him. The developer hires a corrupt scientist to invent a trap called the Slaughter Room in order to get rid of him, but the Man-Thing escapes and kills the leader of the biker gang before shambling back into the swamp.

We sat with our shoulders pressed together and read the book right up until the yard monitor came over to lean under the slide and say that it was time to go back in.

After that, we were friends. I always picked him first for dodgeball, even though he was so bad at blocking and someone always tagged him out right away. He always knew how to fix his bike or my skateboard and didn't care too much when I got competitive about H-O-R-S-E or sounded like I was mad about something when I was really just asking a question.

My dad still lived with us then, and most of the time, he didn't have much of an opinion about my friends one way or the other, but he liked Nate. Ben was too hyper, and to my dad, Eddie might as well have been a cinder block or a potato, but Nate, he would always say, was one to watch. Bright.

My dad didn't care much about good grades, or whether

someone had the right clothes or car, or came from the right neighborhood, but he liked when people were bright.

And Nate was. He was shyer and softer than the other guys we hung out with, but he was smart and interesting and always had the best ideas for how to build a tree fort or make a catapult work. Anyway, it was nice, sometimes, to hang out with someone who didn't always need to be moving as fast as I did.

Nate actually understood what my dad meant when he talked about hailstorms or carburetors, and I liked that. He never acted like it was weird that while other people's parents listened to Neil Diamond or the Bee Gees, my dad listened to bands that came on bootleg cassette tapes with strips of masking tape on them with the names written in marker. The music was angry and screamy, and the bands were called things like the Dead Kennedys and Agent Orange and the Bags. My mom just sighed, got out the vacuum cleaner or the mixer, and pretended she didn't hear.

I didn't like the bootleg tapes as much as my dad did. I was more into the Go-Go's, and sometimes old surfer music like the Beach Boys, or else the Sandals, who did the soundtrack to *The Endless Summer,* but when my dad put on one of his punk bands, Nate lit up like he was hearing something I wasn't. I didn't get what was so great about the music, but it felt good to bring my friends home to someone who liked them. The memory of my dad was hazy and warm.

Now I just had Billy and Neil and no place to feel good about and no one to bring home anyway.

By the time school let out, I was about ready to climb out of my skin. The day already felt a million years long.

I packed up my books, then skated along the cracked blacktop back up to the high school parking lot. Back to the Camaro.

Billy was waiting, leaning on the back bumper and smoking a cigarette. He was looking away from me, toward the pale autumn sky, and I waited to find out which version of him I'd get today.

You never knew with Billy. That was sort of the worst thing about him—how sometimes he wasn't that bad. Especially at first, before I'd figured out what he was like, I actually enjoyed hanging out with him. He picked me up from school sometimes, or let me go with him to Kragen Auto. The problem was, he could be fun.

He didn't treat me the way he treated the girls he went to school with, maybe just because they were older or less willing to stick up for themselves, but I thought it might be something else.

When he took them to parties or to hang out in the Carl's Jr. parking lot with the other wasters from school, it wasn't like a date. And sure, they acted like they were too cool to care about going steady or being someone's girlfriend, but they still tried to get him to come over and meet their parents, or made a big thing of being nice to me, like that was somehow going to impress him. They held their breath, hoping it would mean something, and then a week later, he'd be pulling into the Carl's Jr. with someone else.

It was like he hated them, except he still took them up to Sunset Cliffs to make out. It infuriated me, the way boys acted like girls couldn't be interesting or human and were only good for taking off their shirts.

Billy never treated me that way, though. At first I thought it was because I was younger or because I was his sister, even if I wasn't his real one. But after a while, I started to understand that the reason he treated me differently was because I wasn't like them. I didn't chase boys or wear makeup or even always remember to brush my hair. And for most of my life, the reason had been simple: I hadn't wanted to. But now the rules were different, and it felt more like I couldn't.

Billy talked to me, but in this sly, confidential way, like there was something important he wanted me to understand. It was like he hated me, except for the way he went out of his way to make me just like him. Any hint of softness and he would never let me forget it.

On the ride home, I slouched in the passenger seat, listening to him go on about what a backwater Hawkins was—the hick party scene, the speed limits, the terrible basketball team, the lame girls.

I was staring out the window, watching the countryside flash by—woods and fields. There were so many trees. I knew he wanted me to agree with him and say how much the place sucked, but I didn't see the point, and I told him that—how we were stuck here, so we might as well deal with it.

He turned on me. "And whose fault is that?"

For a second I was sure this was finally it—we were going to talk about what had happened back in San Diego. I didn't want to, and maybe if I kept quiet, we wouldn't have to deal with it.

But Billy had gone brutal and chilly, waiting for me to take the blame. "Say it."

When I didn't answer, he turned in his seat and screamed it at me, his voice a raw, ugly roar. "Say it!"

He gunned the engine and we charged along the two-lane road, scattering drifts of orange leaves. I stared straight ahead and didn't say anything.

In front of us, the road wound lazily through the wooded countryside. We came over the top of a little hill to see a straggly line of bikes. Three boys in brown coveralls with oversize proton packs on their backs. Ghostbusters. They were pedaling down the road, spread out across the right-hand lane.

"Billy, slow down."

"Oh, are these your new hick friends?" Billy mashed his foot down harder. "I get bonus points if I get 'em all in one go?"

The needle on the speedometer was climbing. Ahead of us, the Ghostbusters were still cruising down the middle of the road. They couldn't see us.

"Billy, come on, stop! It's not funny!"

He turned in the driver's seat, looking at me instead of the road. The stereo was blasting and he bobbed his head, thrashing along to the music.

The boys were an interruption in the road, getting bigger. We were coming up on them at an impossible speed, and they finally looked around. I could see their confusion, and I felt the same thing on my own face, because it couldn't mean what it seemed to. Billy wasn't going to run them down, that would be insane. It was the kind of thing people joked about but didn't actually *do.*

I told myself that, but there was no way for me to believe it. In a normal, orderly world, this couldn't happen. But the truth was here, right in front of me: I didn't know what Billy was going to do about anything anymore.

The bikes loomed in front of us. They looked totally destructible.

I knew if I didn't do something, everything after this moment was going to be bad. The fear was in my throat now, a clawing, squeezing hand. I reached across the center console and shoved the wheel. The Camaro swerved out into the oncoming lane.

There was a wild jolt, like everything was sliding. Tires squealed. Then we were around the boys and bombing down the road toward home.

I looked back over my shoulder, in time to see them all lying on the shoulder, bikes tipped sideways in the drifts of leaves.

The danger was behind us now, but my eyes felt hot and too big for my head. It was hard for me to blink, and I stared at the dirty windshield. At the road.

As soon as my hand had touched the steering wheel, I'd known that I was doing something dangerous. I'd crossed some invisible dividing line into a place where bad things happened, and now I would have to pay for it. Billy would scream at me, kick me out of the car and make me walk. Maybe even hurt me.

He didn't even seem to care, though. He just threw his head back and laughed a high, screaming laugh, huge and hilarious, like this was all some messed-up game. "That was a close one!"

He was grinning, drumming on the steering wheel and nodding along to the music. I kept my hand on the door handle all the way home.

I was thinking about something my dad had told me. The trick to being at home in the world, he said, was knowing how to do things. If you had the right tools, you could fix your own sink, find a job, figure out a problem. It was why he cared so much about knowledge and information. It was why I tried so hard to learn the things he taught me.

When you can take apart a hinge or pick a lock, you can always get out.

CHAPTER FIVE

As soon as we pulled up to the house, I got out and went inside.

My heart was beating like a piston in my chest. I needed to distract myself. I went straight to my bedroom and started digging through my boxes, looking for the rest of my costume. It was down in the bottom of the moving box, wadded up under a stack of surf magazines.

Some of the girls in my history class had been talking about trick-or-treating and where to get the best haul. It had made me feel better, a little, to find out that even if it was suddenly deeply uncool to go to class dressed up, the kids in Hawkins still went out on Halloween.

The main part of the costume was an old coverall of my dad's from when he had a very temporary job as a washing-machine repairman. It had been too big for me, and the zipper stuck. I'd been working on my costume since the second week in September, and my mom wasn't a huge fan of the idea that I wanted to be Michael Myers, but she'd still dragged out her sewing machine and cut the coverall down to fit me. That was as far as she'd been willing to go, though. She said I couldn't have a machete, but my dad had come to the rescue. He found a giant deli knife at a swap meet in LA and ground down the blade to look more like the one in the movie.

It was a good costume, and suddenly I didn't care about the kids at school or Billy or whether Neil said I was too old. I was going trick-or-treating.

I pawed through the box and laid the knife and the coverall on the bed next to my mask. It hit me all at once that this was the first time I'd be spending Halloween without my best friends. Then I closed my eyes and reminded myself that even if we'd stayed in San Diego, it wouldn't have been the same. Even before we moved, things had changed.

At least the *Ghostbuster* boys had invited me to trick-or-treat with them. That wasn't so bad. I had a costume and someplace to go.

I put on my coverall and my mask and let myself won-der what kind of candy they gave out here. It was better than thinking about the drive home. I didn't want to picture what would have happened if I hadn't grabbed the wheel. It was over. They were fine.

But my hands felt shaky.

• • •

The thing about Billy was you never knew what was going to happen when he got mad.

The week after school let out for the summer in San Diego, he'd gotten in trouble for trespassing, and Neil had grounded him. There was a construction site across the street from the high school—some kind of apartments or offices—and Billy and his friends liked to hang out there, drinking beers and sitting around on the scaffolding. Then someone from the construction crew must have noticed the empty cans or the cigarette butts everywhere and called the cops.

We were at home in the living room one Saturday night. I'd been supposed to go visit my dad, but at the last minute, Neil had changed his mind and said that I'd been seeing too much of him lately, and I should spend more weekends with my mom. So I stayed in San Diego and baked cookies with my mom and carved *I hate Neil* into the baseboard behind the couch in tiny letters using a safety pin.

I was sitting on the floor watching the NBC weekly movie and eating Count Chocula in my pajamas when the cops brought Billy home. He was dirty and rumpled, with mud on his boots and a cut on his hand, but mostly he just looked furious. The cops said that he and his friends had been up in the scaffolding at the construction site, daring each other to walk across the steel I beams.

I wasn't always good at being careful with people or at making small talk, but I was good at guessing their moods. Even when I was little, I could sometimes tell just by looking who was dangerous or who was lying. My mom would stare at me wonderingly, and once, when I told her the guy she was dating had a gambling problem, she asked how anyone could know that. In that case, it wasn't like I was doing some impossible trick. His pockets were full of lottery tickets and betting stubs. The only reason I knew and she didn't was because she never believed the signs until it was too late.

I hadn't ever told her about Billy, but I should have. I just hadn't gotten to it yet. I kept waiting for her to see without me having to say it. The again, maybe it wouldn't have made a difference.

Neil waited until the cops were gone, then turned with a face like thunder. He told Billy that he could either sign up for junior ROTC, or say goodbye to his car for the next two months. Billy said goodbye to the car.

A week later, I was up on the weedy little ridge behind the house. A creek bed ran along the top of the hill. In the spring, it filled with four and a half feet of dirty, fast-moving water, but now it was dry and would be for the rest of the year.

I'd spent most of my summers hanging out up there with

Nate and Ben and Eddie. We had a little spot, with packed dirt and a table made out of a wooden milk crate, and a mangy couch that Ben and Eddie had found set out by the curb on trash day. It wasn't a clubhouse, exactly, but we'd go up there to shoot BB guns at bottles, or else get Bomb Pops from the Good Humor truck and hang out on the couch, talking about monster trucks or wrestling and sucking on the Popsicles until our teeth turned blue.

Usually Nate would come over at nine or ten. We'd spend the morning reading comics, then take his bike and my skateboard to the park, or else ride over to the pool with Ben and Eddie. But Eddie was in Sacramento for the weekend, and Ben had to mow his parents' yard. Nate was visiting his dad, so I was alone.

I'd been working on our latest project, which was a real working catapult. When it was done, we were going to use it to chuck water balloons at the road. I'd spent the morning getting the firing arm to swing, but now it was afternoon and hot, and I was just sitting on the back of the couch with my shoes on the cushions, looking out over the road that ran along the bottom of the hill.

Billy was inside, hanging around with his friends. Neil had taken his keys, and now the Camaro sat in the garage like a dog in a kennel, waiting for its owner to come let it out. He was supposed to be painting the garage, but he only worked on it when his dad was around.

Wayne and Sid were both from the housing development on the other side of the ridge. They went to school with

Billy and looked scraggly and dangerous, but I got the idea that they mostly just followed him around and let him tell them what to do.

I liked Sid the best. He was tall and sort of pudgy, with big, heavy-knuckled hands and green laces in his combat boots. He was usually nice and could be kind of funny, but he didn't talk very much.

Wayne was louder and skinnier, with greasy hair down to his shoulders and a face like a weasel. Since Neil had taken the keys to the Camaro, they mostly hung out in Billy's room, listening to Metallica and Ratt, but it must have been getting old, because that day Billy brought them out to the hill behind the house.

I wasn't sure I wanted them lounging around in my private hideout. I'd already had to learn how to exist in the same house as Billy, and now he was invading the rest of my life too. Since the night the cops brought him home, he'd been in a rank mood, slamming through the house or locking himself in his room and playing his music as loud as it would go, but that day, the three of them came crunching out to the creek bed and sat down next to me on the couch.

Billy leaned back and lit a cigarette, then stared off at the sprawling neighborhood below. For a while, we all sat and watched the traffic at the bottom of the hill without saying anything.

Sid had a Music City catalog and was leafing through it

looking at guitars. Wayne was jumpy and restless. He kept getting up to pace around in the weeds above the creek, then sitting back down again.

Finally, he threw his arms out and spun in a circle. "This sucks, man. I can't believe your dad jacked your car."

Billy was sitting on the edge of the couch, his eyes fixed on the road. The day had seemed heavy and lazy before, but now he looked tense, like he was waiting for something to happen. He gave Wayne a bored stare, then blew out a long plume of smoke and took out his lighter. It was a silver-colored flip-top with a flaming-skull decal, and I'd always been a little envious of it. Now, though, Billy was staring too hard at the weeds and dry scrub brush that grew all over the hill. The lighter flashed in the sunlight. I didn't like looking at it.

There was a dead cat that had been lying under one of the sweet pea bushes for a while. A mangy orange tom with one white foot. I didn't recognize it from the neighborhood, so it had probably been a stray, but I still felt sorry for it. I figured it must have gotten hit by a car and then crawled up the hill to die.

I'd been interested in it at first, but now I hated to look at it. The way the swarms of flies and beetles crawled over its fur gave me a squirmy feeling. I hated how its sides got flatter and more matted every day.

"Nasty!" said Wayne. He was leaning down with his hands braced on his knees, squinting into the bushes. "Look at this thing. Its ear's all messed up. I bet it used to be a total brawler. Do you think if I got some pliers, we could pull out its teeth for a necklace?"

"Gross, no!" I said, watching from my spot on the back of the couch.

Billy gave me a bored look and then got up and sauntered over to Wayne. The sun looked silver, glinting off his earring. His expression didn't change. "Or we could pay our respects and give it a Viking funeral. What do you think, *Sid*?"

He said it in a hard, bright voice, and I saw that something was ugly between them, but I couldn't tell what.

Sid didn't answer. I was sitting above him on the back of the couch, and he turned to me, holding up the catalog and pointing at an ad for a sleek cream-colored guitar. "This one's a Kramer Baretta. It's got a slanted humbucker, just like the Frankenstrat that Eddie Van Halen plays on 'Hot for Teacher.' See this little plate under the strings?"

I nodded and stared dutifully at the picture, even though I didn't know the first thing about guitars or what a humbucker was.

Over by the body of the cat, Wayne was laughing. "You're the one who said it would be cool to see one. At least Billy's got the balls to be a man about it!"

Sid slouched next to me, staring at the catalog. He folded the corner on the Kramer Baretta and didn't look up. "You mean, do the dumbest thing possible?"

I looked at them, but I couldn't figure out what it was or what was happening. "What's a Viking funeral?"

Billy grinned and rolled his head in my direction. "You really want to know?" He flicked the lighter and held it up, looking at me through the flame. "Ask Sid."

Sid still didn't look up from the catalog, just shook his head. "Seriously, cut it out."

I was hoping he'd explain, but Wayne was the one who answered, popping his eyes wide. "They used to light their dead on fire. Sid knows all about it. He got a hundred on the final history paper. Didn't you, Sid?"

I knew the paper. Billy had gotten a D, and Neil had been irate. Sid didn't say anything.

The cat was mostly decomposed and very dead, but it had still been an actual living, breathing animal. "No," I said. "That's gross. Don't."

It had been lying under the sweet pea for almost two weeks and was starting to get pretty mummified. It would have been dry enough on its own, probably, but Billy wasn't taking chances. He reached into his pocket and took out the little can of butane that he used to refill his lighter.

Without looking away from me, he popped the cap and sprayed the butane over the cat.

I watched as the lighter fluid splashed over the sunken shape of its body.

He and Wayne both leaned down for a closer look. Then Billy held the lighter under the bush. I wanted to jump up and knock the lighter out of his hand. I wanted to scream for him to stop, but it wouldn't have made a difference.

There was a long silence, like we were all holding our breath, and then he flicked the wheel with his thumb.

When the fur caught, it went in a dry, rasping whoosh. Wayne stumbled back, whooping and slapping at the bottom of his vest. The leaping flames had singed the tail of his shirt. Billy watched him with the strangest look—almost like he was satisfied.

The smell of the burning cat was like garbage and scorched hair, and I covered my nose with my hand. I watched it burn and reminded myself that nothing could hurt it now. The cat had probably had a rough life, but this new assault was nothing to it. It was already dead.

The weeds around the ditch were dry and yellow, even though it was only June, and the grass around the cat caught fire almost at once. I watched as the fire raced in a low stripe along the edge of the ditch. It looked almost liquid, spilling through the grass.

"What the hell, man?" Wayne was still cursing and slapping at his shirt. But he was laughing that high, giddy laugh, yelping and clutching his hand.

The fire was the color of a melted Creamsicle. It rushed out from the body of the cat and began to lick its way down the slope of the hill toward the road.

Sid threw down his guitar magazine and jumped up. He crossed the clearing in three lumbering steps and began to stomp hard on the burning grass with his army boots. I watched for a second, then climbed down from the couch and ran after him, stepping on the places he'd missed, kicking dirt over the embers.

It was a little while before we got it under control. Wayne was still skipping and wriggling like a puppy, laughing his high, manic giggle. Billy just watched, standing over the burning cat, smiling that small, tight smile he got when something seemed funny to him.

Finally, everything was extinguished, and Sid trudged back up the hill, breathing hard. The fire was out, but there was a blackened strip of grass for twelve feet along the edge of the ditch. Later I sat on my bed and counted all the places where the soles of my shoes had melted.

All summer, whenever I went up behind the house to the creek and saw that burned place, I would remember the way Billy had looked right before he flicked the lighter. I would smell the dead, burning stink again. A smoky, spoiled smell that sat in my nose like a warning. The cat wasn't a cat at all anymore, just a greasy black spot on the ground. The bush where it had been was mostly burned away, just blackened twigs and ashes.

After that, I knew.

Not that Billy was crazy or out of control, exactly—it wasn't like the cat had been alive. But the fact that he'd done it meant *some*thing.

I was getting good at staying out of his way when he got

mad, but I never seemed to be able to predict it ahead of time. I could never be sure what he was going to do.

• • •

At the corner of Oak and Maple, Billy pulled up to the curb and let me out. My mom had said he was supposed to come with me and walk me around the neighborhood, but both of us knew that wasn't going to happen. He was dressed for some high school party, in a leather jacket and fingerless gloves. It wasn't much of a costume, but I didn't say so.

"You be waiting here at ten," he told me, leaning out the driver's-side window. "If you're not here when I get back, too bad."

I nodded and pulled my mask down over my face.

He flicked a cigarette butt out the window and gunned the engine, already looking off toward something I couldn't see. I stood and watched the taillights go blazing away down the street. They turned the corner and were gone.

The neighborhood was crowded with trick-or-treaters, and I rubbed my arms through the coverall. I still wasn't used to how cold it got at night. Little kids raced back and forth across the road, running from one house to the next, their bags and buckets and pillowcases flapping. The air was crisp and chilly, but no one was wearing jackets.

I stood at the end of the Maple Street cul-de-sac, waiting for the Ghostbusters. I was a little worried that they might not want to see me after what Billy had done, but I'd decided to chance it. Anything was better than sitting alone in my room with no place to go and nothing to do. They'd invited me. And anyway, it hadn't been like I was the one who tried to run them down.

I'd just been the one who'd been right there watching from the passenger seat. Great. Maybe they'd blame me and not show up at all.

But I'd only been waiting a few minutes when, down the street, I saw the familiar shapes of boys in proton packs. There were four of them—Lucas and Dustin, along with the other two who'd been watching me from behind the fence during lunch yesterday. They were all in my science class and sat together in a little block of desks up near the front.

They looked so happy and oblivious, just bopping along, not paying attention to anything around them, and suddenly I had an idea to jump out at them. I wanted to shake things up, not enough to really scare anyone, but enough to make a little bit of a scene.

When I leapt out of the shadows with my machete, it was even better than I'd pictured. They all jumped and screamed high, shuddery screams, and I laughed—really laughed—for the first time since we'd moved to Hawkins. Lucas screamed the loudest. Normally that would have given me a mean, antsy feeling, like I needed to rag on him a little, but in a weird way it was kind of cute.

We headed for the Loch Nora subdivision, which was just off Main Street. At home, that would have meant a bunch of dive bars and walk-up apartments. But even though it was so close to downtown, it was the nicest neighborhood in Hawkins. The street was wide, lined with big two-story houses that all had picture windows and lawns planted with election signs.

My mom didn't usually care much about voting, but this year she'd paid more attention to the election. Before she and Neil were married, she used to talk about Walter Mondale sometimes. Mostly she would just shake her head and say how crazy he was to pick that Ferraro woman to be his vice president, because no man wanted to vote for a woman, even a woman with a law degree. But I thought it was kind of cool. Once, after the wedding, I tried to ask her who she thought she'd vote for, but Neil told me to knock off that political talk at the dinner table. Then he said how Reagan was the best thing that had happened to this country since Eisenhower, and there was no way in hell that anyone in his house was voting for Mondale and that lady. Most of the yard signs in Loch Nora were for Reagan.

We raced through the neighborhood, knocking on doors and holding out our bags for Snickers and Kit Kats. The other two boys were named Will and Mike, and neither of them really looked at me or said much. Mike had thick, dark hair and a pale, serious face. Will was smaller and quieter than the others and reminded me a little of my friend Nate. He seemed like the kind of boy people didn't usually notice.

For some reason, he was hauling around a huge camcorder almost too big for him to carry. He seemed shy and easy to embarrass, like the kind of person who probably felt weird having his picture taken. I wondered if it was easier when he could be the one looking out from behind the lens.

As we ran from house to house, I had to admit I was glad they'd invited me. They were awkward and hyper and a little dorky, but they were being really nice to me.

All except Mike. He sulked along behind us with a sour expression, and every time I glanced back at him, he would look away like he hoped I would just disappear.

The way he kept ignoring me was obnoxious, but there was no point in picking a fight with him. We were supposed to be having fun. So I made a point to have the most fun I could have. Walking between Lucas and Dustin, the night felt warmer, and I could almost forget that I was a million miles away from my friends and my dad and my entire life.

Loch Nora was clean and a lot fancier than anyplace I'd lived back home. By the time we'd cruised both sides of the street, my bag was so heavy that the bottom sagged, full of mini boxes of Nerds and full-size Milky Ways. The town might be the size of a postage stamp, but the candy was top-shelf.

We were standing on the edge of someone's lawn, comparing our hauls, when we looked around and noticed that Will was gone.

The street stretched dark and empty in both directions, and I had no idea how we were supposed to find him, but

Mike was already off and running, darting around the side of one of the big brick houses.

The backyard was lower than the front, and you got to it by going down a little set of stairs next to the house. Mike plunged down them, and we followed.

Will was there at the bottom, sitting in the shadows. The way he was curled in on himself made it hard to see him at first. He looked crumpled and strange, like he was frozen in place.

Mike was crouched in front of him, holding him by the shoulders. "I'm gonna get you home." When Lucas and Dustin crowded closer and tried to help them up, though, Mike shrugged them off and put his arm around Will. "Keep trick-or-treating. I'm bored anyway."

He might have been worried, but he sounded angry. He was talking to all of us, but I had a feeling it was because of me—because I was staring too intently or too long, or maybe just because I was there at all.

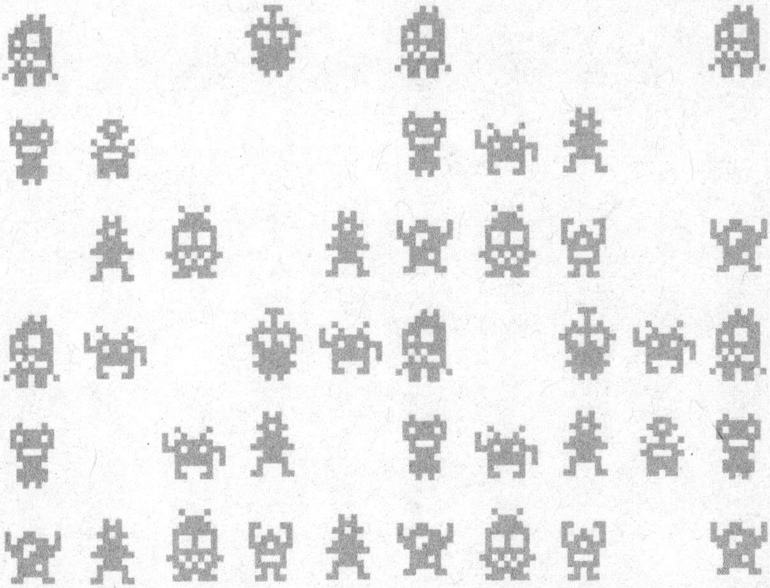

CHAPTER SIX

I walked into the house just past eleven o'clock, with my mask pushed up onto my forehead and my bag of candy slung over my shoulder. My feet hurt all the way up to my knees, and my hands were so cold that I could hardly feel them. So much for the unseasonably warm night. I'd spent almost half an hour waiting for Billy on the corner of Oak Street, but after the porch lights started flicking off and the last trick-or-treaters disappeared into their houses, I knew what I should have known from the start: he wasn't coming.

As soon as I got home, my mom came drifting out into the living room in her nightgown with cold cream on her face. "What in the world were you doing out so late? Where's your brother?"

Neil sat up straighter in his armchair. "I'd be interested to know the same thing."

For a second, I just stood in the middle of the living room, trying to figure out how to answer. I had a sudden urge to tell them that Billy wasn't my brother, even though that seemed like the least important part of the whole equation.

I shrugged and looked away. "Nowhere. There was this guy he knows from school who needed a ride home, so Billy dropped me off first. He'll be back in a second."

The lie was so ridiculous it made my face hot, but it still seemed better to avoid the truth, if I wanted to keep Neil from going ballistic. If I ever wanted to be allowed out of the house again.

My mom was watching me doubtfully, but she nodded. Her eyes were so hopeful, and I could see that she wanted to believe me. It was the same way people like her always got duped. It never mattered what the lie was; they just wanted so badly to believe it.

We were still standing in the living room, facing each other, when the quiet outside was interrupted by the sound of the Camaro. We all turned toward the door.

When Billy came slamming into the house, the smell came with him, rolling like the clouds of smoke and alcohol wafting out of a dive bar. Like bad weather. He was stumbling a little. His eyes were red-rimmed and heavier than ever, and he still had the leather jacket on, but he wasn't wearing a shirt. The light from the stained-glass lamp on the end table made him look deranged.

Neil breathed in through his nose and heaved himself out of his chair. "And where the hell have you been?"

"Nowhere," Billy muttered, and tried to brush past him, but Neil stepped in front of him and stopped him with a hand on his chest.

"What was that?"

Billy ducked his head and mumbled something about a flat tire. I couldn't tell if he was being honest or not—probably not—but as soon as he said it, it was pretty obvious that I had been lying. Whatever he'd been doing, it definitely hadn't been giving a school friend a ride home.

My mom gasped and turned on me with big, hurt eyes. "Why didn't you tell us he *left* you?"

She sounded so mystified, like she truly wanted to know. I had an urge to shake her and tell her she was totally deluded if she thought I'd be safer with Billy than alone, but I just said, "I don't know."

Her mouth crumpled and she pressed her hands to her face, which was greasy with cold cream. "What do you mean you don't know? He was in charge of you, and he just left you! You could have gotten lost. Or kidnapped!"

"Mom." I shook my machete and my bag of candy at her. "It's fine. I'm fine. I mean, have you seen this place? Nobody even locks their bikes!"

She was still looking at me in wounded confusion, like she didn't understand anything about me.

I stared back at her, and she seemed so timid and so small. It made me want to throw down my mask and my candy and shove her as hard as I could. And it made me want to do anything I could to keep her safe and happy and never let her spend a single minute out in the real world.

Neil had stayed ominously quiet, but now he drew himself up and took a step forward so he had Billy trapped against the wall. "I'm curious to know where you learned to be so disobedient."

Billy stared back at him. He was standing with his chin down and his jacket open, looking mutinous. He smelled like beer and the dry-skunk smell of Nate's brother, Silas, and all the other eighth-grade boys who got stoned behind the baseball diamond back home. It was the smell of not caring. "Bite me, Neil. I'm not in the mood."

My mom and I both tensed and moved closer to each other. Usually Billy kept it under control at home. He might have been a total jerk the rest of the time, but he never talked to Neil like that.

For a second, they just stood looking at each other.

Then Neil spoke in a low, dangerous voice. The air was heavy and metallic, like right before a thunderstorm. "I don't know where you've been or what you've been up to, but you will show me some *respect!*"

He shouted the last part. His voice sounded much too big in the smallness of the living room, and I winced, even though I was willing myself not to.

My mom clasped her hands to her collarbone, clutching

the lace on her nightgown, but her expression was already flattening, eyes sliding out of focus like she was slipping out of her own body. I knew what happened next. She would flinch and gasp and look away, but she wouldn't do anything to stop it.

I picked up my machete and put the mask back on. Then I turned and walked back down the hall to my room.

Safe on the other side of my door, I shoved my flannel blanket against the crack at the bottom. It made the shouting quieter, a little.

I dumped out all my candy in the middle of the floor and sat with my back against the footboard of my bed, counting the different kinds and sorting it into piles. Snickers with Snickers, SweeTarts with SweeTarts. The stalker boys had been right. The haul from Loch Nora was excellent. Inside the mask, my face felt hot and slick from my own breath.

Out in the living room, Neil was tuning up. For a while, it was just a rumble of voices, softer sometimes, then louder. There was a short, sharp cry and then a flat, meaty sound, like punching the pocket of a baseball glove.

I pretended it was nothing and I was someplace else. Sitting on the floor of my dad's apartment, maybe, watching *The A-Team*. In a minute the buzzer would sound, and the guy from Little Caesars would be standing in the hall. He'd hand over a pizza with peppers, mushrooms, and three kinds of meat. The smell would waft through the whole apartment, and my dad would put away the puzzle he'd been working on. We'd sit on the floor with the pizza between us, eating our slices straight out of the box. I'd pick off the peppers, he'd pick off the mushrooms, and we'd drink Dr Pepper and watch TV until the late-night movie was over and the test pattern came on. I closed my eyes, and I could almost pretend it was true.

From the other side of the wall, there was the sound of something falling over, but I couldn't tell if it was furniture or a person.

Inside the mask, I was no one, blank as an empty window. Billy seemed faraway, someone I didn't even know.

That's what I told myself, at least—and that he was a jerk. I didn't have to worry about him and his stupid life and his mean, awful dad.

But the truth was worse and more complicated. I did know him. I couldn't help it—I'd been watching him too closely and too long not to.

I repeated the lie anyway, like if I said it with enough force and enough times, I could make myself stop caring.

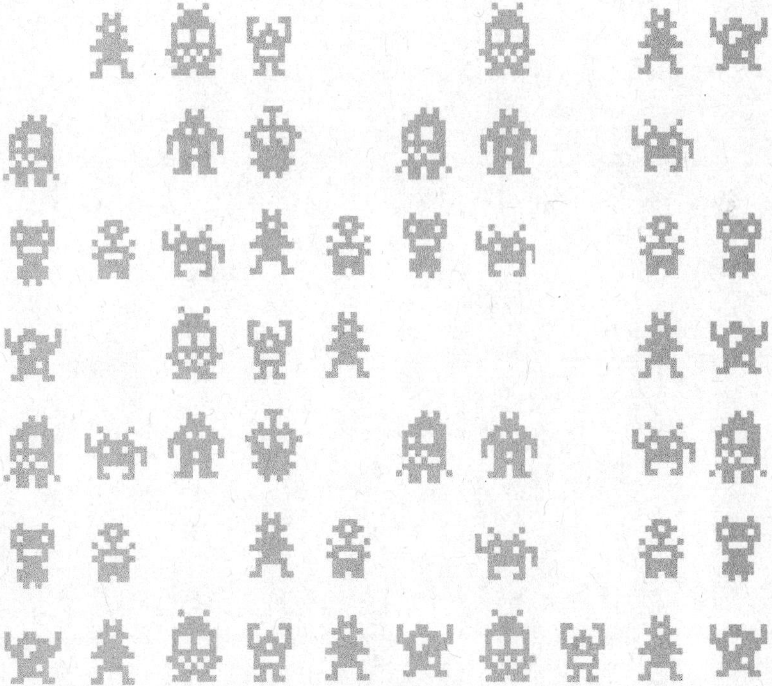

CHAPTER SEVEN

As I got out of the Camaro on Thursday and skated up toward the middle school, I was feeling more optimistic than I had since we'd come to Hawkins. The scene last night had been pretty bad, but now it was morning and I was ready for class, armed with Halloween candy and the idea that maybe I was actually going to like it here. I pushed through the double doors, squeezing past a pair of girls dressed in heavy knit sweater vests and eating a handful of M&M's.

I made it to my locker before the bell and was putting away my board when Lucas showed up. He was alone this time, wearing his normal clothes and looking awkward.

I raised my eyebrows. "Hey, stalker."

The look he gave me was impatient and a little embarrassed, but he didn't argue. He seemed fidgety, though, like he had something else on his mind. Just then, the warning chime rang. I shut my locker and we started for science class together.

It felt weird to be walking down the hall with a boy. A nice boy, with a wide, earnest smile and clean hands. I wasn't going to be all giddy and ridiculous about it, though. Back home, I was always hanging around the halls with Nate, or else Ben and Eddie.

Walking with Lucas felt different. He kept glancing over at me, and it took him a minute to get to what he wanted to say. I thought maybe he was going to tell me why Mike had such a huge problem with me—but it turned out he was mostly just worried about what I thought about Will having a breakdown. The way Lucas was acting, it was like he thought I would freak out about it. That wasn't really my style, though. Sure, I was mouthy sometimes, but I wasn't going to tease Will or go around telling everyone. There were just certain situations where it was better not to be a jerk.

Still, I'd heard things. In the two days I'd been there, it was pretty clear that if there was a Weird Kid in the class, Will was it. Hell, I was the new girl, and I still wasn't even the most interesting thing at Hawkins Middle.

The things people said about him were stupid or ridiculous and totally all over the place. A girl in my history class named Jennifer Mack had said that last fall his mom had reported him missing because he'd been lost in the woods, and it took him forever to find his way back. In my PE class, the general consensus was that his dad had kidnapped him for a week, and some of the boys in English had been elbowing each other and drawing cartoons of him with X's for eyes. They said he'd come back from the dead, which really didn't explain why they were being such jerks, because you'd think if they actually believed that, they'd be nicer about it. It seemed like a bad idea to make fun of a person who'd been raised from the dead, since he was clearly some kind of superhero.

Lucas was looking at me in a hard, unhappy way, like he was trying to make me understand something but couldn't say the words out loud. His breath smelled like Skittles.

His version of the story was pretty much the same as Jennifer Mack's, except he actually knew the details. He said the reason that everyone at school called Will zombie boy was because the whole town had thought he was dead—they'd had a funeral and everything—but his explanation wasn't really doing it for me. Even if Will had really been gone for as long as everyone was saying, a week was way too soon for a funeral. Even if you were searching for someone, getting scared that you might never find them, wouldn't you still try to convince yourself they were missing way before you'd assume that they were dead?

In science, I sat at my desk and stared at the back of Will's head, trying to see him the way Lucas did. Even without really talking to him, I knew the type. He was exactly the kind of boy that other boys always made fun of. It was one of the ways that he reminded me of Nate.

The idea of him as some kind of undead monster was so ridiculous it was actually a little scary, like the twist ending to a story. I'd learned from movies like *Psycho* that sometimes people were dangerous even when they didn't look like it. No matter how hard I stared at Will, he just looked tired and shy and a little bit worried.

Dustin wasn't in his seat, and I figured maybe he'd decided to ditch first hour to sleep in, or else hang around watching reruns and eating Halloween candy.

I was wrong.

He came barreling in late, flustered and out of breath. When I'd come in late on the first day, it had given me a tight, squirmy feeling when everyone turned to look at me. But he didn't seem to care. He flopped down at his desk, totally unfazed by the scene he was making. He ignored Mr. Clarke, leaning across the aisle to whisper to the other stalker boys in the noisiest, most obvious way. Like they had some kind of force field around them, and no one else could see them there. Even when Mr. Clarke finally got annoyed and told him to pay attention, he barely acted like it mattered.

I watched from the back of the room, trying not to feel left out. Dustin was still leaning sideways in his seat, whispering excitedly at Lucas, Mike, and Will. Then he turned to me and mouthed the words *A/V club. Lunch.*

I desperately wanted to know what was going on, but after the whole scene with Will the night before, I was still highly aware that I didn't really know them at all, and maybe they didn't want to know me. I'd come to school that morning half-ready to spend another lunch hour watching the girls over on the four-square grid and messing around on my skateboard. I'd resigned myself to lunch alone with a tuna sandwich and a handful of fun-size Charleston Chews, and it still felt hard to believe I might have found friends in a place like Hawkins.

But the way Dustin had turned and mouthed the words at me was so effortless, and I was ready to spend my lunch someplace that wasn't sitting alone on the steps behind the gym.

• • •

The A/V room was dim and cluttered, all shelves and no windows, more like a closet than a room. There was a big desk in the middle, stacked with loose papers and a computer and a ham radio, and the walls were lined with cubbies full of cords and microphones. It had a stuffy, adult feeling, like it was off-limits to students, but you could tell from how casually the boys let themselves in that they spent a lot of time there.

Dustin was standing at the desk, bent over the ghost trap he'd made for his Halloween costume. It had a pair of mechanical doors that opened on a hinge and were striped with electrical tape. The only thing I knew about why we were there was that he wanted to show us some weird animal he found in the trash on Halloween and then carried to school in the ghost trap for safekeeping. The rest of them were gathered around Dustin, and I squeezed in too.

The ghost trap wasn't like a real trap that you could catch anything with, but it still had a little switch to work the hatch, and he pressed it.

The thing inside was gross and kind of amazing. It was wriggling around in the bottom of the trap like a fat, blind tadpole, only it was about the size of a hamster and covered in slime. I'd heard of rescuing kittens out of dumpsters, but this was on a whole different level.

For a second, we all stood in silence, looking at it. It gave me an uneasy feeling. I wasn't scared of animals—even the creepy-crawly ones. I'd hunted for snakes in the weeds behind my house. Snakes were dry and scaly, though, and even kind of graceful. The thing in Dustin's trap was slippery and lumpy like snot.

Its body was basically a blob, with a pointed tail and two stubby little front legs. Dustin scooped it out of the trap, and I squinted at it, studying its bulbous head. I was looking for the eyes, because it didn't seem to have them. I'd never seen anything like it.

Dustin bent over the table, gazing at the creature in his hands like it was the sweetest, most adorable thing. He kept calling it a *he,* even though it was so weird and shapeless that how could you tell?

When he saw me staring, he asked if I wanted to hold it, and I shook my head, but he turned and tipped it out of his cupped palms and into mine.

It felt cool and squishy, heavier than it looked, and I passed it to Lucas fast. Lucas handed it off to Will, and it made its way around the circle. I was a little relieved to see that I wasn't the only one shrinking back from it. Will was looking at it like it had some kind of disease, and even Mike didn't exactly seem thrilled to touch it. He was the bravest, though, and held it up for a closer look.

The way Dustin was so excited about a giant tadpole was a little intense. He was telling us all kinds of random trivia— that it was a terrestrial pollywog and he'd named it Dart and it liked 3 Musketeers bars but hated light. The whole thing was totally bizarre, like a big, complicated game, and I wasn't sure I was even really part of it.

Still, it was fun to watch Dustin leaf through a stack of books about amphibians that he'd brought from the library, and it was nice to have something be fun and exciting again. It had been months since I'd had a chance to be part of something.

The way Will had stared at the tadpole, so tense and wary, was weird. I wasn't planning to cuddle it or anything, but it wasn't actually scary. It was just gross and a little slimy, small enough to hold in your hand. He was watching it like he was frozen, and I wondered again if this was turning out to be some kind of real-life *Dungeons and Dragons*, but he didn't seem like he was pretending.

After lunch, we headed to class. Dustin was on a whole big thing about how he'd discovered a new species, how he was going to name it after himself, and what he was going to do when he was famous. I listened, but it still sort of felt like we were playing a game. Or else they were playing a game, and I just happened to be hanging around with them while they did it, I just didn't know the rules.

I went along with it anyway. Dustin was so excited about the tadpole, it was almost cute. And even though the whole thing was kind of dorky, it wasn't like we hadn't had our own games at home.

Back in San Diego we'd hung out in the hills behind my house every day after school and run wild there all summer. Even before I learned to skateboard, I was in love with how it felt to ride fast and reckless on the back of Nate's BMX, balanced there with my hands on his shoulders and my feet on the pegs. We zoomed down Wakeland Road with our eyes closed, the wind against our faces. We took our feet off the pedals and let go of the handlebars and never cared how many times we wiped out.

When I thought about the life I'd left behind in California, it felt bright and faraway, almost like a dream. I kept catching myself turning nostalgic for it, remembering the very best parts—afternoons at the go-kart track or the beach. Summer nights looking for toads in the warm, dusky silence of Eddie's mom's garden.

The Harrises' house was a pretty little bungalow with morning glories growing over the gate and toads that hopped clumsily across winding stone paths. We chased them through the rosebushes and caught them in an old colander. We always had this big plan to name them and keep them as pets, even though they smelled like fish guts, and half the time they peed all over your hands when you picked them up. We put them in a cereal box and fed them crickets until we got bored and they got mad. Then we'd let them go again under the roses.

The garden was as big as an Olympic swimming pool— bigger than my whole yard—but we didn't hang out there very much because Eddie's mom was always buzzing around after us, making trays of celery with peanut butter and handing out napkins. It was annoying and a little weird to have a grown-up actually pay attention to what we did.

The rest of us had parents who never seemed to notice we existed. Nate's mom spent the afternoons slumped in front of the TV, and Ben's dad dropped us off at the rec center or the roller rink sometimes but was usually too busy running his roofing business or rebuilding the dune buggy that was sitting out in his driveway. My mom was less checked-out and definitely more functional than Nate's, but she never came out to the ditch behind the house.

We lived our daily lives in places where no one would

poke their head in and want to know what we were up to, but on nights when the smog was down and the moon was up, we would all go over to Eddie's. We'd sit cross-legged under the roses or lie on the little strip of lawn between the flower beds and the house, looking up at the night sky, breathing the warm, dizzying smell of the flowers.

We didn't pretend things, because we didn't need to. Our games and inventions were actually real. When we built machines, they worked. And when we wanted something to feel magical, all we had to do was lie in the Harrises' garden and look up.

• • •

As the last bell rang, turning us loose for the day, I was feeling pretty good, bouncing along on the thought of spending an afternoon with friends. I had an idea that maybe I'd even go out to the parking lot and tell Billy I didn't need a ride.

Then reality sank in, and I lost some of the bounce. When you started counting on other people to include you, or started assuming you had after-school plans without having to check, that was a danger zone. There was no point in getting excited about something that wasn't even real.

As I stopped by my locker to drop off my math book and pick up my skateboard and my backpack, I reminded myself that even though Lucas and Dustin had been friendly, I shouldn't count on them too much. After all, at home my social life had been built on seven years of schemes and projects and adventures. And in the end, it had turned out that even the friends I thought would always have my back . . . didn't.

"Hey, Max!"

I turned, tucking my skateboard under my arm. It was Lucas.

For a second, I could hear Billy somewhere in a dingy corner of my mind, telling me that Lucas was going to get bored with me. He would forget about me, just like my friends at home had forgotten about me, because I was that much of a drag. It was stupid to think that because we went trick-or-treating once, they'd want me around the rest of the time. I was this weird, unlikable girl, and no one wanted to hang around with the weird girl. I told myself all that, in Billy's low, flat voice because it felt truer than using my own. Billy could be out of control and was a total jerk, but he was usually right.

Lucas was standing in front of me, looking expectant. He smiled, and Billy's voice was interrupted by the voice of my better self. *Stop it, Max.*

Lucas didn't seem like the type to be friendly in a just-being-polite way, and it was pretty obvious that he was going out of his way to find me. If he was inviting me along, it was because he wanted to, not just because he was checking up or worried what I would tell the other kids in our grade about them. For one thing, their secrets just weren't that interesting. And anyway, I didn't talk to any of the other kids.

Lucas had stopped smiling, but his gaze was easy and direct. He made a *hurry up* gesture. "Come on, we're taking Dart to show Mr. Clarke."

When Dustin said anything to me, it was always more like he was talking *at* me, like he was mostly worried about how to make himself seem interesting or impressive. I kind of got the feeling that he wasn't actually thinking about much at all. Whereas Lucas sounded less fawning and more impatient. His voice was low and abrupt and a little hoarse. I liked that. My mom was always so sensitive about how people spoke to her, like the tone was all that mattered. They could be saying the most awful things in the sweetest voice and she would melt for it. But even when Lucas sounded irritable or impatient, I didn't mind. He never seemed like he was trying to talk me into anything.

I shoved my homework into my backpack and slammed my locker door. "What's Mr. Clarke supposed to do about it? Is he some kind of tadpole expert?"

Lucas shrugged. He didn't seem bothered that I never knew how to sound soft. His eyes were dark and steady, like I was someone worth learning about.

I thought I might have the same way of watching things, a little. My mom was always telling me to stop giving her that bug-eyed look. She said the way I stared at people, it was like I was trying to pull them apart piece by piece.

Lucas looked at people too, but he did it in a level, intent way, like he was just trying to see. He looked thoughtful, not hostile, and when he smiled, it was wide and sheepish.

It had been forever since it felt like someone was actually going out of their way to try to see me.

"Come on," he said again, and I followed him.

In Mr. Clarke's room, we stood in a little circle around the desk as Dustin got ready to take Dart out of the ghost trap.

I was pretty interested to see what Mr. Clarke thought. Maybe he was an expert on giant slimy tadpoles? Dustin was taking his time about revealing Dart, though, making a production out of it.

We were all watching in anticipation when Mike came sprinting in. He was wide-eyed and breathing hard. Without any warning or explanation, he grabbed the trap out of Dustin's hands and shouted to Mr. Clarke that the whole thing was just a dumb prank. Then he took off, bolting out of the room with Dart and the ghost trap, leaving Mr. Clarke looking totally baffled.

Lucas and Dustin only hesitated a second before chasing after him. After a beat, I shrugged and followed them.

Back at the A/V room, they all crammed inside, but Mike stopped in the doorway. I went to push past him, and he stepped in front of me, blocking my way.

"Not you." Then he turned and shut the door in my face.

I heard the lock click, and then I was alone in the hall.

For a second, I just stood there, staring at the closed door. I was getting used to Mike's moodiness, but this was ridiculous. Apparently, I was allowed to tag along after them, but not to be in on any of their plans or secrets. I dropped my backpack, still hearing the echo of Mike's voice: *Not you.*

After pounding on the door for a minute, I sat out in the hall on my board. I thought about starting on my homework, but it was hard to concentrate knowing that I was being left out, and that even though Dustin and Lucas were friendly enough to me when we were eating lunch or messing around during the passing periods, they were still totally on board with Mike when it came to keeping me out.

I could trade fun-size Snickers for Clark Bars and walk to class with Lucas or Dustin, but as soon as their party was all together, I wasn't part of the game.

And maybe it wasn't fair to expect them to just scoot over and make room for me, but it wasn't fair to invite me into the party and then kick me out again whenever they felt like it. I didn't have to stick around and keep trying to earn my way in. I could go home or head downtown to the arcade and play *Dig Dug,* whatever I wanted. Nothing was keeping me there.

I waited anyway.

The truth was, I still had a small, stupid hope that maybe after they were through with whatever covert business they were up to, we'd all hang out together. And even more than that, I wanted to know what was happening in the A/V room. I was more and more curious how that blind, slimy tadpole had turned into some huge secret.

The hall was empty. All the other kids had gone home, and most of the teachers were grading papers in their classrooms or making copies in the front office. The whole place had taken on a spooky, abandoned feeling.

I'd only been sitting there for a few minutes when I got the uneasy feeling that something was happening. The door to the A/V room wasn't soundproof, and I didn't even have to put my ear against it to hear the noises coming from inside.

At first, it sounded like the normal scuffling sounds of boys arguing over comic books or baseball cards, and I didn't think too much about it. Then I heard Lucas say something in a tense, irritable voice, and there was a commotion of banging and thumping.

I reached into my backpack and grabbed a paper clip. My dad was always telling me that you should never go any-where without the tools to pick a padlock or a doorknob. I straightened the paper clip in a fast, fluid jerk, even though part of me was still whispering that maybe this was all just a game.

The noises on the other side of the door were mak-ing me nervous, though. I jammed the paper clip into the doorknob and felt around for the tumbler. From inside the A/V room came a whole bunch of chirps and squeals, and someone yelled. It sounded like Lucas.

There was a loose rattle, then a click, and I held the paper clip steady and turned the handle.

As soon as the door swung open, something came scram-bling out with the boys all flailing after it. Lucas tripped and went sprawling next to me, but Dustin crashed straight into me, and we both landed in a tangled heap on the hall floor.

I looked around wildly. "What *is* that?"

Mike stood over us, his eyes wide in exasperation and alarm. "Dart! You let him escape!"

I stared up at him. I'd had just enough time to register the shape of the creature as it bolted from the A/V room. It had squat, froggy legs and a huge, yawning mouth, and it looked hardly anything like the lumpy blind tadpole Dustin had showed us this morning. It had squirted past me down the hall, feet paddling frantically on the linoleum. And now it was gone.

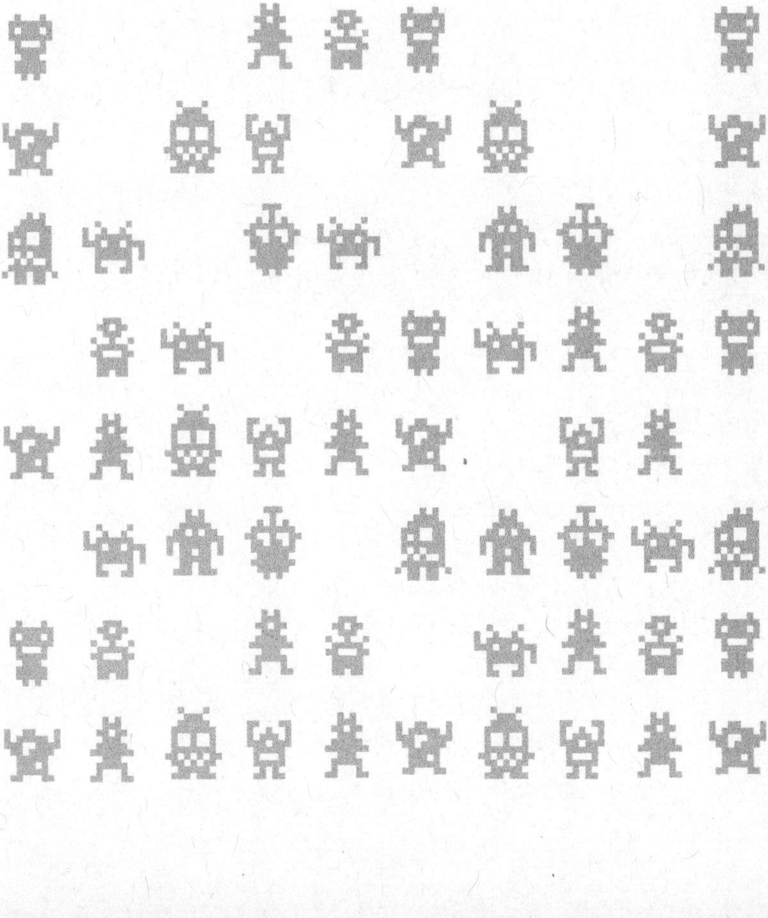

CHAPTER EIGHT

The hall stretched empty in both directions. Dart was nowhere.

The boys decided that we should spread out to search the school. As we all headed off in different directions, I had a sinking feeling that I had ruined whatever chance with them I might have had.

I made my way through the athletics hall, checking the classrooms and the equipment closets. I didn't want to feel bad about Dart. If they hadn't locked me out of the A/V room, none of this would have happened. But I had a guilty feeling that I needed to fix it anyway. It didn't matter whose fault it was; I was still the one who'd let him out.

I was poking around in the locker rooms off the side of the gym, searching through empty lockers and trash cans, when there was a howl and someone leapt out behind me.

I whirled around, but it was only Mike, waving a mop and staring at me like I'd done something offensive just by being there. I figured now that it was only the two of us, we'd have to talk about the awful way he kept treating me, but he just turned and walked away from me, back out into the gym.

I wasn't about to let it drop, though, and I followed him.

"Why do you hate me so much?" I said it in a hard, matter-of-fact way.

It was the kind of question you weren't supposed to ask, but I'd learned that sometimes you could get a straight answer just by being more up front than the other person. I'd never had a problem telling the truth, but some people didn't like to say things if they thought it was going to make you mad. So being direct was the easiest way of dealing with them. Like, for example, sometimes it was the only way to get a straight answer from my mom.

Mike glanced quickly over his shoulder without really looking at me. "I don't hate you."

The way he said it was clipped and stony, and I didn't want to believe it, because the alternative was that he was telling the truth and just treating me terribly anyway.

• • •

For pretty much my whole life, I'd been really bad at talking to people. It wasn't because I was nervous or shy. I didn't worry about being bullied or worry that no one would think I was cool, but the idea of me actually being popular was absurd. I didn't know how to make people *like* me.

It should have been easy, or at least doable. My dad made friends with everyone, like making friends wasn't even something you had to *do*. More like it was a commonplace natural element, waiting for him as soon as he walked into a room, easy as breathing.

Anywhere we went, he collected people. It was like his superpower. I mostly just made them want to strangle me.

It was one of the visitation weekends right after the divorce, back when I still got to see him twice a month. For two days, we'd been hanging around the apartment. He'd been running a little sports-betting thing on the side and had spent all of Sunday afternoon sitting at the counter, calculating point spreads and who owed him money, while I flipped through the same four channels on TV over and over and messed around with my skateboard. But now it was getting dark, and I was starving.

"There's no food," I said, opening the refrigerator and staring inside.

Even on the thinnest days, there were usually a few baloney slices or a carton of leftover Chinese food, but now the shelves were bare. I sighed and shut the door. There wasn't anything sadder than a refrigerator with nothing inside except a naked yellow lightbulb and a jar of relish with rust and black stuff caked on the lid.

So my dad took me down the block to the Black Door Lounge and bought me a hot ham and cheese. I ate it while he talked to some of the scuzzy guys in the back, taking bets on the Dodgers game and playing a few rounds of pool.

Everyone at the Black Door loved him. As soon as we walked in, they would all shift around on their stools and clamor for his attention. That was how it was everywhere—a crowd of people falling all over themselves, shouting *Sam! How you been?* and slapping him on the back. He was good at the kind of teasing that people liked. Whenever I tried it, I just sounded harsh and confrontational.

That night, he was in a big, expansive mood. He made his way toward the back, grinning and high-fiving, while I trailed along behind him trying to look invisible so no one would ask me when I was going to learn how to hustle darts like my dad and how old I was now and whether I had any boyfriends yet.

My dad always let me tag along with him and treated me like his coolest, proudest thing, but I wasn't slick or friendly like he was, and I had no idea how to fake it. The way he could just slide into a room and make everyone love him was like a magic trick. I didn't get it. My mom always said that he could charm the spots off a ladybug. I couldn't even order fries or ask for directions without sounding like I was about to take hostages.

The hot ham and cheese was greasy and not very hot.

I sat at the end of the bar with a basket of fries and a glass of Coke on a paper napkin, practicing on the little padlock from a pink patent leather diary my mom had given me. It was a cheat: the lock was so easy you could pick it with the end of a ballpoint pen, and the strap that held it to the diary was flimsy enough that you could probably just peel it off.

I was popping the shackle for the third time when a leathery-tan woman in a sequined top crossed the lounge and sank onto the seat next to me.

"What a cute little diary," she said, leaning close so that the stiff bird's nest of her hair brushed my arm. I could smell beer and honey-roasted peanuts on her breath. "A lot of secrets in there?"

I hunched over the book and shook my head. When I twisted the paper clip, it made a soft *snick,* and the lock popped open.

The woman fumbled a lighter out of her purse and lit a cigarette. She was watching me in bleary curiosity, with her elbows on the bar, letting her drink dangle from her hand. The glass was half-full of something dark brown and decorated with a pair of cherries on a plastic sword. I wondered if I could figure out a way to pick the diary lock with a cocktail sword, then decided it would probably break. And anyway, I didn't want to ask the woman for hers.

She was leaning on the bar, staring at the side of my face, and I tried not to look at her. I wanted to tell her to buzz off, but I'd already spent enough time in bars to know not to argue with drunk people. It never went anywhere good.

She downed the rest of her drink in a long swallow and reached over my arm to grab the book. I tried to tug it away from her, but I didn't feel like getting into a wrestling match over it, and in the end, I let her have it.

"Let's have a look," she said in a bright voice, pronouncing all the words too clearly, the way drunk people did when they wanted to sound sober. She was wearing so much makeup it was caking in the creases around her eyes.

Then she leaned back on the stool, holding the diary above her head. "We're having a dramatic reading," she called, looking around the bar. She didn't wait for anyone to answer, just slid clumsily off the stool and turned to face the lounge.

The rest of the regulars glanced at her. They all looked deeply bored. There were a few snickers, but most of the guys at the pool tables were completely uninterested in whatever pink, girly thing we were doing.

I sat on the stool with my chin stuck out. My mouth felt angry and small. The woman was trying to make a spectacle of me, and I had to remind myself that it didn't really matter. She opened the diary and held it up in front of her like she was about to recite a speech in a school play. Then she stood there with her mouth open and her cigarette smoldering in her free hand.

The book was blank, of course.

My dad was watching from the back pool table, and he smiled at me. He didn't put down his pool cue or say anything, but the way he was smirking made me smirk a little too. I was Sam Mayfield's daughter, and maybe we liked our word games and puzzles and notes in code, but that was as far as it went. His rules were simple: you never showed your hand, you never gave away your time or your talents, and you never wrote down your secrets.

The woman lowered her head and handed me the diary. With a heavy, phlegmy sigh, she sank back onto the stool, like looking stupid in front of a bunch of barflies who didn't even care was somehow my fault.

It was disgusting, the way people always wanted to embarrass girls or tease them about their feelings. Like the very fact of having something that you cared about was worth laughing at. They all wanted me to be this certain soft frilly way, just so they could make fun of me.

The woman mashed out her cigarette in the bottom of her empty glass. There was so much lipstick on the filter, you'd have thought her mouth was bleeding.

She gave me a long, baleful look. Her face seemed saggy and tired. "I guess you think that's pretty cute."

I shrugged and kept my expression blank, but my skull felt hot behind my eyes. I hated that I was supposed to be her punch line. "No, I think it's pretty smart."

• • •

In the gym, Mike stalked away from me like he had someplace to be, but I could tell he was just trying to avoid looking at me. I followed him. I already knew I wouldn't be able to win him over the same way my dad would, though. My dad was a pro when it came to lightening the mood. He never had to ask people why they hated him.

Mike was stomping around like he had some personal grudge against me. Even if he didn't hate me, he was still acting like I'd ruined his life, and I wasn't letting him leave without an explanation. "Yeah, but you don't want me in your party."

He spun around to face me. "Correct!"

"Why *not*?"

"Because you're annoying!"

He said it in a hard, exasperated voice, like that would be enough to hurt my feelings or make me back off. Like I was so sensitive and delicate that being called annoying was the worst thing anyone could say to me, when I had to live with Billy every day.

I hadn't expected it, though. It left a raw ache in my chest, but I stared back and got my face under control. At least we were getting somewhere.

He was on a roll now, listing all the ways they didn't need me, how every one of them belonged to the group and had a purpose and I didn't. The stuff he was telling me wasn't real, just all this fantasy role-playing about paladins and clerics. Then he said something that made no sense at all. "El was our Mage."

When he said it, something happened on his face that I didn't understand. There was no one else, no fifth party member, and it took me a second to really get that he was talking about someone who was gone.

He went on, trying to seem like he was bored and above it all, but I knew what he was *really* saying. I was being shut out by the memory of this other person, this girl who was on the inside of the circle and knew secrets I didn't. A girl who wasn't *annoying.* Who didn't take up too much space or say the wrong thing. Who wasn't even around anymore. All he was saying was that I wasn't allowed to be part of the group because once there'd been another girl. A better girl.

He was looking down, like he was trying to tell a story but didn't know what words to use, or maybe he was just embarrassed by how it felt to say them out loud. It was a story that was obviously important to him, but the parts he was saying didn't mean anything to me, and I had to bite back the jab that kept forming inside my mouth.

Hearing someone's most important thing was a little too much like seeing them without their skin. Sometimes the total unguardedness of it made me want to be mean. I had a quick, unhappy anger in me that made me feel like the woman at the Black Door trying to embarrass me over the possibility that I might have feelings. I didn't want to hurt him. It was what Billy would have done, and I wanted to be better than that. It was just so hard to be gentle when you knew someone's weaknesses.

Instead, I followed him through the gym on my board, gliding across the basketball court. When I coasted around him in lazy circles, with my arms held out, he smiled, even though it looked tense and he was trying to act like he wasn't. The gym floor was polished to a buttery shine, and it slipped like grease under my wheels. I was showing off, but sometimes you had to show off to get boys to see you as a real person and not just *another girl*. I needed him to stop acting like I was somehow stepping on the memory of a girl I'd never met.

He was watching me as I cruised past, laughing even though he looked a little like he was still trying not to, when something strange happened.

There was a heavy feeling in my chest, like the air had gotten thicker. The board jerked out from under me as suddenly as if someone had grabbed the nose and pulled.

I hit the basketball court with a thud that made my ears ring. The impact echoed through my ribs.

Mike stood over me, looking puzzled. He held out his hand and reached to help me up. "Are you okay?"

I nodded, holding my side where I'd landed. I was looking past him, toward the doors—there was nothing there. I started back across the gym for my board, trying to shake the eerie, creeping feeling that someone had touched me.

But the place was empty. It was just the two of us.

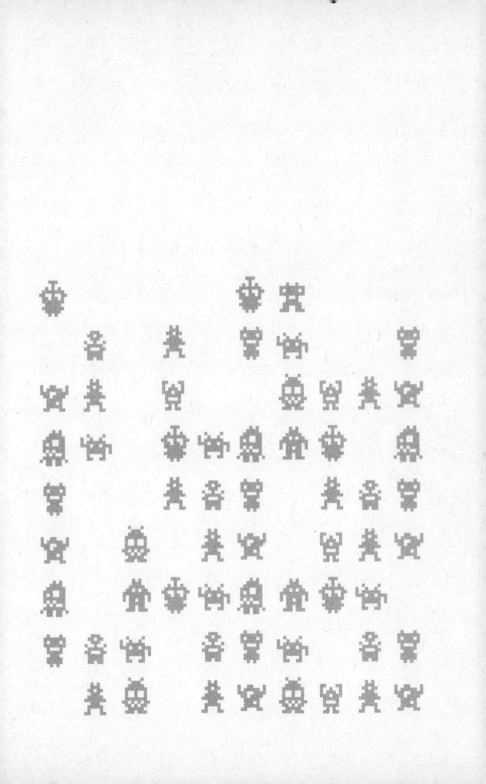

CHAPTER NINE

The next morning, I woke up with a bruise down my side where I'd fallen and a strange, unsteady feeling that everything was changing. I just didn't know what it was changing into.

Yesterday afternoon had been wild. After Mike had finally started being honest with me in the gym, we'd had to accept the fact that Dart was nowhere. The search had been cut short anyway, because as soon as Mike helped me up and we left the gym, Will had had another episode. He'd been standing out in the field behind the school, pale and rigid, when his mom showed up to get him.

She was small in stature, with dark hair and a worried

face, and I recognized her as the woman from the afternoon downtown when I'd wiped out on my board and she'd run out to see if I was okay.

She'd understood right away what was happening with Will, and after he finally came back to himself, she took him home.

The way the rest of them acted when we found him out there was weird—like they were frightened for him but not particularly shocked. Almost like they'd been expecting it. I was a little surprised that he was still allowed to come to school if he was in such bad shape. I figured it was like Jamie Winslow in my class at home. She had one of those rare kid-cancers and had to wear a wig. She still came to school when she could, and I figured even when they were in bad shape, sometimes people just wanted to feel normal.

After we'd called off the search for Dart, everyone went their separate ways.

It was no surprise when I got out to the parking lot and Billy was gone. And the next morning, he left without giving me a ride to school. He said it was because he had to be there early for some basketball thing. I knew he was still trying to punish me for making him wait, though. I didn't care how long the walk was. It was still better than being trapped in the car with him.

Mike and Lucas were standing around out front when I got there. I'd expected they'd want to hang out in the A/V room again, but they said they were waiting for Dustin so they could search for Dart some more. We started without him, digging around in the dumpster by the back steps, in case Dart had magically decided to make his way back to the habitat he'd been living in when Dustin found him. I was pretty sure we weren't going to have much luck, but we searched anyway, hauling out the trash and going through it with a couple of old mop handles.

I still wasn't sure why Dart was such a big deal, but they were bent on finding him, and since I was the one who'd let him out, the least I could do was help look for him.

I could see how someone would be upset about losing an important discovery, and if your pet went missing, you'd definitely want it back. But their level of concern for a mutant frog was a little bizarre—showing up to school early, rooting around in a dumpster—and I wondered what they'd been talking about when they locked me out of the A/V room. They still wouldn't say what was so special about him. No matter how you looked at it, though, when Dart had escaped, I'd seen a pair of back legs when he hadn't had them just a few hours before. In less than a day, he'd grown a whole new set of body parts, and that definitely wasn't normal.

Will wasn't at school, and the boys were anxious and preoccupied. Still, things seemed to be going okay, right up until lunch.

We were sitting out on the steps, eating our sandwiches and talking about how they did the ectoplasm effects in

Ghostbusters. Mike had gone to use the pay phone to call Will's house; then all of a sudden he came running back, yelling that we needed to talk right away in the A/V room.

Lucas and Dustin both jumped up, and the three of them headed inside. When I tried to follow, though, Mike turned and gave me an exasperated look. "Party members *only.*"

It wasn't as if I'd thought that our stupid heart-to-heart in the gym made us best friends, or that now Mike was suddenly going to welcome me with open arms, but I'd thought we'd maybe worked out some kind of truce.

Lucas and Dustin both acted embarrassed, like they felt bad about it, but a few muttered *sorry*s weren't enough to make up for the way they hadn't stuck up for me.

I'd been loyal to the party, even though I didn't understand half of what was happening. I hadn't told anyone about Will's latest episode, or their stupid missing frog, or even asked about their missing Mage. I dug around in trash for them.

That afternoon was long and dismal. In history, we were studying for a quiz to name all the presidents in order, but I didn't pay much attention. I'd already had to memorize them last year.

When I asked the girl next to me if I could borrow her eraser, she looked right past me like I was nowhere, like I was a person-shaped hole and she was looking through me.

The way I could disappear while I was still standing in a room reminded me of things I tried not to think about.

The way my mom and dad had just decided to stop loving each other and pass me between them like a spare garden hose or lug wrench. Except, even that had changed. First with Neil, and then with the move. Instead of being able to count on a trip to my dad's every couple of weeks, what used to be an agreement had turned into my mom wanting to keep me away from the one person who actually understood me.

Sure, there were things that weren't so great. Although my dad was usually pretty good with commitments and schedules (when he tried), sometimes he'd get all excited about me coming up from San Diego and start making plans to change out the wheels on my board or promise to take me to Knott's Berry Farm. Then he'd get so distracted drinking beer and working on one of his side gigs that he'd lose track of time, and we'd wind up just sitting around his apartment all weekend.

Later he'd always be sorry, but letting me pick the horses for him at the track wasn't really an apology. It never made up for the feeling that I was ignorable, forgettable. Unnecessary.

After school, I was dropping off my books and collecting my skateboard when I was interrupted by the sound of Lucas calling my name. I closed my locker and walked out of the school without looking at him.

The doors wheezed shut behind me and he followed me, but I was done with the way he thought he could just keep pretending he was my friend without ever bothering to include me or explain anything.

When he caught up to me in the parking lot, I spun around and lit into him. Here he was, acting like I was the one who was being totally unreasonable, and I wasn't going to just smile and nod and stand there for it.

Lucas spread his hands and blurted out a parade of excuses: It wasn't like that. They did want me around, but it was just too complicated to talk about. There were things they couldn't tell me, for my own safety.

That last one was so ridiculous I couldn't keep the incredulity off my face.

"My own *safety*?" My voice spiked in disbelief. What he was saying had no bearing on anything about my actual life. "Because I'm a girl?"

He stared back, shaking his head, but he had no real answers for me. I was just supposed to believe all his vague secrecy and stop asking questions. The idea that he could protect me from anything was ridiculous. If he actually believed that, it just proved that he didn't know the first thing about my life or what I needed. It was infuriating that someone was trying to save me from things I didn't need to be saved from.

Billy was waiting for me down in the senior lot. There were so many things that no one in my life had ever protected me from.

• • •

My mom was basically useless when it came to being fierce or protective. I'd read that mother wolves and bears and lions would mess you up if you came near their cubs, but she didn't have that instinct. She was always mousing around or apologizing, acting like she didn't know what was happening in our house.

Sometimes, though, she had an eye for things I didn't. Sometimes she took me by surprise.

The garage at home in San Diego had been attached to the house. It was big enough to park two cars next to each other, even though we never did, and you could get to it from inside through a door at the back of the laundry room.

Billy hung out there a lot, with his friends or by himself. He kept a transistor radio on the workbench and a bench press in the corner. On weekends and afternoons, I'd find him out there in the shade of the open garage with the music blasting, lifting weights or working on his car.

I'd been changing the wheels on my skateboard, and when I went out for an Allen wrench, Billy was in the garage with the door up. He was in his undershirt, working under the hood of the Camaro with a cigarette clamped between his teeth. He'd finally gotten his keys back from Neil.

Before he and Neil moved in, the garage was just where we kept the Christmas lights. My mom mostly parked her car in the driveway, and I never went out there except to look for the Allen wrench—and no one ever smoked. Now there was always a jumbo Folgers can on the corner of the workbench, full of ashes and cigarette butts. Before, I hadn't cared about the garage one way or another, but now I felt weirdly protective, like it was just one more conquered territory in a house that had been mine and wasn't anymore.

I sat on the concrete step with the door to the laundry room open behind me and watched Billy for a while. The hood of the Camaro made an aggressive angle, smoke puffing up from underneath.

I leaned forward with my knees on my elbows and cupped my chin in my hands. "At the health assembly in school, they told us that we're not supposed to smoke."

Billy straightened and closed the hood, wiping his hands with a rag. "And do you always do everything your teachers tell you?"

That idea was so wrong it was hilarious. My grades were usually okay, but my conduct cards were a mess. I was always in trouble for something—talking back, or drawing cartoon hot rods on my desk with a felt pen. I laughed and shook my head.

That seemed to make him happy. He smiled in a slow, lazy way, then pulled the pack of Parliaments out of his shirt pocket. He held it out to me and waited, watching my face until I took one.

I'd never smoked before, and the cigarette felt weird in my hand, but the actual mechanics of it seemed pretty simple. I'd watched Billy plenty of times. I stuck the filter in my mouth and held still while he leaned over and lit it for me.

I sucked in, feeling the first dry billow of smoke, hot in

the back of my throat. It tasted like batteries and burning newspaper, and I coughed so hard my eyes teared up.

Billy was leaning against the Camaro, laughing with his head back and his eyebrows raised, and I was pinching the cigarette awkwardly between my fingers, trying not to choke, when I heard a gasp behind me.

"Maxine!"

My mom only called me that when I was in trouble. She marched down the garage steps and grabbed the cigarette out of my mouth. I'd only taken two or three puffs.

Billy was still leaning against the side of the Camaro laughing, and I had a crazy urge to laugh too, just to show him that I wasn't freaked out by the way the smoke burned the inside of my nose or how red-faced and guilty I must have looked. That I was in on it.

My mom was staring at me in total horror, and I was sure she was going to ground me, but most of her anger seemed to be pointed at Billy.

She turned on him, looking outraged. "Do you think this is funny?"

"Come on, Susan. It's just one cigarette. Relax."

My mom stared at him. *"Relax?"* Her voice was high and furious. "Look, mister! You can fill your lungs with crud or wrap yourself around a telephone pole in that death machine, or whatever else you want to do to yourself, but the party ends there! You are not dragging my daughter down with you!"

It was the first time I'd seen her truly mad in a long time, and I suddenly felt really sorry. I'd only taken the cigarette because it seemed like the cool thing, the obvious thing. I hadn't even considered how my mom would feel about it or what she'd think.

Her mouth was so thin she must have been biting the inside of her lip, and I hoped she wasn't going to cry, the way she sometimes did when she got mad. Her eyes had a wide, wounded look, but her cheeks were a bright, angry red.

Billy had taken out another cigarette, and now he lit it. He was smirking in that bored, insolent way he always did when he was trying to get a rise out of her. The flick of the lighter seemed to break something inside her, and her anger crumbled into helplessness. It was always so easy.

The three of us were standing in the garage when Neil got home. He parked his truck in the driveway and came striding toward the house, then stopped.

He stood in the open garage door, looking tall and face-less with the sun at his back. "What's going on in here?"

We all stood frozen in the shade of the garage, not know-ing what was going to happen next. I braced myself, waiting to see what Neil was going to do. My mom was huddled near the back of the Camaro with her arms folded around herself, and I waited for her to tell him that Billy had given me a cigarette and then talked back to her when she tried to reprimand him. Instead, she just smiled and glanced away like she was nervous.

In front of the Camaro, Billy was standing at attention, looking angry and defiant.

The air felt electric, like the cloud of blue smoke after a firecracker, and it tasted worse. I pressed my lips together to keep myself from coughing and tried to look normal.

My mom dropped the cigarette into the coffee can and shook her head. "Nothing."

Right then, standing in the garage, I hadn't gotten it. I'd thought my mom was too scared of Billy to tell Neil what he'd done. Later, though, once the novelty of having a stepdad had worn off, and I got to know Neil—the real Neil—I understood what my mom must have already known: Sure, she could be nervous and oversensitive, and she apologized too much, but she wasn't dumb. She hadn't been scared of Billy, she'd been scared *for* him.

• • •

There were things I wished I could be kept safe from, but none of them were the kinds of things Lucas could do anything about. The way he seemed to think he could help me by keeping me out gave me a hollow feeling.

Even though I'd been in Indiana for less than a week, I'd been starting to think that things were looking up. That I'd found a place where I fit. I'd done everything I could to make a space for myself, and it still wasn't enough. I was never going to be part of their club.

Even Lucas, who acted like he thought I was cool, and who almost always said what he was actually thinking, wouldn't say the truth about that. Every conversation between them was some hush-hush secret meeting, with me on the outside. I might be good enough to go trick-or-treating or eat lunch with, but I still wasn't one of them.

All week, I'd been twisting myself in knots trying to figure out a way to belong here, but now I understood that it was pointless. Hawkins wasn't some magic solution or an answer to a question, and wide streets and Halloween decorations didn't make it home. There was no place for me in a tiny, sleepy town full of cow pastures and sewing machine repair shops.

My only place was in the passenger seat of that stupid Camaro.

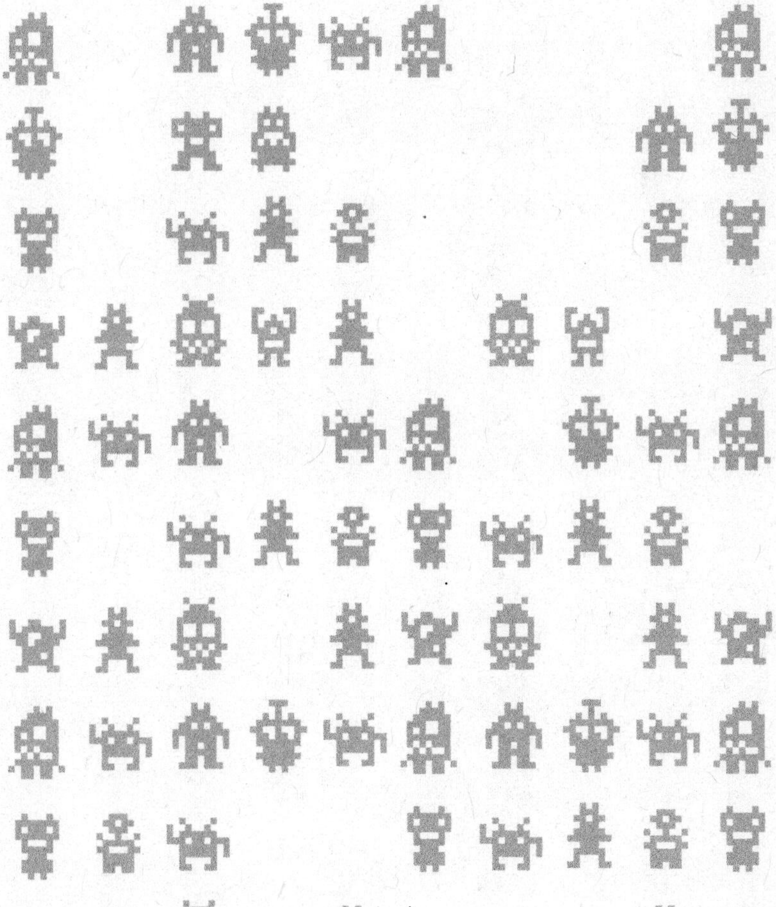

CHAPTER TEN

When I stalked away from Lucas, Billy was waiting for me, leaning against the fender of the Camaro. "That kid you were talking to, who is he?"

"He's no one." I got in and slammed the door.

Billy slid into the driver's seat and lit a cigarette but didn't start the car. He was staring out across the parking lot. "Why was he talking to you?" His voice was dangerously even, and I was gripped by a horrible sinking feeling. I knew what came next. "He causing you trouble?"

"Why do you care?"

"Because, Max, you're a piece of crap, but we're family."

I threw up my hands and rolled my eyes. "Whatever would I do without—"

He reached out fast and caught me by the wrist. "There are people in this world that you stay away from."

He was leaning close, staring right into my face, and he sounded serious and scary. He was acting like he was looking out for me, but I knew what he really meant. We weren't just talking about being friends with boys. Neil—and, I guess, Billy—had a lot of opinions about anybody who wasn't white and Lutheran and a man. Neil said it was just that different kinds of people belonged in different worlds. That it was about property values, or crime, or a million other coded things, so that he didn't have to say what he really meant. People like *that*.

I stuck out my chin and stared back at Billy, but when I tried to jerk away, he held on. His fingers dug into my wrist. After a second, he let me go and started the car.

It pissed me off that he could even act like he had any right to judge a person by looking at them. The way he'd stared after Lucas made me very nervous about what he might do next, but right away, that was canceled out by another thought. I didn't even have to *try* to stay away from Lucas, because that was over now. They didn't want me around. I meant nothing to them. I stared out the window and tried not to cry.

When Billy got mad, it was scary, but I was used to it. The way he could make fun of my hobbies or my friends or call me names was bad sometimes; I mostly tried not to take it personally. It was nothing. It was like the little rhyme we used to sing on the playground about sticks and stones. I could handle it. Yeah, it felt awful, and I hated the way Nate and Ben and Eddie had looked at me sometimes, like they were sorry for me, but there was no other option. I had to handle it.

Sometimes, though, Billy acted like we were in on some big, crucial secret together. Like we understood each other, like he was so worried about me. And that was worse.

I knew he wasn't really worried. He'd just found one more way to mess with me.

• • •

Since their big Halloween blowup two days ago, standing in the living room when Neil and Billy were both there was like standing under power lines—so high-voltage you could hear the hum.

Back in San Diego, they'd been angry with each other, but it had usually stayed under the surface. Now I was starting to understand that it had only been that way because Billy was hardly ever home. Here in Hawkins, he had nothing but time. Since we'd moved into the house on Cherry Road, he'd certainly tried to fill that time with parties and girls and the basketball team. But the girls here all had curfews. And there weren't that many parties and that many places to go.

Neil was in a similar rut, or maybe that was just how

grown-ups always were. He left for work in the mornings and came home after five like always, and when he walked in, he would ruffle my hair or hand my mom some flowers, but underneath, he was like a box of dynamite. I spent my time waiting for the explosion.

It was important to be ready, because if Neil and Billy got into a disagreement, Billy would take it out on me. And if by some miracle the explosion didn't come, he would take it out on me anyway, just to blow off steam.

That morning they'd had a strange, wordless argument over breakfast. Billy had taken the orange juice from the middle of the table, and Neil reached over to take it back, but Billy didn't let go. Neither of them said anything. The carton hovered between them, their hands flexed, fingers digging into the waxed cardboard. Then Neil pulled so hard the carton jerked out of Billy's hand. Neil's elbow swung around and knocked my mom's little red sugar bowl onto the floor. Now the bowl had a chip in it.

I'd spent the last seven months collecting signs of danger, and that—that one little chip—was the clearest sign of all. It was so small, only about the size of my pinkie nail, but it seemed to explain everything.

• • •

I'd never been scared of blood. That wasn't some exaggeration or me trying to be tough, it was just the truth.

I'd gone off BMX ramps on Nate's bike and played street

hockey and wiped out on my board so much that my mom had started buying three of everything when she went shopping for my school clothes.

I'd watched boxing and WWF with my dad, and I'd seen football players destroy their knees on TV, and sometimes there were fights at school and someone got a bloody nose. The trashy boys or the rocker girls would flail around until the vice principal or the gym teacher waded into the crowd and pulled them apart, then told us all to go back to class. I watched horror movies—as many as I could—and never got tired of the bloody parts.

My dad understood me better than most people, and even he didn't really get what I liked about monsters. He was more into spy flicks, but he liked that I was interested in something he hadn't taught me.

His friend Ron had worked on a movie lot for a while and knew all the secrets to a really good splatter-fest. He told me they made the blood out of colored corn syrup and that was why it looked so fake onscreen. I nodded, but the truth was, even the football injuries and the school fights never seemed real. The blood always seemed a million miles away.

The first time I saw Neil beat Billy, it wasn't like any of those things.

The day I met him, Billy was already angry and out of control, but after they moved in with us, it got much worse. Or maybe he had always been like that, and now I was just close enough to see it.

He had been driving around Mission Valley and had gotten pulled over. When Neil found out, he became very quiet, and his eyes went cool and steady in the way I'd learned to be nervous about.

I was sitting at the kitchen table with a bent paper clip and a bottle of nail polish remover, cleaning the bearings on my skateboard, while my mom leaned on her elbows at the counter, flipping through a home decorating magazine.

Billy was standing at the open refrigerator, drinking out of the milk carton because my mom hated when he did that, and when Neil came in, holding the ticket like a flag, we all looked up. "This is how you spend your time? On this reckless, irresponsible nonsense?" Then he crumpled it up and threw it at Billy.

Billy turned to face him, letting the refrigerator door swing shut.

I stared hard at the label on the nail polish remover.

Since that day in the garage with the cigarette, things had been tense. Billy had always been rude and nasty to my mom, and it had been worse since the Hargroves moved in. He got mouthy with her when he thought he could get away with it, but I'd never seen him talk back to his dad. And in this moment he didn't say anything.

When Neil hit him, I didn't understand what had happened at first. It looked like something in slow motion.

For a second, we all just froze, like no one knew what was supposed to come next.

I looked over at my mom, sure that she'd be horrified, and needing her to fix it the way she had that day in the garage. The scene was bad, but it would all be okay, because she'd go to Neil and use her sweet, let's-all-get-along voice and make it stop.

But she didn't. She was standing at the counter, staring down at her magazine, her hair falling in a brick-red curtain over her forehead, hiding her expression. What was happening on the other side of the kitchen was bad enough, but the way she stood there looking at her hands, it was almost like she expected it.

When Neil hit him, Billy stumbled, but he didn't back away. Neil wound up to hit him again, and my mom still didn't say anything or try to stop it. This time, Billy fell back against the little wall shelf where my mom kept her recipe box and her painted teacups. The forget-me-not blue one smashed on the floor, and she didn't even look up.

Suddenly I understood in the worst, clearest way that this wasn't a surprise. Or at least, it wasn't so much of a surprise that she would leave. The idea that you could see someone hit his son like that and still pick him was terrible. My dad was forgetful and a slacker and kind of shady, but at least he never acted like a psycho. He never hit anyone. And still she'd left him and saddled us with whatever angry, twisted thing Neil was offering. She'd *picked* this for us.

Billy was trying to stand, slow and unsteady. He got his legs under him, but he was still bent over, with one hand on the floor and his feet apart, like he was trying to keep his balance in an earthquake. There was blood on his bottom lip, a little, and a puffy half-moon around his eye.

"You are going to learn respect," Neil said, moving to stand over him. "Respect, and responsibility."

My mom got up and went into the other room. She did it in a vague, vacant way, like she'd just remembered there were cookies in the oven and she needed to take them out.

With one hand, Neil undid the buckle on his belt, and for a second, I didn't understand. He was standing over Billy, staring down at Billy's bent back as he yanked his belt out of the loops. The way his eyes slid out of focus, it was like he wasn't even seeing Billy anymore.

I could almost forgive my mom for leaving. I'd never been squeamish about anything, and still I had an urge to look away. I was so wildly sure I wasn't supposed to see this, I wasn't supposed to be here. I still half believed that any second he'd glance around and remember I was there, and it would all stop. He'd see me sitting at the table with my paper clip still in my hand and that would be enough to make him catch himself and put down the belt. He just needed to remember I was there.

But Neil didn't even glance at me. He stood over Billy, folding the belt in half, doubling it over in his hand. I held my breath and waited.

The sound it made was thick and ugly. I felt it in my teeth.

Billy hunched his shoulders, but he didn't yell or try to duck away, and that was worse. I knew, in a deep, unhappy way, that this was wrong, I just didn't know how to stop it. I'd always known my mom was timid and kind of a pushover. I hadn't really believed she would let something get this bad, though. I'd never thought that she was weak before.

I wondered for the first time if things could be too scary for grown-ups to deal with. My mom was gentle and soft. She always complained that I was too callous and too much like my dad—that he had me in his pocket. But that was nothing compared to her. Neil had her in his fist.

Neil let the belt dangle, swinging it in a loose, lazy way, like he was winding up. I set my teeth and winced, imagining what it would sound like when it landed.

Billy watched the end of it with a resigned look, like a dog I saw in the back of the animal control van once, staring out of the wire mesh with this helpless mix of fear and fury.

Neil planted his feet and raised the hand with the belt. "Are you ready to take your punishment?"

"Stop it!" I shouted it. I hadn't known I was going to say anything until it came tearing out of me. It felt jagged, like I'd been holding something inside.

Neil turned, and for a second, looking into his eyes was like looking right into the sun, blank and dazzling. Then he smiled a tight, mechanical smile and turned back to Billy. "Is this the son I raised? A worthless loser who needs a little girl to fight his battles for him?"

He said it with so much wonder and disgust that I felt my face get hot and my eyes fill up.

In that second, I believed it—that he was right, that I was no one, just a little girl and there was no way to stop someone like him. He was a grown-up.

Neil set his jaw and swung the belt. He did it without hurrying, like it wasn't a big deal. He did it the way Mrs. Haskell down the street beat the dust out of her rugs. When he was done, he didn't look at either of us or say anything else. He just turned and walked out of the kitchen.

I sat with my hands clasped, fingers locked together like we were about to say grace.

Billy was still on the floor. He was on his hands and knees under the shelf where my mom kept her teacups. The blue one was in pieces around him. It looked like a broken Easter egg.

When the silence had lasted too long to deal with, and I was sure Neil was gone, I pushed my chair back and got down next to Billy. I knelt on the floor, sweeping the broken cup out of the way. Some of the fragments stuck to my hand, and I brushed them off on my pants. "Are you okay?"

It was such a stupid question. Billy was kneeling on the linoleum with his head down. He was so very far from okay. I thought he'd ignore me, or maybe tell me what a moron I was. Instead, he just stayed like that, staring at the floor. "Get away from me, Max."

The place around his eye was puffing shut, and I leaned to get a closer look. The skin was turning from beet-red to purple. If he put a frozen TV dinner on it, maybe that would take the swelling down.

I knelt there, remembering what he'd said to me in the parking lot of Captain Spaulding's and the nervous, hopeful feeling I'd had then, like we were in some sort of secret club together—like we could be on the same team.

"Do you want me to get you some ice?"

He looked up then, and I could see all the ways he hated me. His mouth twisted, and he turned on me like a snapping dog. "I *said,* get away from me."

The sound of his voice was the sound of an animal, horrible and savage. This time, I did what he said.

CHAPTER ELEVEN

Already, Hawkins was starting to feel small, like I was bumping around inside a fishbowl. Every day, I saw the same faces, walked into the same classrooms, waited for the bell, and then walked out again. I passed the same people in the same little cliques of threes and fours, and they always glanced at me, stared a beat too long, then looked away again.

I tried hard not to be mopey or think about the A/V boys anymore. It had been fun while it lasted, but they'd made it clear I didn't belong with them. No matter how much I wanted the company or how hard I tried to earn it, they didn't want me around. And as terrible as that felt—being shut out by the only people who'd been even a little bit friendly to me—I had to remember it was better that way. Being on my own was nothing compared to what Billy would do if he found out that I'd made friends.

Saturday was usually my favorite day, but with nowhere to go and no one to hang out with, what was the point? I tried to think of something to do, but everything felt like one big letdown. I could skate around the shabby downtown again, or else spend an hour or two alone at the arcade. Video games seemed a little lonely now, but at least it would pass the time. I was ready to burn through some quarters and forget about my real life for a while.

• • •

The Palace Arcade was full of loud, sweaty high school boys, and the carpet was crunchy and smelled like nachos. Still, blowing up a few monsters would make the day go faster. When I came up to the *Dig Dug* cabinet, though, I stopped short. There was an OUT OF ORDER sign taped to the screen.

I stood in the aisle between rows of games, looking at it. This was it, the story of my life. One more thing that had been nice while it lasted.

I was about to go look for a *Galaga* or a *Pac-Man* instead, or maybe just turn and walk out altogether, when the tall, oafy guy who ran the counter came over to me. He was always working when I came in, and didn't seem particularly friendly, but he'd obviously noticed that this was my game.

He was eating Cheetos out of the bag and looking how he always did—inscrutable. "Sorry about that, Road Warrior."

I must have seemed pretty desperate, because he shoved another Cheeto into his mouth and said, "Fret not. I got another machine up and running in the back."

The back office was basically just a storage room. I stood and waited while he unlocked the door. When he pushed it open, though, I saw that I'd been set up. This was a mom-and-pop arcade in a tiny town in Indiana: there was no backup *Dig Dug*.

Instead, Lucas was waiting for me, fiddling around with a broken *Asteroids Deluxe* machine.

The manager waved me inside and nodded to Lucas. "Keep things PG in here." Then he winked and left me there, feeling totally stupid.

I was supposed to have known better. After all, I'd encountered a whole parade of untrustworthy guys, able to trick my mom in a thousand ways. It was new, and unsettling, being the one who fell for things.

Lucas's face was open and anxious, if totally sincere, and I wanted to know exactly what was so important that he was ready to fake a broken game just to talk to me.

I marched into the office and sat down. He was perched on a stack of boxes, looking so serious I was a little worried.

The story was a real whopper.

According to Lucas, back when Will had disappeared, he wasn't actually lost. Or at least, he wasn't lost in the woods in some basic, normal way. He'd been gone, all right, but he was someplace else. At first, I didn't get what Lucas meant, but then I started to understand that he was talking about another *place,* not like lost in the city or the airport, but . . . lost. Somewhere no one had ever heard of or knew how to get to.

I just looked at him, shaking my head. When he'd told me the story before, I'd been skeptical, but whatever. It wasn't totally out of the question that someone could disappear. I was a whole lot less convinced that someone could disappear into an undiscovered world, and as Lucas talked, I got madder. My face felt flushed and prickly.

The story got more and more outlandish from there. The place where Will had gotten lost was not just any old world, but a world full of monsters. Not only *that*—Dart was one of them.

Yes, Dustin had found a baby monster and taken it to school in a homemade ghost trap, and then waited around to see what would happen, while it just kept getting bigger, but somehow it was my fault because I'd let it escape.

The whole thing was so ridiculous that I wanted to laugh. I wanted to shove him backward off his seat for telling me such an insane story.

But it didn't even end there! No matter how ridiculous I thought the story had gotten, Lucas was ready to one-up himself. They couldn't let me in the club because there was some huge government conspiracy and there was a special program, and men from a secret lab who would come after us if they knew we knew, and this whole alternate plane of existence full of monsters and we would all be in deep trouble if anyone found out we knew. There was a creature called a Demogorgon. There was a girl with magical powers who fought it and saved the town, maybe the world, then disappeared back through a hole in the wall, and no one had seen her since.

When he said that part, I thought I understood. The girl in the story was the same one Mike had talked about in the gym—El, the Mage.

It all sounded so fake, like a comic book or a make-believe game they were playing.

It was one thing to leave me out, have their secret meetings in the A/V room, and go on their stupid fantasy adventures without me. But it was another thing to try to trick me just to have something to laugh about. And if they were so determined to make me feel like an idiot, maybe they should have picked a better story instead of this wild, impossible fantasy that no one with half a brain would ever believe.

My dad didn't lie to me, but he had no problem lying to other people, and he was usually smiling when he did it. I'd gotten good at spotting liars. But Lucas wasn't even trying to seem slick. His eyes were wide and plaintive, like he was begging me to believe him.

When he was finally done with the story, I leaned back in my chair, keeping my face cool and amused. It seemed better not to care. I was sure it was all some big joke and it seemed very important, suddenly, to show how seriously I wasn't taking him. It was better than letting him see how mad it made me to have him treat me like an idiot. Like I was that gullible.

As soon as I stalked out of the office, he followed me, still spouting his elaborate story. But I was done listening.

Out in the arcade, I stopped and faced him. "You did a good job, okay? You can go tell the others I believed your lies."

As I turned to go, he caught me by the arm. "We have a lot of rules in our party, but the most important is, friends don't lie. Never ever. No matter what."

"Is that right?" I peeled the OUT OF ORDER sign off *Dig Dug* and waved it at him. Whatever noble rules they lived by in their little club, it had nothing to do with me. I wasn't part of their party. They'd made that abundantly clear.

He sighed. "I had to do that. To protect you."

That was it. I couldn't keep my voice low anymore, and I started to list all the random stuff he'd told me about the government and the monster and the girl.

Lucas lunged forward and covered my mouth with his hand. "Stop talking. You're going to get us killed." His face was earnest and unhappy, and in that second, I stopped being thoroughly convinced that he was laughing at me and started to think maybe he believed it.

"Prove it."

"I can't."

"What, so I'm supposed to just trust you?"

"Yes."

Suddenly I froze. The rumble of the Camaro echoed from the arcade parking lot.

I'd gotten used to listening for it. Back home, it had been the sound that meant the fun was over. I'd be hanging out at the rec center for drop-in floor hockey after school, or at the roller rink for teen-skate, and the Camaro would start revving up outside, and I'd know it was time for me to go.

Before I had time to think, I reached over and clutched Lucas's hand. "Don't follow me out." His hand was warm in mine, but all I could think about was what Billy would say—what he would do—if I came out to the car and he saw Lucas.

I dropped Lucas's hand and he opened his mouth to say something else, but I didn't wait.

Outside, the Camaro was idling in the parking lot. I climbed into the passenger seat, trying to seem like everything was normal. The engine ran rough in the cold, and the heater was blasting against my face. Even the rush of hot, dry air smelled like cigarettes.

Billy was looking past me. "What did I tell you?"

At first I didn't understand. Then I glanced toward the door and saw Lucas retreating back into the arcade. When I checked Billy's face, I understood with a sinking feeling that things were about to get bad. Lucas must have come and stood in the doorway, and Billy must have seen.

I'd been so careful not to let Lucas follow me. Unbelievable. This whole time, he'd been practically begging me to listen to his story, but he hadn't trusted me enough to stay inside, where Billy couldn't see him.

Thinking that made me feel like a hypocrite, though. I hadn't told him why he needed to stay.

I was talking way too fast, trying to convince Billy that there was nothing going on. And there wasn't, not really.

"Well, you know what happens when you lie." He said it in a light, matter-of-fact way that still sent an arrow of fear through my chest. His voice was brutal underneath.

I did know.

We drove in silence. Billy was drumming along to Metallica, his cupped hand thumping on the steering wheel.

I was still thinking about Lucas. His story was impossible. Not just wild, but actually impossible. There were no monsters. At least, not the kind he was talking about.

Billy was the closest thing to one that I had ever known. If Lucas wasn't careful, he was going to get hurt, and I wouldn't be able to do anything about it.

I told myself that it wasn't my fault. That this was what it meant to live with the monster standing right behind you. Even though it's yours—you're the one it's after, the one standing in its shadow—it will still take a wide, nasty swipe at anyone who gets close enough.

The Halloween movies understood that; the message was very clear. Even in the sequels, Michael Myers is just stalking his way through Haddonfield, on a mission to find his baby sister, and when he does, he's going to kill her. That's it, his whole plan. His obsession. He wants to kill her so bad that he broke out of an institution to find her. The thing is, he's a merciless killing machine. He might have an end goal, but he's not particular about how he gets there. And along the way? It's everyone else who dies.

• • •

The day everything changed, Nate and I were hanging out in the ditch behind my house.

We'd been working on our bike ramp all week, building it out of plywood and scrap lumber down in the bottom of the creek bed. When it was done, it was going to be the biggest one we'd ever built. Ben had brought some leftover house paint for the supports, and Eddie brought a posthole digger from his mom's garden shed that we'd used to sink the supports deep in the crumbly dirt so the ramp wouldn't wobble when we hit it.

The ground where the dead cat had been was still burned black at the top of the ditch, but the bushes were already turning green again, and the weeds were starting to grow back.

It had been overcast since noon, but the afternoon was hot, and the hill buzzed with the sound of grasshoppers and cicadas whirring in the grass.

Nate was sitting up at the top of the ditch with his note-book, drawing out plans, figuring out the angles for the struts. We had some framing nails and Nate's dad's toolbox and a pile of scrap wood we'd bought for seven dollars at the hardware store.

I was hot and sticky, and the palms of my hands were raw and sweaty from the rubber grips of the posthole digger, but I worked anyway, sinking the supports and patting the dirt down around them. We had picked the widest, deepest part of the ditch to build our ramp. When it was finished, it was going to be big enough to launch us into space.

"Where's the hammer?" I asked, lining up a pair of boards and trying to hold them steady with one hand while I felt around in the pile of tools with the other.

Nate made a note in his book and didn't look up. "Under the plywood, I think."

I found the hammer and retrieved it from the pile of loose boards lying in the dirt around the tool belt.

The air in the bottom of the ditch was still and quiet. There weren't even any mosquitoes. I was glad that today it was just the two of us, but it felt a little strange, a little off. "Where are Ben and Eddie?"

Ben and Eddie had been pulling weeds for Mrs. Harris in the mornings, but they usually showed up at my house by two or three. We hung out together almost every day, and for the last three years, they'd spent almost as much time in the bottom of the dry creek as Nate and me. But in the last week or two, they'd been around less and less. It wasn't like they'd been avoiding me, exactly, because we were still friends. I'd just seen them at the pool on Friday and we'd taken turns cannonballing off the diving board, but they'd pretty much stopped coming over, and I was starting to wonder if maybe they just weren't interested in building ramps and waterballoon launchers anymore.

"Are they too cool for me or something?"

That made Nate stop writing and look up from the book. His forehead wrinkled, and he frowned. "No, not like that. They just had other stuff to do, I guess."

"Better than this?"

He shrugged but didn't say anything.

I gave him a hard stare. "What?"

He just ducked his head and wouldn't look at me.

"What?"

"They're not mad at you or anything. They just don't want to hang around your brother."

I narrowed my eyes and didn't answer. Billy was a constant part of my life, but he wasn't my brother. At first he'd been my idol and then, almost as fast, my new problem. And in the months since the wedding, he'd been turning into something even sharper and more jagged.

Nate kept his head down, looking like he wanted to apologize. "Don't get pissed off at them. They know it's not your fault."

"I'm not pissed off. They can just go build their own ramp if they want, and good luck finding someplace with a slope this good."

But I couldn't help feeling like it kind of was my fault.

For the rest of the afternoon, we worked on the ramp,

digging postholes for the struts and nailing boards into X's for the supports. We didn't talk about Billy, or the new weirdness with Ben and Eddie. If we had, maybe the day would have turned out differently.

We had just finished anchoring the supports when Billy and Wayne showed up.

They came crunching down into the creek bed in their motorcycle boots. They looked overheated and bleary-eyed. Billy's hair was artfully messy, curling over his forehead, and I knew he'd sprayed it that way on purpose. Wayne was wearing a red flannel shirt with the sleeves cut off. They looked weirdly lopsided together, like a car with a missing wheel. My friends weren't the only ones MIA. I hadn't seen Sid since the afternoon of the dead cat and the fire.

Billy and Wayne ambled over to the couch and sat down to watch us. The couch was still in its spot at the top of the ditch. It had been sitting there all summer, and the upholstery was getting pretty ratty.

Nate stayed sitting in the dirt with his legs crossed and his head down, trying really hard to pretend they weren't there. I straightened up and glared at them. "Go away. This isn't your creek, so go hang around somewhere else."

Wayne looked at me wide-eyed, then laughed in a high, jittering whinny that made my skin crawl. "Max is playing doctor with her boyfriend and doesn't want us to watch."

I refused to acknowledge his comment. Nate and I had never once done anything like that, but I could feel myself blushing anyway.

Even back before school let out, things had been getting that way. Everyone was starting to pair off. It was beginning to seem like the only thing anyone talked about was who was going out with who, who'd done under-the-shirt stuff and gotten to what base, and who was starting to get bigger up top. While I wasn't paying attention, it had gotten so that if you were a girl who hung out with boys just because you wanted to, no one believed you. It always had to mean you were someone's girlfriend.

Billy was watching me in a strange, thoughtful way. He leaned back and kicked his boots up on the milk crate, giving me a chilly look. "Is that true, Max?"

Over by the pile of scrap boards, Nate was still sitting in the dirt and staring at his notebook, but I could tell that he was listening. It made me furious that even up here in the ditch, Billy could just show up and mess around with my life. He was ruining everything.

He began to tap down his cigarettes, drumming the pack on his knee and staring at me. "I said, is that true?"

I picked up another nail and tightened my grip on the Craftsman hammer. "No."

"Then you need to be more careful who you hang out with. Unless you want people to think you're easy."

I raised the hammer and held the nail in place, but I was too mad to aim straight. The hammer came down at a bad angle and glanced off the tips of my fingers. I swore and hopped in a circle while Billy laughed.

I wanted to rearrange his face with the hammer. It wasn't

enough that he'd moved in and set up camp inside my life. In less than six weeks, he'd chased away Ben and Eddie. He'd taken over my spot behind the house. And now he was going to take Nate away too. He had to ruin anything I liked.

I wanted to act cool and over it, but my face was burning. "You just think that because the only time you hang out with girls is if you know they'll screw you."

As soon as I said it, I knew it was a bad idea. The way he looked at me was dangerous, and I understood that whatever happened next was going to hurt. He stood up. He looked very tall standing in front of the ratty old couch at the top of the creek bank. Then he was down in the creek bed with me so fast I flinched, so close I could feel his breath on my forehead. His boots were almost touching the toes of my Vans. "You need to worry a little more about what people think of you."

I clenched my jaw and tightened my grip on the hammer.

Billy's gaze flicked to my hand. I thought he'd be furious, but instead he laughed. "What are you going to do with that hammer, Max?"

I didn't answer.

Above us, in the shade of the sweet pea bush, Wayne was still sitting on the couch. Billy stood over me, smiling, his eyes never leaving the hammer. I thought he was going to grab it out of my hand, but he only leaned closer, his voice sly and wheedling: "What are you going to do, Max? Are you going to take a swing at me?"

I stuck out my chin and shrugged. "Thinking about it."

Nate put down his notebook and stood up. "Come on, Max. Let's go down to the park or something. We can work on the ramp another time."

I shook my head. "This is my spot and my ramp, and I'm not going to sit around the picnic shelter and do nothing just because Billy's a jerk. It was mine first."

I was talking to Nate, but I was still looking at Billy, so I saw when his face changed. In a second, he'd gone from bored and kind of amused to dangerous.

He shook his head sadly and smiled a wide, fake smile, but his eyes didn't change. "Ma-ax, don't be selfish, now. You gotta learn to share. We're *family*."

The word was a loaded one, sweet and sick like poison.

I didn't answer, just squared my shoulders and glared at him, still holding the hammer. I was clenching my teeth, blazing and furious, but I didn't know what to do. I wanted to be able to use a smirk or a stare or a single word the way he did, filling up space as some kind of weapon.

Billy gazed down at me, smiling, always smiling, and I stared back at him.

Nate had crossed the packed dirt. He stepped closer, and this time, he sounded angry. "Leave her alone!"

It took a lot to make Nate mad. He usually kept his mouth shut and put his head down until it was safe to come out again. When he did get mad, it was righteous.

The way he cared about what was right and fair reminded me of the Man-Thing. Nate was short and shy and skinny, and the dry creek bed wasn't anything like a murky swamp in the Everglades, but the way he was glaring at Billy with his head down had the same unarticulated fury. For the first time in a long time, I thought about motorcycle gangs and real estate developers and the Slaughter Room. The way the Man-Thing had vanquished all of them. I was glad someone would defend me, even though I knew deep down there was nothing Nate could do.

Wayne was still hunched on the couch, watching and laughing his crazy laugh. It was higher now, and nervous.

Billy didn't laugh. He grabbed Nate by the elbow and shoved his arm behind his back. At first Nate didn't struggle or make a sound, and then he did. His eyes watered, and he gave a short, sharp cry. His face was going red.

Billy shoved harder, and Nate pressed his lips together, closing his eyes. Wayne had stopped laughing and gotten to his feet. Now he just looked sick and helpless, standing there in the weeds.

"Stop it, Billy!" I said it in a hard, flat voice, already sure this wasn't happening, so horribly sure that it wouldn't turn really ugly, because it couldn't.

Billy grinned, forcing Nate's arm up so high his hand was jammed between his shoulder blades. "Stop it? Stop what, Max? Stop this?"

Afterward, all I could think about was how his voice had sounded so bright and cheerful. It didn't match what was happening on his face. His eyes were full of a terrible nothing—chilly and faraway.

The sound was loud. It was like water poured over ice, or the sudden crack when a rock hits a windshield. Then Nate gave a howl and collapsed on his knees in the bottom of the creek bed, holding his arm awkwardly at his side. Billy stepped back, and at first I didn't understand. I thought that would be the end of it—it was obnoxious and ugly, but it was over. And then I saw the reason Nate's knees had given out. His elbow was bent the wrong way. His face went white in a way I didn't know happened in real life, like all the blood had dropped right out of him. We could see the pale knob of the bone jutting underneath his skin.

For a long time, none of us moved. Then Wayne turned away and struggled up out of the ditch. His boots sent a rain of dirt and gravel sliding down the bank to land in a little drift at my feet. He started in the direction of the street with his head down and without looking back.

Billy was still watching me in that strange, avid way that always made me feel like I was being x-rayed. His face was blank, but his eyes were full of a bright, glittering light, the way Mrs. Haskell's German shepherd Otto got when he was looking at a cat.

Billy breathed in through his nose and leaned closer. "What are you going to do, Max?"

I didn't say anything. Nate was slumped forward with his head bent, making a low wheezing noise, but I didn't go to him. I was suddenly sure that showing any kind of tenderness in front of Billy would make it worse. I'd seen what had happened to Billy when I tried to help him. Neil had mocked him for it, and that was bad enough. But Billy had *hated* me. I wanted to be a good friend, but I couldn't do the right thing, the brave thing, not even to help Nate.

Billy was standing over me, blocking my way. "You're going to be a good little girl and keep your mouth shut. Right?"

Behind him, Nate was crying now in soft, hitching gasps, holding his arm against his chest.

Billy leaned very close to my ear and said it again: "Right, Max?"

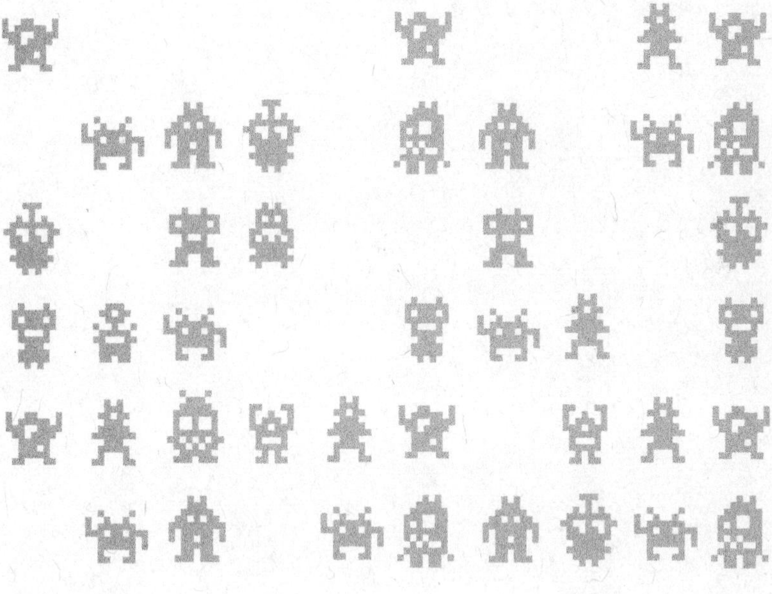

CHAPTER TWELVE

He said it was an accident. That's what he told his dad and my mom and the paramedics when we all stood out in the driveway after the ambulance came.

He'd been showing Nate a Hulk Hogan wrestling move and his hand had slipped, was all.

His smile when he said it was weird and empty, and I was so sure there was no way the grown-ups would be able to look at him and think he was telling the truth. I hadn't accounted for how hard they wanted to believe he wasn't a psycho. I was tempted to give up and tell them everything, but there was no guarantee the truth would make a difference. Nothing would magically fix Nate's arm. It seemed better just to nod along.

Even Nate didn't argue. He sat stone-faced on the stretcher and didn't say anything, even when they braced his arm with bandages and padded boards and loaded him in the back of the ambulance.

I called him when he got home from the hospital. I wanted to say that I was sorry, but the words wouldn't come out right. I sounded careless and too bright, like nothing mattered.

"My place was crazy after you left," I said. "But it's mostly cooled down. I just didn't think he would actually do that, you know?"

Nate should have shouted at me, or at least told me to stop acting so normal. Instead, all he said was, "I know."

After that, though, he didn't come over to work on the ramp anymore. The frame sat half-built, boards bleaching in the sun. After a while, when I finally accepted that none of them were coming back, I finished it by myself. My dad had taught me how to cut mitered corners and I was good with the handsaw and the level, but I was still just one person, and the sheets of plywood were heavy. It took me four days.

School in San Diego started two weeks later, and I went back not knowing if I had friends at all anymore. On the first day, there was Nate, sitting over at the group table on the other side of the room, with his arm in a cast. At lunch, everyone crowded around to sign it—even Mrs. Mallard the

French teacher, who hated me, and kids who never used to talk to us. I felt too awkward to sign it myself, and he didn't ask me to.

It was better that way. At least, that's what I was starting to believe. I had a bad feeling that putting my name on it wouldn't be a friendly gesture, but more like I was admitting to something.

Nate still picked me first for dodgeball sometimes, and when I got in the cafeteria line behind him or sat next to him in shop class, he didn't tell me I couldn't, but his eyes were always looking past me now.

Billy was dangerous, and he would keep getting more dangerous until someone got hurt. I could do my best to try to keep him happy, but not forever. Maybe not even for long. There was a time when I'd actually believed I knew how to handle him. I wouldn't make that mistake again. The whole point of movies was that monsters could be beaten. The point of the sequels was that they always got back up.

I knew what Billy had done to Nate was no accident, but I didn't know how to stop it.

Billy's rages were like the storms that blew in sometimes during fall. They happened suddenly, after days of clear blue sky. It would have been easy to say that he'd learned the trick from Neil, but Neil always wanted you to think that everything he did was so reasonable. He got satisfaction out of being the one who always seemed in control. Billy liked chaos better.

After Nate, I thought for sure that Billy had really messed up. He'd get sent to military school or wind up in jail or something. He was out of control in a way I didn't know how to deal with, and finally everyone else would see it too. But Neil and my mom wouldn't even say out loud what he'd done. They acted like they didn't get it.

Even later, when they'd already decided we were moving to Indiana, they never talked about the real reason, and when I tried to get them to say it, they gave me made-up ones instead. It would be good for us. It would give Billy a fresh start, away from his trashy, friends and other bad influences. It would give me a place to run and jump and play, with clean air and wide streets and less traffic.

They acted like it was this favor they were doing for us. Like Billy wasn't the ringleader of every kind of trouble he and his scuzzy loser friends got into, and I was six instead of thirteen. They still wouldn't admit the real reason: Billy was completely out of control and we were skipping town and hoping things didn't get worse.

I'd been an idiot before, when I'd believed in family and security. I knew the truth now: The world is a big, chaotic place, and you're totally on your own. You might as well keep your monsters close. That way, they never take you by surprise.

The night everything actually changed and we found out we were moving, I'd just gotten home from playing *Pac-Man* at Joy Town.

Neil was standing on a chair in the living room, taking down the row of framed travel postcards my mom had hung over the back of the couch.

For a minute, I stood and watched him lift each one off its hook and set it in the growing stack on the coffee table, but I didn't think it meant anything big. Of course he was taking them down. This was Neil, who didn't like any lamp or clock he hadn't picked out himself. He'd already reupholstered the old footstool and gotten rid of the rug in the hall, and now he was just ruining one more part of my old, familiar life. After all, he'd already ruined everything else.

"What are you doing with those?" I said, half thinking that maybe if I didn't seem like I wanted them too much, he'd let me keep them in my room.

He glanced down at me, but instead of answering, he turned and called, "Billy, come on in here. Susan, you should be here for this too."

My mom came in from the kitchen and stood in the doorway. We all waited, not talking, until finally Billy came slouching in, looking bored. He dropped down next to me on the couch, and Neil got down from the chair.

He stretched and then dusted his hands on his pants, even though the postcard frames hadn't been dirty. "Susan," he said, but he was still looking at Billy. "Do you want to tell them?"

My mom smiled weakly. "We have some big news, you guys."

She was trying to sound cheerful, but her voice wobbled and then went up at the end, like she was asking a question. My first thought was that they were going to have a baby, and right away I started to factor in one more hostage to worry about. One more soft, fragile thing that would need to be kept safe from Billy.

After a second, though, I decided that wasn't it. My mom looked nervous, but not happy or excited. I waited.

"We're moving," she said. "The bank offered Neil a transfer. There's a branch in Indiana, and—"

The room was folding in, getting smaller and brighter and way too hot. She went on, talking in that same high, bright voice, like this was all part of some great adventure. But I didn't really hear anything after *Indiana*.

Billy stood up. His face was furious and hazardous. "This is such crap."

I put my hand on the arm of the couch, feeling how shabby and worn-out the upholstery was, how rough.

Neil turned to Billy, and his tone was icy. "You're going to want to take some time in your room to cool off."

The edge in his voice told me that, underneath his calm, reasonable mask, he was itching for a fight, and I waited for things to get worse. Billy just turned his back on Neil and stalked off down the hall. On his way, he cursed and slammed his fist against the wall. My school picture from fifth grade shuddered and fell. It wasn't the same as taking a swing at Neil, but it was close enough. I waited for Neil to react the way he always did, to blow past talking and go straight to discipline. To the belt. Instead, he just watched Billy go with that bland, bored look.

"There's a putty knife in the garage," he said, turning to me. "Run and get it, and I'll pop these picture hooks out of the drywall."

I didn't want to run and get anything for him, but I did it. My heart felt like it was too big for my rib cage and was crawling up into my throat. My face was tingling.

I was almost to the laundry room, passing the dark doorway to Billy's room, when he stepped out into the hall and reached for me.

I tried to twist away, but I wasn't fast enough. He caught me by the arm, and it wasn't the first time he'd ever touched me, but other times had always been to push me out of the way in the kitchen or flick the end of my nose. This time, his fingers closed hard around my elbow. I gasped.

He leaned down so his mouth was right next to my ear. "You did this."

I held very still. There was a smudge on the wall behind him, and I stared at it.

Billy's voice was so low it seemed like I was feeling it, not hearing it. His thumb was pressing into the crook of my elbow so hard my hand was starting to go numb. "Look at me."

When I still didn't look away from the smudge, he gave me a little shake, talking through his teeth, low and dangerous. "Look at me, Max."

This time, I did.

His face was close to mine. His breath was hot and metallic. I could smell stale cigarettes in his hair. "I'm going to destroy you for this."

His eyes were a dead, dull color I'd never seen before, like looking into a black hole. My mouth was very dry.

Maybe back at the start of it all, standing in front of the Skee-Ball stalls at Fort Fun, I would have thought he was joking. Even after he burned the dead cat, and gave me the cigarette just to annoy my mom. Even after all the times he'd done crazy, reckless things and the times Neil had punished him for it, I would have told myself that was just Billy. It was just a game. But now all I could see was the sick, busted angle of Nate's arm.

"I didn't do anything."

He leaned down so his forehead was almost touching mine. "You've got a big mouth, Max."

His voice was low and ominous. I could feel it in my teeth. I shook my head, fast and breathless. There was no version of things that wouldn't have ended with my mom calling the ambulance. It wasn't like we could have left Nate there. He couldn't have just gone home without anyone noticing. "What was I supposed to do?"

Billy gave me a long, level stare. Then he raised his chin and let me go. "You're lucky I'm around to watch out for you. Remember that."

He left me standing in the doorway to the laundry room. There was a hot, achy place on my arm, throbbing in time with my heartbeat. When I looked down, there was a red mark the size of his thumb.

"Maxine," Neil shouted. "Did you get lost in there?"

"No, sir," I called back.

After I'd brought Neil the putty knife, he got back up on the chair and pried the picture hangers out of the drywall. I went in my room and opened my dresser. Since the wedding, Neil and my mom had been getting kind of weird about letting me see my dad, and now they were going to take me away from him altogether—take me halfway across the country with Billy. I put some socks and underwear and two pairs of jeans in my backpack. The next night, I took a twenty-dollar bill out of my mom's jewelry box and did the only thing I could do.

I left.

• • •

At home, Billy pulled into the garage so he could change the Camaro's spark plugs with the door up and the music blasting. I stayed out in the driveway with my board.

I was practicing my kick flips, when my mom called to me from the screened-in porch. "Max, could you come and help me hang this picture?"

I sighed. "Can't it wait? I'm busy."

Neil was climbing the front steps, carrying a box of power tools. "Put down that skateboard and do what your mother tells you, Maxine."

I wanted to roll my eyes at him, but I dropped my board and went to help her with the picture.

We were just making sure it was straight, when out in the garage, we heard the music shut off and the Camaro rev up. A second later, there was a huge, brittle crunch, and I knew what it was even before I looked.

Billy had backed over my board.

I leapt down the front steps and raced to see, hoping I was wrong. But it was just the way it had sounded. He'd crushed the deck with his back tire and the nose had splintered off completely.

I stood over it, looking at the damage. This was my punishment. It had to be. The price for being seen with Lucas.

"You jerk." I said it in a flat, furious voice. My cheeks were prickling in a hot, humiliating way, like I was going to cry, and I bit the inside of my lip hard.

The look Billy gave me was bored and heavy-lidded. "What do you want me to say, Max? Maybe if you didn't leave your stuff everywhere, it wouldn't get broken."

"You jerk!" This time I yelled it, stomping hard on the concrete.

We were facing each other in the driveway, standing over my broken board and shouting at each other, when Neil came back outside. He stopped on the steps, looking back and forth between us. "What's going on out here?"

"He wrecked my board!"

Billy threw up his hands. "She left it in the driveway!"

Neil gave both of us a hard, level stare. Then he turned to Billy. "Looks like you'll be giving your sister rides from now on."

Like we hadn't already been stuck with each other all week. I didn't want to get in the car with Billy. I never wanted to see him again, but Neil was giving us both a dangerous look, and I didn't say anything. I picked up the pieces and went inside.

• • •

I was frightened now. Billy's moods were bad enough, but I didn't like the way he'd looked at Lucas. He'd broken the board just to show me that he could, and that meant he might be planning to break other things. I knew beyond a doubt that this was too dangerous and messy for me to handle on my own.

I needed a grown-up, someone to step in and take over the situation for me. But my mom would never be able to keep Billy in line even if she tried, and Neil's way would just make everything worse. I needed someplace far away, where things were easy and laid-back and I wouldn't have to think about it anymore.

I needed my dad.

The problem with that was, no way in hell would my mom and Neil willingly send me back to California. The only way to get there was to go on my own, and the fallout would be bad if I got caught. If they'd freaked out about me running away when we were back in San Diego, it was going to be ten times worse now. I tried to decide if I could leave without them knowing. If I was brave enough to take the Greyhound all the way to LA from Indiana.

I was pretty sure I could handle it, but the trip was going to be a lot longer than the one from San Diego, and I'd have to do it without my mom noticing I was gone before I'd even gotten out of town. And the biggest issue was how much it was going to cost.

I wished I were a grown-up. Every problem would be so much easier with a bank account and a job. But then, if I were a grown-up, none of this would even be an issue. Grown-ups didn't have to deal with friends who abandoned them or with dangerous stepbrothers. When things got out of control, they could just leave.

The solution to all my problems came sooner than I'd expected, though.

After dinner on Friday, my mom was in an exceptionally good mood. She was bent over the newspaper with a pen, circling things in the Sears ad.

"Honey," she said, glancing up from the housewares section. "Neil and I are going up to Terre Haute tomorrow to see about getting some things for the house."

Billy made a disgusted noise. "What a joke. Hawkins doesn't even have a Sears."

My mom was still bent over the newspaper, talking in a vague, dreamy voice, like she hadn't heard him. "There's supposed to be a new mall opening in town soon. Star Land?

170

Star Court? But that's months from now. We need some new sheets and towels, and a snow shovel before the weather gets bad."

The shopping list was so fantastically boring I couldn't tell if she was saying it to us or to herself. I was considering my options, trying to shake the nagging sense that this whole idea was insane. The feeling I got when I imagined leaving was like the feeling I got from standing on the end of the high dive. Pretty soon, there was going to be snow. I'd never really seen snow, except on TV. I told myself that it was no big deal, just a sprinkling of frozen water. An unflavored shave-ice. I tried not to think about how I'd be missing it.

My mom glanced up from the paper like she could see what I was thinking, and I half expected her to ask me if there was anything I needed to tell her. But she just smiled her small, nervous smile. "I was thinking if you wanted, we could take you shopping for some new clothes? I bet the girls dress differently here."

They did, but they dressed like choir directors, and I was not about to start showing up to school in beige turtlenecks and plaid skirts. I was already talking myself through what came next. Terre Haute was at least an hour away. The shopping trip would mean they'd be gone all afternoon and I'd be alone in the house.

Alone except for Billy.

I knew that telling her I didn't want to go to Terre Haute was going to hurt her feelings, but it was my best chance.

In a day or two, her feelings were going to be pretty hurt anyway.

"No thanks," I said, trying to sound casual, and not like I'd rather be dead than walking around in a matching blouse-and-sweater set.

She looked kind of shattered, but all she said was, "Okay, maybe some other time?"

Even now that I knew when my opening would be, there was still another layer to the problem. Bus tickets cost money, and I didn't have any. Or at least, not the kind that would get you more than a round of *Pac-Man* and a slice of pizza. My mom almost never let me buy anything without asking Neil first, but I had an idea and I'd have to try. There was no other way.

I found her in the utility room, folding laundry out of the basket on top of the washer. I picked up a sock and started poking around in the basket, looking for its matching one.

She smiled in a bright, distracted way. "How thoughtful of you!"

I fiddled with the sock and immediately felt guilty. I didn't usually help her with the laundry. I needed to talk to her when Neil wasn't around, though, and he never helped with the laundry.

We stood facing each other in front of the washing machine. She smelled powdery and sweet, like perfume and fabric softener, and for a second, I felt really bad about what I was going to do next.

"I have to ask you something, but it's private. You can't tell Neil."

She was watching me, wide-eyed, and I realized I was scaring her a little. "What is it, honey?"

I took a deep breath and tried not to look as guilty as I felt. "About the school clothes. I do kind of want to go shopping?"

She looked at me with something so earnest and open it made me shrivel inside. The expression on her face was hope. "Really?"

I nodded. "I just was wanting to go by myself. The eighth-grade girls here are all nuts for jelly bracelets and lace tops, and they have some really cool ones in the window at that Cozy Closet place. I was thinking I could go down there and pick one out. With my friends." I had to be careful not to push it too far. Hopefully she'd believe in a version of me who was into jelly bracelets and had friends. "And . . . I was wondering if maybe I could get some volumizing mousse too. They have it at the drugstore?"

By that point, she should have been deeply suspicious, but she was looking at me in this warm, open way, like this was all she ever wanted, her rambunctious daughter turning into one of the good girls, nice and sweet and normal.

Her beaming smile gave me a shaky feeling, like I was slipping out of focus. I wanted to make her happy, but none of the things that would make her happy were things I could be without lying. When my mom looked at me, she saw a problem that needed to be solved. She saw someone too prickly and rude to feel good around, and too much like my dad to really understand.

It wasn't until I was back in my room, the bills in my hand, that I had time to feel guilty. It was a lot of money for her to spend on me, even if I had been telling the truth, and the part where I wasn't going to use it for the lace top made me feel really bad. I didn't know what else to do, though.

Someone should have told her I was too much like my dad to trust. But Billy was spinning out again, and things would be so much worse if I stayed. I didn't have any other options.

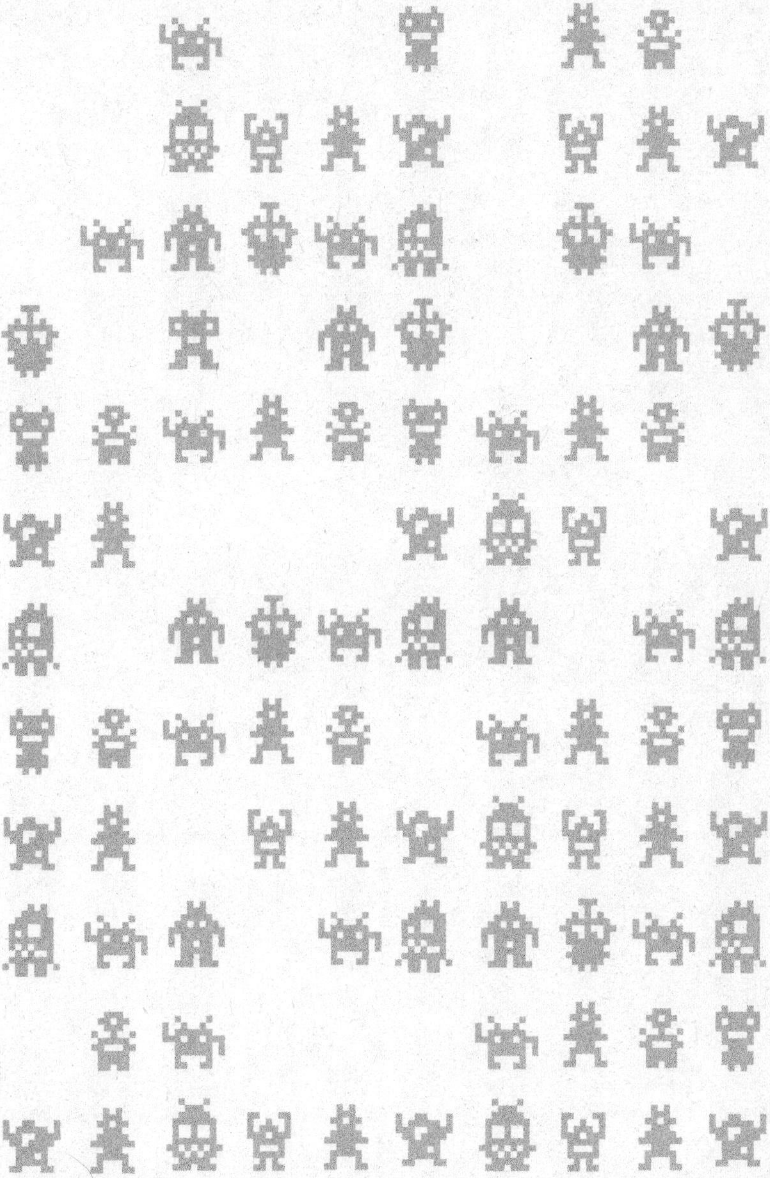

CHAPTER THIRTEEN

On Saturday, I got myself a box of Club crackers, two cans of Squirt, and my toothbrush and locked myself in my room. I packed the snacks in my backpack, along with socks, underwear, and an extra pullover. It wasn't much. I wished I had some Twinkies, but I'd have to live without.

My mom and Neil had left for Terre Haute that morning, and now I was just waiting for Billy to go out so that I could make a run for it.

He was camped out in the living room, lifting weights. The bench press was the same one he'd kept in the garage back home, but since the move, he'd been keeping it in the house. The garage here was cold and spidery and full of boxes.

He was doing curls with the barbell and drinking one of Neil's beers, with his music blasting and a cigarette jutting from his mouth. He'd always been intense about working out. Lately, though, whenever he was home, it was pretty much all he did.

I sat on the edge of my bed, trying to fix my skateboard deck and waiting for Billy to get tired of his workout routine. The backpack sat on the bed, packed with everything I planned to take with me. I'd have maybe three hours to get into town and find my way to the bus station. Then I'd figure out the schedule and catch the next bus for California.

At the very least I knew the ride would be long and boring. But it was hard to imagine the specifics. Once I got to LA, the rest of the trip was easier to picture. I'd find a pay phone and call my dad. He'd be confused at first, maybe even annoyed, but he'd understand. He wasn't supposed to have me full-time, but he was cool about stuff. If I explained the situation, he'd come and get me.

I pictured my new life in his apartment, sleeping on the pullout couch and eating cold takeout for breakfast. He'd stay up way too late calculating point spreads and working on weird inventions and spend all his nights and weekends at the bar or the track. But I could deal with that. I'd get used to it.

I stared at my backpack. Sneaking away meant taking barely anything with me, but I'd be fine without my stuff. I didn't need my comic books, or even most of my clothes. All I really cared about was my board, and it was in bad shape. Once I got to my dad's, maybe he'd be able to fix it.

My dad was good at the kinds of things they never taught us in school. My mom called him a jack-of-all-trades, but he actually only had three or four. When they were married, he used to hustle pool sometimes, and once he sold black-market tape decks out of the garage. Since the divorce, though, he'd gotten more careless. He'd keep a job for a couple months, usually as a repairman, or the cashier at a payday loan place, before he got fired. Or else got bored and quit. But his real job was getting people things they needed.

He could find old concert bootlegs or new license plates, if that was what someone was looking for. And he ran all kinds of betting, even the illegal kind.

He wasn't big on housekeeping or home decorating. His apartment was shabby and dark. But the kitchenette faced east, and he'd sit at the counter and drink his coffee in the mornings with the sun coming in through the shades in stripes, lighting him from behind. Sometimes if I was the first one up, I'd sit alone in the kitchen and picture how I must look, the sun coming through my hair like I was bursting into flames.

My favorite thing was watching him make fake IDs. He'd spend an evening sitting at the counter in his kitchenette, peeling the backings off old California driver's licenses, squinting down at the names and birth dates through a magnifying glass. There was something almost magical about watching him match the old pictures to new names, like watching people become someone else right in front of me.

He'd sit with his head bent and his fingers working to assemble the pieces, making new identities for people doing things he wouldn't tell me about. A lot of the jobs he did were things he wouldn't tell me about.

He didn't make the IDs very often. When he did, though, he would always let me watch.

I didn't know the exact word for what he was, but I knew enough not to tell my mom. He never said who they went to, just that he wasn't selling them to high school kids. I'd watched enough spy movies with him to know the score. A fake ID was for helping people disappear.

The last time I'd stayed with him, I'd stood at the counter in my stocking feet with a can of Coke and leaned next to him. He was gluing down a color photo the size of a stamp, setting it carefully in the corner of the ID with tweezers. The man in the photo was dark-eyed, with a stringy mustache. I knew him from the Black Door Lounge. He always came in to watch boxing on the weekends, and when I was younger he used to give me the cherries out of his old-fashioneds. His name was Walter Ross, and he hung out at the lounge with the rest of my dad's scuzzy friends. The ID was for someone named Clarence Masterson.

"That's Wally from the bar. Why does it say his name is Clarence?"

My dad smiled but didn't look up. "Because you need a really specific name to sell a new identity. Nothing sounds faker than *John Smith*. Two steps left, sweet pea. You're blocking the light."

I moved out of the way, watching as he lined up the photo with a careful finger, then pressed it flat and held it there. I wondered where Wally was going and what he had done to make him want to be someone else.

Of course my dad would understand why I'd come. He was the kind of person who would get how it was to be in the place everyone said you should be and still just need to leave.

• • •

I was sitting on the edge of my bed, winding duct tape around the broken nose of my deck, when the doorbell rang.

Billy was out in the living room, ten feet from the door, but he didn't answer it and the bell rang again, an impatient double chime like someone was stabbing it with their finger. He dropped the weights and yelled for me to see who it was. I sighed and got up to go check, half-convinced it was just going to be some perky middle-aged lady going door-to-door selling Avon.

But I knew it wasn't. Ladies who sold Avon were uptight and fussy, even in Hawkins. They never really came out to Cherry Road.

When I opened the door, Lucas was standing on the steps, wearing a canvas jacket with a fake sheepskin lining and looking serious. My whole face felt cold.

I could see his bike behind him, keeled over on its kick-stand on the side of the road.

"I have proof," he said.

At first I wasn't totally sure what he was talking about. He was wearing a camo bandana tied across his forehead like Rambo, which didn't prove anything about anything, it was just weird.

I was a little freaked out by him showing up at my house. Any other time, I would have been happy to know that even after everything I said to him at the arcade, he still wanted to hang out with me. Now all I could think about was what was going to happen if Billy saw him. I didn't know how much time we had, but I needed him to leave.

Before Billy could turn around and see Lucas standing on the porch, I stepped outside and closed the door behind me. "Proof of what?"

He shook his head. "You have to come with me now."

It wasn't an answer to my question, because he *never* answered my questions, and I could feel myself starting to get angry again. "Where?"

Lucas pressed his lips together before answering. "You just have to trust me."

For a second, I stared at him. The longer we stood there, the more I started to think that we'd still be standing there when Billy came to see what was going on. The door would open, and he'd come up behind me, and then the scene would really get bad. "You have to leave."

Lucas was looking at me in that open, exasperated way

he had, where every particle of his attention was fixed on me, impatient, but completely, 100 percent honest.

"My window," I said finally. "Around back. It's the one with the firewood rack underneath. Meet me in thirty seconds."

I turned around and shut the door before Billy could come out and find Lucas there.

Billy was still in the living room, but he wasn't lifting weights anymore. When he reached for his beer and demanded to know who it was, I didn't let my face change. The way he was looking at me was sharp-eyed and too steady, like he knew something was up, he just didn't know what. Lucas had told me a story about monsters like he believed they were real, and I knew that it was true. Just not the way he meant.

After all, there was one in my house right now.

With my expression as blank as I could make it, I walked down the hall to my room and shut the door behind me. The backpack was sitting where I'd left it, waiting for me to scoop up my board and my jacket and make a break for it.

This was my shot, but suddenly getting back to my dad didn't seem like much of a solution to anything.

When Lucas came coasting around the side of the house on his bike, I was waiting at the windowsill. There was a part of me whispering that I was giving up what might be my best shot at California. I was going to miss my opportunity and regret it forever. But another, louder part of me insisted that Lucas was here for something important. If I didn't go with him now, I'd never have another chance.

I left the backpack sitting next to my broken skateboard.

Lucas had come all the way out to Cherry Road because he wanted to show me something, and whatever it was, I was pretty sure he believed it. I didn't really think it would be convincing—maybe not even any proof at all—but suddenly I needed to see it too.

I opened the window and climbed out.

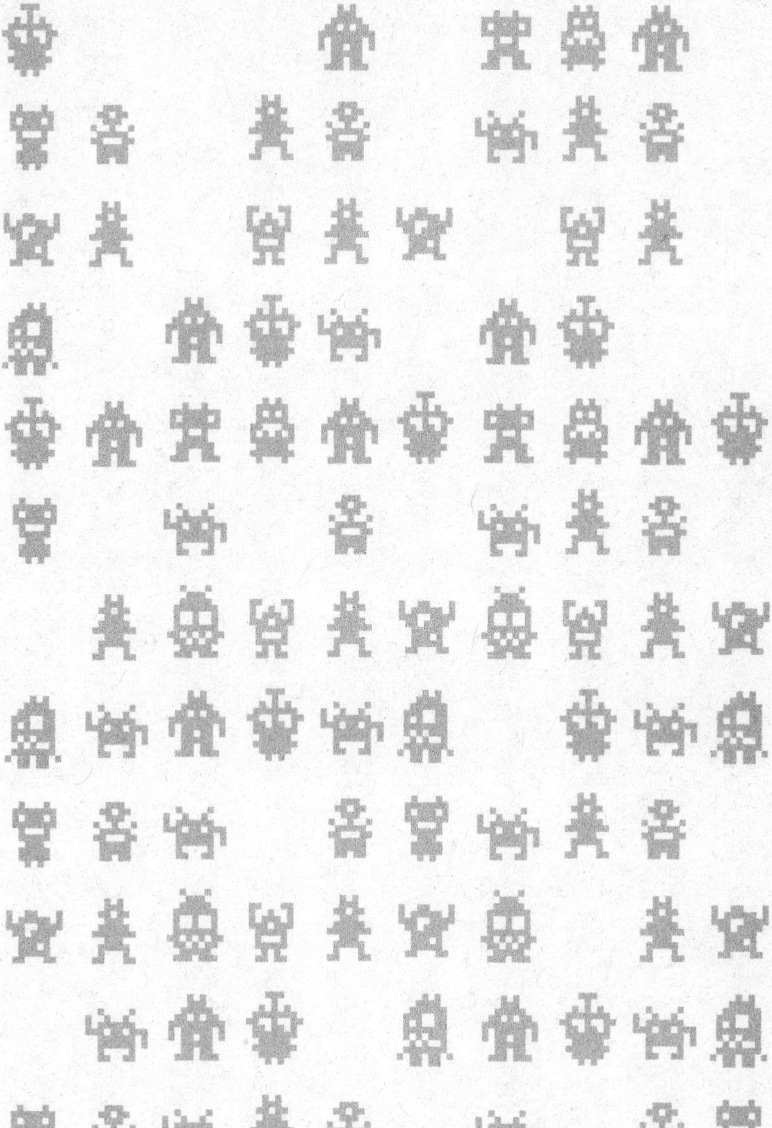

CHAPTER FOURTEEN

Lucas rolled up on his bike, and I jumped down from the top of the wood box and got on.

He cut across weedy gravel driveways and through yards, staying off the road. I perched behind him on the back of the banana seat and held on to his shoulders. The afternoon was quiet and peaceful. It was gray and chilly out, and all the neighbors were inside. I should have been worried about where we were going or what kind of proof he meant, but the whole time I was listening for the Camaro.

I felt twitchy and breathless, expecting it to come roaring after us at any second. I knew that if Billy actually stopped working on his pecs for two seconds and noticed I was gone, he'd catch us in a heartbeat. He'd pull up next to us, give me that hard stare, and I'd have no choice but to get in. Everything else would fall away, and all I'd be able to see was the yawning mouth of the passenger seat.

But it wasn't just how easily I'd cave that made my throat hurt. I didn't know what he'd do if he found me with Lucas. Or, I knew, I just didn't know exactly how bad it would be, and that scared me worse than anything. The feeling it gave me wasn't like worrying about bus rides or disappointing my mom or whether I ever made friends again. It was a freezing, bottomless fear, and it covered everything.

Even without knowing the full situation, Lucas was careful not to go near the main road, though. We rode through the silent neighborhood, my hands on his shoulders. The canvas coat was rough under my fingers, and the shape of his shoulders was different from the bony, familiar way Nate's shoulders had felt. I could feel how the muscles in his back moved as he pedaled and how warm he was through his jacket.

We rode fast, not talking. I told myself that I'd only agreed to go with him in order to keep him away from Billy, but it wasn't quite true. That fear was being steadily overridden by another feeling, warm and glowing in my chest. He'd come to get me. And I was glad.

As Lucas put more distance between us and my house, I stopped worrying about Billy and started to be increasingly curious about where we were going. We weren't headed into town after all. Instead, we followed a weedy road up through a spindly stand of trees, and stopped at the top of a hill. We got off the bike, and Lucas took hold of the handlebars and walked it over to the other side of the slope.

We were looking down into a junkyard.

Lucas had a smug expression, and I was ready for him to explain why he'd brought me to the town dump. "What's going on? What are we doing here?"

Below us was a sea of rusty old cars with their taillights busted out and their doors torn off, mixed with ancient refrigerators and rusty sheets of corrugated metal. The whole place was a jackpot for building supplies.

Then I saw we weren't the only ones here.

At one end of the junkyard, Dustin was standing near a rickety old bus with an older guy, probably Billy's age. He looked irritated and kind of preppie, with a giant swoop of hair like someone in a new-wave band. They had a gas can with them and a baseball bat pounded full of nails, and weirdly, a bucket of meat. They were dropping the meat in a trail on the ground.

I turned to Lucas. "What are they doing down there?"

He jerked his head at Dustin and shrugged like it should be obvious. "Looking for Dart."

"In a junkyard? That doesn't—"

He held up a hand to cut me off. "I know, I know, that doesn't make sense. But you just have to trust me."

The whole thing was so supremely weird that I was tempted to stick around to see what happened next. I didn't really believe him, but I was kind of curious to see where this was going.

Lucas stashed his bike, and we headed down into the junkyard.

We cut a path through the weeds toward the bus. Everything about the scene was straight out of a horror movie, except that no one in horror movies wore Members Only jackets. I was pretty sure that the junkyard was abandoned—maybe out of commission five or ten years—and also that Lucas and Dustin had been here before.

"Steve," Dustin was saying as they stood in the center of the clearing. "Steve, listen to me. Dart has discerning tastes. It does *so* matter where we put the bait, and I'm telling you, this is the perfect spot."

The other guy just gave him a bored look and dumped out the rest of the meat in a pile.

The sun was setting, and I didn't know what I was doing there or when my mom and Neil would be getting back. I didn't have a coat, just my warm-up jacket, but I knew the icy, creeping feeling on my neck wasn't because of the dropping tempature. I was gripped by an eerie certainty that something was going to happen.

Lucas and Dustin had gone off to whisper about something—probably me—behind one of the dead cars, and I was left standing awkwardly in the clearing with Steve. I began to wonder where Mike and Will were, since Lucas hadn't mentioned anything about them and they were nowhere to be seen in the junkyard.

I waited for Steve to make some crack about my hair or my clothes, or act like a jerk the way high school boys always did, maybe even tell me to get lost, that this was private secret monster business.

But he just went over to one of the junk piles and started picking through it, pulling out sheets of scrap metal and lugging them across the clearing. I watched as he fitted pieces of battered plywood against the doors and windows. He was shoring up the bus.

After a minute, he turned and looked at me with one eyebrow raised. "Are you going to give me a hand, or what?"

I trotted after Steve, and together we started covering the smashed-out windows of the bus with mismatched sheets of plywood and scrap metal.

He held a square of aluminum siding in place and glanced over his shoulder. "So you're new in town?"

I nodded. It was the kind of question a retired neighbor or the lunch lady would ask you, weirdly adult, and I didn't know what else to do. Steve just nodded back and started pulling dented sheets of aluminum out of the drifts of junk and tossing them in a heap.

The whole afternoon had turned blurry and surreal, and everything about it was the strangest part.

Lucas and Dustin were still crouched behind the broken-down car, having some sort of very intense discussion that didn't include me. It was infuriating that no matter how hard I tried to understand their game, they would always be playing it without me.

Steve yelled for them to come help, and we worked in silence, dragging the scrap metal over to the bus and layering it to cover the windows.

The bus was a mess inside, the vinyl seats half-rotten and tilting on rusted legs.

Steve looked around like he was taking inventory. "We need to figure out some way to board up the windows and still be able to keep a lookout."

There was a hatch in the ceiling, square like a trapdoor. I glanced up. "If we can get on the roof, it'll be easy to see from there."

Steve looked down at me and raised his eyebrows. I thought he'd wave me off or say that it was a little kid's idea, but instead he nodded and clapped me on the arm. "Good thinking."

I hunted through the heaps of rusty buckets and warped boards until I found an aluminum ladder lying in the weeds. It was a little shaky, covered in tattered spider-webs and dry grass, but it seemed sturdy enough. I hauled it into the bus and leaned it so it jutted through the opening in the ceiling.

When I climbed up top, I could see all the way to the rooftops of the big Hawkins Lab compound—almost all the way to town. Another time, I would have gotten into the game. I would have felt excited about the whole afternoon, satisfied that we'd just built a pretty sweet fort. The more I watched the others, though, the more obvious it was that Lucas had been serious. None of them seemed very much like they were playing.

The roof of the bus was faded from the sun and speckled with rust. From up here, you could see in every direction, but it felt too exposed. Over in a weedy corner of the junkyard was a big pile of tires. I got back down and we searched through them, picking out the sturdiest ones, then rolling them over to the bus one by one. The rubber was so old it was cracking, and the tires left big smears of black stuff on my hands. We wrestled the tires up the ladder and stacked them on the roof in an overlapping pattern to make a sort of bunker.

Steve was down in the center of the clearing, pouring the gas in a wide circle around the heap of meat. It was completely weird to watch, but the meaning was obvious enough: he was going to lure out whatever they were hunting, and then set the trail of gas on fire.

The bus was rickety and rusted out, but after we were through, it was so heavily armored it looked like something from *The Road Warrior*. With the reinforcements in place, Lucas straightened his bandana and climbed on top with his binoculars to keep watch. It had been a good call, bringing the binoculars, but I had no idea what he was watching for.

Steve and Dustin both followed Lucas into the bus, and even though neither of them bothered to explain what we were supposed to be doing, the meaning was clear: it was time to hunker down.

We sat and waited. The inside of the bus smelled like leaves and mold. The amount of preparation we'd put in seemed like overkill. Dart was about as big as a guinea pig the last time I'd seen him.

I tried my best to sit still and be patient, but I was getting restless. The air was colder now and the sun had set completely. Steve sat on the floor with his back against the ball of the bus, flicking the wheel on his lighter and then flipping the top down to put out the flame.

Dustin was more animated. He fidgeted in the cramped little space behind the driver's seat, shifting from foot to foot and telling me all about the monster that had terrorized them last year and how Steve had fought it. The whole thing sounded ridiculous. Steve didn't exactly look like a hero, just a guy who'd spent all afternoon poking around the salvage yard with his collar popped and his sleeves pushed up.

"And you're, like, totally one hundred percent sure it wasn't a bear?" I knew I was pushing it, but it was still hard to believe this could be anything but a joke. No one came out to an abandoned salvage yard to light a monster on fire with a flip-top lighter and a can of gasoline and actually meant it. That was kids' stuff. Fantasy.

Steve just nodded, leaning there with his lighter, but Dustin turned on me angrily. "What are you even doing here if you don't believe us? Go home!"

I knew he only meant it in a mean, petty way, like he could punish me for daring to question the outrageous stories they kept handing me. He didn't know the hardest part about going home was that I'd been trying to. The problem was, no matter how much I wanted to be there, my real home might be too far to get to. For the first time, I let myself consider the possibility that it might not exist at all anymore, if it ever really had.

There was a blue-violet square of sky showing through the hatch in the roof, velvety and studded with tiny pin-prick stars. I climbed the ladder and clambered out onto the roof with Lucas. As we sat in the dark, waiting for whatever strange horror was coming, I still couldn't help thinking that this was all some giant practical joke. The small, sneaky voice in my head whispered that I was being tricked, but I had no idea how anymore.

The most obvious explanation for everything was that they actually believed it.

I still didn't know whether I did. Whether I *could*. The way I was going along with it didn't feel like belief, exactly, but still, the fact was I'd chosen this instead of a two-day bus ride. I'd chosen this over everything. It dawned on me that I would rather sit in a freezing-cold junkyard, waiting for some kind of monster to show up, than be safe in my living room with a plate of Oreos and a glass of Quik, watching *T. J. Hooker*. It was ridiculous, but it was true.

The roof of the bus was cold through my jeans. Lucas was crouched behind the wall of tires with his binoculars, scanning the junkyard.

A layer of fog had rolled in, thick and low to the ground. I watched it, remembering the smoke that had drifted around the men at the bar in the bus station. The creepy goblin story waiting to happen. Since morning, I'd been thinking more and more about that night in the bus station. I'd been so sure that I belonged there, hiding my face, running, that I'd been ready to do it again.

Now, when I really let myself imagine it, it scared me a little, how close I'd been to stepping right off the edge of my normal everyday life, with no net to catch me. How easy it had seemed.

I forced myself to actually imagine what it would be like once I was on the bus, probably sitting next to some sleazy burnout, and also once I got there, trying to find my way from the bus station all the way out to my dad's apartment in East Hollywood.

Even my dad was just playing a game, telling me about padlocks and secret messages because it was more exciting than the truth—that he was a small-time bookie with a bitter ex-wife and a daughter with an attitude.

That was what I'd been headed toward. A pullout couch in a cramped one-bedroom with dirty windows and a sticky floor. A small, grimy life in a place that barely even had room for my dad. And that was only if he didn't freak out and send me straight back here.

I still had a stubborn idea that he wouldn't do that, but it might have just been wishful thinking. I *wanted* to belong to him, but if I was being honest, I wasn't sure he had room for me. Not in the way I needed him to. Not every day. And when I was being *really* honest with myself, I admitted that I'd known that and had just been pretending.

I wondered how many people were playing a game

without really knowing that was what they were doing. For weeks I'd been telling myself that all I wanted was to go back to my dad, but when the chance came, at the last minute I'd picked the great unknown instead.

The fog didn't look so much like cigarette smoke in a bus station anymore. It looked like the ocean.

It was good to sit up here in the crisp, cold air with the stars spread out above us. I knew that no matter what, none of the people in my life were going to swoop in to help or make things better.

My mom tried, but she wanted me to be someone else. Billy was never going to fix anything. What he wanted for me was a fast, flashy world, bigger and more honest than my dad's, but violent and chaotic. The only things he liked about me were my worst parts.

Lucas was watching me, his eyes kind and expectant, like he was waiting for something. I wanted him to understand, but when I tried to say any of the hard parts out loud, I could only manage the simplest version. My eyes were blurry and wet suddenly, and I hated it. When I talked about my life, it felt like he was seeing too much of me. I didn't want him to think I was just some random girl who cried at stupid things.

He didn't act weirded out, though, or like crying made you weak.

He didn't say anything about it at all. "You're cool, Mad Max. I like talking to you."

The woods were full of noises—chirps and squeaks

and chittering—but they weren't the cries of birds, even whatever weird, unfamiliar birds lived in Indiana. We were sitting in the nest of tires, looking at each other, when there was a strange rustling below, and we both froze. Down in the junkyard by the edge of the clearing, something was moving.

At first, I didn't trust what I was seeing. The shape was dark against the pale backdrop of the fog. It had a sinewy body and a strange pointed head. It couldn't be Dart; there was no way. It had to be a trick of the light, and I was just seeing a dog or a coyote. A cougar, even. Not the hungry, angular thing that came slinking over the dry ground.

The monsters I understood were all just men underneath: Michael Myers, Jason, Leatherface. They loomed huge and hulking, hiding their faces behind masks, but they were still just flesh and blood.

The thing that had appeared down in the junkyard, slinking between the broken washing machines and dead cars, was not like anything I'd ever seen on TV or in the movies. All the monsters I had ever known were ordinary underneath. Even the mummies and vampires were actors in makeup when you looked close enough.

The meat was still lying in a gooshy heap in the clearing, surrounded by a circle of gasoline. The creature didn't come to it. When Steve opened the door to the bus and stepped out into the junkyard, I didn't understand what he was doing at first. Then I got it. He was using himself as bait.

He stood over the pile of meat, holding his spiked

baseball bat and waiting for the thing to charge him. Instead it just stayed slow and low to the ground, like it was stalking him.

That was when we saw the others. They slunk through the salvage yard from all sides. One had climbed up onto one of the rusted-out cars, and it was much closer. Dart; had brought friends.

The junkyard echoed with clicks and trills, like the calls of creatures in a nightmare. And then we were screaming at Steve, trying to get his attention, telling him to look. To run.

Steve heard the urgency of our shouts and turned just in time. One of the dark, wiry shapes lunged, and he barely got out of its way, throwing himself across the hood of a junked-out car. As soon as he hit the ground, he set his feet and swung like he was batting for the fences. The bat connected with a *thunk,* and the creature fell back. So it might have been faceless and expressionless, but you could hurt it.

Then Steve was running, pelting back toward the bus, with the creatures scrambling after him. When they moved over the misty ground, I knew with horrible certainty that I was seeing something that did not belong in the natural world. Steve flung himself back inside, and Dustin slammed the folding door just in time.

We all flinched as the beasts threw themselves against the sides of the bus. I crouched between the seats, just trying to feel like there was some kind of barrier between me and them. A fortress around me to protect me from the monsters. I'd seen them, I'd heard their high, chittering calls, but another part of me was trying hard not to believe my own senses.

Suddenly there was a heavy clanging noise overhead. Something had clambered up onto the roof of the bus and was moving slowly toward the open hatch. For a terrible moment, we all looked up.

I stood in the dark, mildewy-smelling bus, at the foot of the ladder. The thing peered through the hole in the roof, and then its head seemed to split, peeling open like the petals of a strang, poisonous flower, revealing a huge, hungry mouth filled with hundreds of teeth. I let out a high scream, like every terrified girl in every horror movie. I'd seen all kinds of monster flicks and slashers, but I'd never really understood the girl in the horror movie before.

Then Steve was in front of me, shoving me out of the way, squaring up with the bat like he'd face down the whole world and take a chunk out of it before he let anything get to us. Next to me, Lucas moved closer. He reached for my hand, and without meaning to, I was already reaching back.

The thing on the roof bent its awful alien head. I had a crawling sensation, like the whole world had come into sharp nightmare focus, and all this time I'd only been squinting at it through a dirty window. The thing threw back its head and let out a long, bone-chilling roar. Then there was an answering sound, echoing from someplace off in the distance. The thing on the roof raised its head to listen. All at once, it turned and bounded down from the bus and into the woods.

We stood frozen in the abrupt silence. Lucas was still beside me. His hand felt warm and comforting in mine. I squeezed it, and he didn't pull it away.

Lucas glanced at me, his eyes very wide in the dark, and I let go of his hand in a hurry. I was half-sure he'd reached for me by mistake, but I couldn't help thinking how good it had felt to hold on to him. It seemed ridiculous that three hours ago, I'd been worrying about the distance between Indiana and California, when the universe was so impossibly big.

CHAPTER
FIFTEEN

The sky was completely dark now, scattered with all the stars I couldn't see in San Diego. The Milky Way stretched over us, delicate and alien. The woods seemed to drift by. Every tree and branch stood out sharply for a second and was gone again almost as soon as we passed it.

I followed the others through the thick underbrush of the woods, and then along the railroad tracks, like I was walking in a dream. We followed the sound of the monsters, a roaring through the trees like an angry wind.

I'd always been ready for any big adventure, perfectly happy to be dragged along with my dad on his schemes and scams and projects. You had to move fast to keep up with him. I'd thought that made me ready for anything. Everything Lucas had told me in the arcade came rushing back: The mysterious other world, the monsters, the secret lab. Will getting lost in a dangerous, impossible place. The Mage. Now the story was all happening around me, and I didn't know where it was going or how it would end. I had to just keep moving my feet and roll with whatever happened next.

When the sound came again, the others all started after it, plunging away from the tracks into the woods. After a second, I followed them.

• • •

The lab was a huge concrete building like a hospital, except the whole place, including a gatehouse, was behind a high fence with barbed wire along the top. We stood up on the wooded hill above it, looking down at the road. A beat-up old car was sitting at the gate with its lights on. It seemed like a strange thing to find when the lab was closed and the whole place was dark. A slender girl and a shaggy-haired boy had gotten out of the car and were staring up at the fence. They looked like they were probably in high school.

When we stepped out of the trees, the two of them whipped around like they were on high alert, then stood staring in surprise. *"Steve?"*

As soon as we came crunching out of the woods and down to the gatehouse, it was obvious that everyone knew everyone else, but no one had expected to find the others here. The shaggy-haired boy turned out to be Will's brother, Jonathan, and the girl was Mike's sister, Nancy, and they'd come out to the lab to check on Will. As they all discussed what was going on, I learned that Will and Mike were supposedly inside the lab and very much in danger. With the gate locked, though, there was no way to get inside. During the day, there was probably a guy in a wheelie chair sitting in the little gatehouse to buzz people in, but now it was empty. Everything was very quiet.

We stood in the middle of the road while Dustin and Will's brother messed around in the gatehouse, trying to figure out how to open the gate.

We were still just standing there when all the lights came on at once and the gate slid open. Jonathan and the girl got back in their car and drove into the compound to look for Will. The rest of us waited.

While we did, Lucas told me about Will and the lab, how they were monitoring him after the time he'd spent lost in the otherworld. We didn't talk about the junkyard, but I kept remembering the awful, gaping mouth studded with teeth. I kept remembering how it had felt to hold Lucas's hand.

We were still in the middle of the road, trying to figure out what to do next, when suddenly a blaze of headlights came rushing toward us, and we all scattered out of the way. We stood watching as the lights got closer and Jonathan's car came roaring past us up the drive, followed by a hulking Blazer with a Hawkins Police Department shield painted on the side. The Blazer skidded to a stop in front of us, and the driver leaned across to the passenger-side window.

He was a big burly man with a lot of stubble. "Let's go."

I'd been warned my whole life not to get into cars with strangers, but I figured maybe that didn't count if it was a police car, and anyway, there was nothing left to do.

The drive from the lab was very quiet. None of us talked about it, but I knew from the way the cop was staring into the dark that something terrible had happened. The look on his face was too grim to mean anything else. I could still smell the rancid stink of the monsters in the junkyard, —or maybe the smell was on him, too, seeping into everything.

We drove along a narrow two-lane road that wound through the trees. The house was tucked deep in the woods, even farther outside of town than ours. It was small and shabby, with a sagging porch, not much different from any of the little one-story bungalows I'd lived in with my mom back in California.

When we pulled up to the house, the other car was already there, and I finally got a good look at everyone else. Mike and Will had been at the lab, along with Will's mom. The big, grim-faced man was named Hopper, and he was the chief of police. The girl we'd met at the gatehouse was Nancy Wheeler, and she was Mike's sister.

I had about a thousand questions, but I mostly stayed quiet. The only thing I knew for sure was that I'd thought our standoff in the junkyard was the strangest thing that would happen all night—maybe the strangest thing that would happen in my whole life—but instead I'd stumbled smack into the middle of something even bigger and more bizarre. There was no *Previously, on* . . . segment or voice-over to catch me up. The story was happening, and had been for a while. They were all part of it—not just Steve or the boys, but everyone. Will's mom and brother, Mike's sister, Hopper. Lucas and Dustin didn't seem even a little surprised to find them there.

We piled out of the cars and went inside. I'd expected a cozy, messy atmosphere, run-down maybe, but normal. When we stepped inside, though, the whole place looked deranged. It was full of drawings, hundreds of them, taped all over the floor and the walls. Each one was part of a bigger whole, branching and forking like veins under the skin of something huge.

They laid Will on the couch, but he was completely zonked out. I still wasn't sure what was wrong with him. All they'd told us was that they'd had to break out of Hawkins Lab, which was abandoned now and full of monsters. They were keeping Will sedated, which had something to do with Dart and the hungry, slinking monsters we'd seen in the junkyard.

As we sat at the kitchen table, I started to piece together the story from things the boys were saying, but the picture I was getting was wild. They kept calling the animals in the junkyard something that, at first, sounded like *demon-dogs*.

But as they kept talking, I realized they were saying demodog. The place Will had gotten lost in was where the monsters came from, and even though he was back now, something that lived there had gotten inside his head. Or his body. The difference was hard to figure out. Mike and Dustin called it the Mind Flayer, but the important part was that it had found a way to use Will like a puppet so that they were always connected. It would be able to find him. And if it could find him, it could find us.

That was why they were keeping him full of some kind of heavy-duty tranquilizer, with shots in his arm and a backup syringe loaded with an extra dose: so the thing that had set up shop in his brain wouldn't have a chance to look out through his eyes and see us.

It was awful to see how hard Will's mom had worked just to keep him safe, and even though I'd never thought he was scary before, the thing inside him had made him into something terrible. He was part of the monster now, and still, she was ready to do anything to save him.

We sat and waited in the dark house, while out in the shed his family was doing everything they could to learn how to stop the Mind Flayer before it found us.

It was no good, though. When Hopper came charging inside, ordering us to get ready, the dogs were coming, I wanted to let myself believe they could protect us from whatever happened next. I was a little comforted at how quickly everyone readied themselves. Mike's sister, Nancy, was in high school, but she seemed way different from the high school girls who went around with Billy. She was preppie and skinny, with large, cautious eyes and dark hair cut in a bob. She looked like the kind of girl who mostly liked Swatch watches and Bonne Bell lip gloss, but when Hopper had handed out weapons, she'd been the one who took the rifle. Her eyes were wide and scared, but she held the gun like she meant it.

I was so afraid that none of it was good enough and we were going to die here in the little brown house, surrounded by monsters. Next to me, Lucas stood with the pocket of his slingshot pulled back. All the weapons seemed small and too ordinary to do much good.

Nancy was standing in front with Steve and Hopper, and she was frightened and delicate like the girls who always screamed the chilling scream in all the stories, but she was fierce, too.

I'd always believed that it wasn't too hard to be strong. That people like my mom just weren't trying hard enough. I knew that girls could be as badass as boys, but before I'd always thought the only way to do it was by being just like them. Nancy didn't seem to be trying to be Steve or Hopper. She was dangerous and brave and frightened all at once. When she lifted her chin and raised the gun to her shoulder, it looked like it belonged there.

We stood in the cramped little living room and waited. The dogs were coming for us, but at least I wasn't facing them alone. For most of my life, I'd been like a balloon tied to a railing somewhere, unprotected. I'd gotten so used to the feeling that it was hard to realize it was gone. The others were all around me now. They didn't even know me, and still, they'd put me in the middle of their circle. They weren't about to just give up and let the world roll over us, the way my mom did.

Outside, the woods had come alive. There were snarls and rustles as the bushes shook below the window. They were coming for us. I wondered what it would feel like to be torn apart by rows and rows of little bristling teeth. It made sense that something would only have a huge, savage mouth like that if it was built to eat everything it touched.

The map of drawings lay in a snaking tangle on the floor, a guide to somewhere terrible and impossible. We'd come close to outsmarting it, but the Mind Flayer had found us anyway.

There wasn't much hope in what we were about to do, but now I thought I understood why they could stand to face it: no matter what happened, they had each other. Most of the time, my mom didn't have anyone. If I was really being honest, most of the time she didn't even have me.

The demodogs were out there, hunting through the woods in a frantic pack. I could almost feel them rushing toward us. And then, without warning, something happened. There was a colossal thump, and a dark shape crashed through the living room window and slid bonelessly to the floor.

Then the door swung open, and it wasn't the army or the State Patrol or a bunch of lab men in hazmat suits.

It was a girl. She stepped into the living room, and I knew, just knew, beyond all question, that this was the girl Lucas had told me about. El, the Mage, had come back.

She stood in front of us, dressed in black with her hair combed back tightly from her face. As soon as Mike saw her, all the misery and the pinched meanness he'd been walking around with seemed to drain out of him. He looked raw and lost and very young. He went to her and hugged her hard, like he knew without question she would hug him back, and it didn't even matter that we were all watching.

The way he reached for her filled me with a weird kind of gladness so unexpected it almost hurt. I had never been that sure about anyone.

CHAPTER SIXTEEN

When I'd first moved to Hawkins, I'd thought it was small. I'd thought it was the kind of place where nothing ever happened, and the streets were wide and quiet, and the best part about them was they all led out of town. Now we were trying to figure out what to do about a creature from another dimension tearing a hole in the skin of the world.

The situation seemed impossible, but El said she could close the gate. She sounded so sure, so determined, and finally Hopper agreed to take her to the lab. The rest of us stayed behind in the ramshackle Byers house.

Mike was pale and tight-lipped, but I understood his

moods a little better now. I was getting better at knowing how to recognize sadness when someone was being a jerk. It didn't make the way he'd treated me all right, it just made it easier not to take personally.

The grown-ups and the older kids had all gone, except Steve. He was helping Dustin pack up the body of the creature that El had tossed through the window. It turned out that the name Dustin had given them was demodogs, and as helpful as it probably was to get the dead one off the floor, it felt like we should be doing something more important. I was a tomboy and a daredevil and I mostly tried to be brave, but that was nothing compared to how it hard it must have been to be the girl whose job it was to close the gate on a world full of monsters. It was a kind of brave that didn't even seem possible. They'd barely escaped from the lab, and now they were going back in.

The longer we stood around doing nothing, the more restless and wrong it felt, like we were hanging El out to dry. True, she'd ignored me when I'd introduced myself, as if I'd done something wrong, but maybe it didn't matter that much. I tried not to let it get to me.

Steve wasn't about to let us go running off to help her, though. We were all arguing with him about what to do next, when outside there was a low, snarling rumble.

I knew that sound like I knew the sound of my own voice, and I ran to the window. Billy's Camaro came tearing through the trees and roared up the driveway. He'd found us. Found me.

It had been dark for hours by now. Of course Neil and my mom would have gotten home from Terre Haute and freaked out when they found me gone. They'd sent Billy to bring me back. But I honestly had no clue how he'd figured out I was here.

Lucas was right there next to me, leaning against the couch to look out the window. His arm beside mine was warm, but it didn't get rid of the icy feeling creeping down my neck.

When Steve came up behind us and saw what we were looking at, he put his hand on my shoulder. "Don't worry, I'll take care of it."

I didn't try to stop him, but I was plenty worried. He just gave me a reassuring smile and stepped outside into the gravel driveway to meet Billy.

Billy got out of the Camaro, a cigarette jutting from the center of his mouth like always. The cherry glowed a wicked, itchy red, even from the window. Steve was talking to him with a bored look, like nothing about Billy impressed him. Billy was smiling, but I could see from the loose, easy way he moved that he was going to go right through Steve to get to me.

The way they watched each other made me think that maybe it wasn't even about me. Or at least, not all of it. They were looking at each other with the kind of fixed stares you only get when it's personal. Suddenly Billy shoved Steve in the chest, hard enough to knock him backward. Steve went sprawling in the dirt, and Billy raised one booted foot and stomped hard on Steve's ribs. Then he stepped over Steve and up onto the porch.

He came slamming into the house, scanning the living room for me. "Well, well, well."

Then his gaze shifted to find Lucas, and I knew what came next.

"You know what happens when you disobey me!" Billy's face was twisted with rage. "I break things!"

His voice sent a shudder through me. I could almost hear it—the sound of my skateboard deck splintering, the sound of Nate's arm breaking. Billy didn't look like a real person at all anymore but like a grinning, snarling monster. He went straight for Lucas, and I understood that he was going to do something terrible that couldn't be taken back. The moment would stretch on forever. We would never stop living it.

He stalked through the dim, cluttered living room, backing Lucas against the bookcase in the corner, and I waited for the loud, sickening snap.

Instead, Lucas kicked Billy square in the groin.

I was horrified and deeply impressed. My heart was in my throat, sure, but I had wanted to do that for months. When Billy turned on Lucas, he looked ready to murder him. The whole thing felt flat and too bright, like it was happening to someone else.

Suddenly Steve charged back into the house and decked Billy. The punch connected with a dull smack, and Billy threw back his head. He was laughing. I was struck by how creepy it was when you hit someone and they just let you do it, laughing like it's everything they ever wanted.

Steve was still trying to talk to Billy, like maybe this could all just be civil, but Billy wasn't having it. He'd come here to fight. He took a swing at Steve, and then they were shoving each other around the kitchen, slamming into the counter. Billy reached out, fumbling along the drain board. His hand found a plate, and in one fast, fluid motion, he smashed it into the side of Steve's head. Steve staggered, and then Billy was on top of him, swinging his fists in huge, bludgeoning arcs, beating Steve's face into hamburger.

The boys were screaming for him to stop, but I knew that wouldn't make a difference. The dreamlike feeling was falling away. Every crumpled drawing and drop of blood was getting clearer and more real by the second.

I'd always known that when Billy lost his temper, it was different from how other people got mad. It had still seemed survivable, though. Manageable. He was out of control, but if you stayed alert, you could weather him like a storm. Now I was horribly sure that if someone didn't do something to help Steve, Billy was going to kill him.

He had Steve pinned to the floor. The others were just staring in total disbelief, but I'd seen what he could do. Every day, I walked around knowing what he'd done to Nate. I'd seen what happened when Billy stopped trying to control himself, and now if no one did anything, I was going to see someone die.

When the demodogs had come, El had shown up at the last minute and saved us. There was no one to sweep in and save us or work miracles this time. The others might be acquainted with monsters, but they hadn't seen one like Billy.

I remembered how it had felt the first time I'd watched the Hargroves in action. Neil standing over Billy with the belt in his hand. Neil calling me a stupid little girl for having the guts to try to stop him. Making it so clear that he thought I was small and weak and pointless. And knowing Neil believed that still wasn't as bad as the way Billy had hated me for trying to help him. He was damaged. Broken, maybe. And even if he'd been coherent enough to argue with, it wouldn't make a difference. I understood now that Neil was in his head, and that meant he was just as dangerous as his father. Worse, because Neil was cruel and frightening, but he cared how things looked on the outside. He still wanted people to think he was reasonable.

Billy was crazy.

Under Billy's pounding fists, Steve was fading, going limp. His head rocked back.

The others were all watching in shock, like the sound had been turned down. The living room was dim and claustrophobic. Everything seemed very close, like being inside a cardboard box. Somebody needed to do something.

That backup syringe from the lab was sitting on the corner of a little sewing table. It was full of something colorless. Whatever it was had been enough to keep Will completely out of commission, and I grabbed it.

There had been times when Billy had seemed exciting, almost fun, but we were so far beyond that now. I uncapped the syringe, already reeling at what I was about to do.

It felt like I'd spent my whole life thinking about how things worked, figuring out the rules for locks and people, memorizing my escape routes. Billy had never been a problem that was solvable; he was just something I had to live through. Tonight, though, I was done with monsters.

The syringe felt small and weightless in my hand, the kind of thing that was more dangerous than it looked. The needle was sharp, just waiting to end up somewhere.

Holding it like a knife, I shouldered my way between the boys. I crossed the floor in two quick strides and jammed the syringe into the side of Billy's neck.

There was a smooth, bottomless feeling when the needle slid into the skin. I'd been expecting some kind of resistance, but there wasn't any. I clenched my jaw and pressed the plunger. For a horrible second, I was sure whatever was in the syringe wouldn't be strong enough. Billy was too angry and too ferocious to stop. He would whip around and grab me by the throat and squeeze till I was dead.

Then he froze, and his eyes slid out of focus. He got to his feet and turned to face me. The syringe was sticking out of the side of his neck, and he went to pull it out, but it was too late.

"What the hell is this?" His face was dumbfounded and slack.

He staggered and fell back, limp and boneless, like he was tumbling into a swimming pool. He was laughing in a slow, drunk way, trying to look at me, but his eyes kept fluttering closed. He was trying to fight it, but the drug was in his blood now.

Steve's bat was leaning against the wall. It looked like a weapon out of a Texas chain saw torture shed, covered in a spiky layer of nails, perfect for killing monsters. When I grabbed it up and hefted in my hands, it felt serious— heavier than I'd expected.

I stood over him with the bat, watching a blurry comprehension come into his eyes.

He stared up at me, trying to focus, and for a second, I wondered if he was even seeing me.

After being abducted, Will had turned into something terrible and frightening, but even with the Mind Flayer working through him, he was trying not to let it. His mom was terrified pretty much all the time, but she was ready to fight for him, no matter how scary he was, no matter how hard it got or how dangerous. He'd almost gotten us killed, but you couldn't even blame him, because he didn't ask for this. He was trying so hard to stop it.

Billy lay on the floor at my feet, moving his arms in useless little jerks, like they weighed too much to lift.

I gestured with the bat. "From here on out, you leave me and my friends alone. Do you understand?"

Billy was trying to sit up. He looked up at me, dazed and resentful. "Screw you."

I slammed the bat down as hard as I could. The nails bit into the floor half an inch from the crotch of his jeans. "Say you understand!"

It came to me that we would never be here in this room, in this awful, impossible moment, ever again. It was a miracle. A gift. And I needed to make it count.

"Say it!" I shouted, holding the bat like I was standing over home plate.

I couldn't protect the girls who went around with him. They were drawn to him in their own whacked-out ways, for their own reasons. Maybe it was what they wanted—or what they thought they wanted. I'd been drawn to him too, and it wasn't what I wanted, but it was what I thought that I deserved. Or else, maybe I'd just believed it was all there was. Maybe that was how it was for everyone.

When I stood over him with the bat, I had a fierce, glowing feeling like a comic-book hero: righteous. I was doing this for the girls he messed around with, for the way he grabbed and sneered and talked about them later with his friends. For my mom, who, no matter how many times she got burned, was always ready to believe that the worst, most despicable parts of people didn't define them. For myself, because I understood that things were messed up and dysfunctional and just rolled with it anyway since I'd spent so long believing there were no other options.

The bat was heavy in my hands, but it belonged there.

The universe was very big. I mean, there were places where the fabric of reality opened onto whole other worlds!

The boys were all standing behind me, huddled against the wall. I bent down and yanked the keys from Billy's pocket. I had nothing but options.

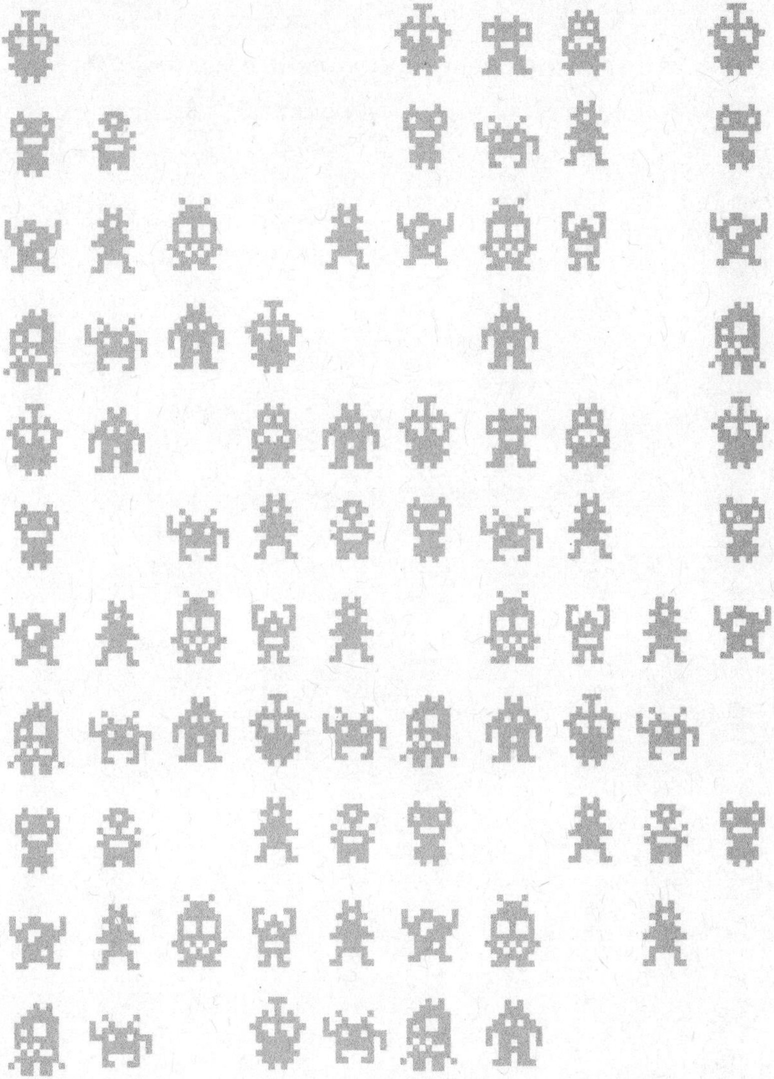

CHAPTER
SEVENTEEN

A month before this, I wouldn't have been caught dead getting ready for the Snow Ball. The whole time I'd been in California, I never went to a dance. At least, none except for the last week of day camp in fifth grade, when they forced us to do square dancing.

Now I was standing in front of the bathroom sink, in my good sweater and my salmon-colored pants, getting ready for the winter dance at Hawkins Middle School.

My mom stood behind me, fixing my hair. I forced myself to hold still, trying to get used to the weird, cautious feeling of her fingers in my hair. She tugged gently, braiding the front of my hair back from my face. I watched us in the mirror. The strangeness of having her so close made me restless and twitchy.

"Ow!" I said, even though it didn't hurt that much.

When she'd pinned the braid in place with a barrette, she clasped her hands and stepped back to inspect my sweater. "Are you sure you wouldn't rather wear a dress?"

"No, this is good."

She frowned a little. "Won't all the other girls be in dresses?"

"I don't know. Probably?"

She looked sort of surprised by that, but she smiled. "Always my little rebel, aren't you, marching to your own drum."

I grinned, even though I wanted to roll my eyes over being called little. "Yep."

When she was done giving me the once-over, she put an arm around my shoulders and stood next to me in front of the mirror. Our reflections were similar, freckled and redheaded, but her hair was a shade or two darker. I'd always just assumed that I was more like my dad, but so much of me was my mom. She looked wistful and a little worried, but proud, too. She looked happy.

With a distracted sigh, she turned to me and tapped a thumb against my mouth. "What about some lipstick? Just a little dab?"

I made my eyelids heavy and gave her a long look. "Don't push it."

But I could feel myself smiling.

I wasn't going to magically turn into her ideal daughter, but I wasn't disappointing, either. It felt weird to be dressed up, trying to look pretty just for a dance, but it wasn't the same as giving up the person I was the rest of the time. I was still me. I would always be myself, even with my fancy braid and my sweater and my mom's fingers in my hair.

She was always going to be my mom, even when she made herself small and gave away all her time and attention to guys like Neil. She would keep choosing him, making dinner and excuses for him, and there was nothing I could do to fix it. I couldn't change the men she picked and the things she put up with, but I could love her without feeling obligated to make the same choices.

Deciding to back away from the monster was easier, knowing that I wasn't alone here in Hawkins. That there were a whole lot of people who would show up and fight for each other. If I trusted them and if I let them, maybe they'd show up for me, too.

When I glanced over my shoulder, Billy was standing in the doorway, watching me and my mom. Since that night at the Byers house, he'd been careful to stay out of my way. There was still a dark fury in his face sometimes, when I took the time to look for it. He hadn't come after me or any of my friends, but I knew I wouldn't be safe from him forever. He was the same person he'd always been, and that empty, glittering rage still flashed across his face at random times. I thought I saw it in the center of his pupils, blacker and emptier than before. I needed to be careful.

For a long, uneasy moment, we looked at each other, but neither of us said anything. After a second, he turned and disappeared down the hall.

There had been times in my life when he was the coolest, most exciting thing that had happened to me, and times when he'd been the worst. Now, though, I thought I could just settle in and live with him until I didn't have to anymore. Since coming to Hawkins, I'd seen things so wild and fantastical that the hugeness of it made Billy seem smaller somehow. Less real.

After I'd jabbed him with the needle, we hadn't stuck around. He was passed out on the floor, and it was crucial to help El and Hopper in whatever way we could. With Steve out of commission after Billy had bounced his head off the floor, there'd been no one to stop us.

I'd driven us all out to a pumpkin field in the Camaro and then followed the others underground into a winding network of tunnels. Not the place where Will had disappeared to, but a dark, sprawling nest that the monsters had made for themselves in our world.

We'd found the demodogs and drawn their attention until El could do whatever big, dangerous miracle it took to close the gate. We'd done it because we needed to. Because El was some kind of magician or a mutant—a real superhero, maybe—but she was still just one person. She had the power to save us from the monsters, but she didn't have to do it alone, and when the whole world was on the line, her friends were ready to do whatever it took to help her.

• • •

At school, the halls were decorated with posters and banners for the dance, painted in icy blues and silvers. The gym was transformed, dripping with tinsel and streamers, with a disco ball and a punch bowl. Nancy Wheeler stood behind a folding table, handing out refreshments, while Jonathan took photos against a marbled backdrop. The whole place was full of boys in khakis and girls with feathered hair and dresses filled out with shoulder pads.

Lucas and Mike were both looking awkward and uncomfortable in collared shirts and sport coats. Most of the other boys were dressed pretty much the same, but Dustin was wearing a bow tie and had combed his hair into a huge, curly pompadour. He looked ridiculous, but comforting and familiar, too. The fact that he was wearing high-top sneakers with his dress slacks made me feel less like an idiot in a costume and more like I was just trying on a new version of myself. If it didn't fit, I could still take it back.

The version of me who wore a shiny barrette in her hair and let her mom touch her face didn't feel so terrible, though. Maybe I would keep it.

A slow song came on. Lucas was looking at me with kind, steady eyes. Usually he was unflinchingly direct, but tonight he was having a hard time getting the words out. He kept making it halfway through a sentence, then picking a different one and starting over. After I got tired of watching him stammer and squirm, I grabbed his hand and tugged him onto the dance floor.

It was easier to understand the hugeness of all the secrets he'd had to keep from me now, and to appreciate how hard he'd tried to explain them anyway. When I thought back to that night, it seemed almost like something I'd imagined, like remembering a dream. The clearest parts were also the most impossible—hiding from the demodogs in a junkyard, arguing over how to close the gate on the Mind Flayer. Stabbing Billy with a syringe full of drugs. I had taken his keys. I had *driven his car*. We'd all gone underground together in a last-ditch effort to keep the horde of demodogs away from El long enough for her to save the world.

Certain things were burned into my mind so clearly I could still see their outlines when I shut my eyes, but I didn't know if there was any way I'd ever be able to say them out loud to someone who didn't already know.

Now here I was, with Lucas's hands on my waist, his face inches from mine. I darted forward and kissed him. It was fast and awkward, but his mouth was warm and the feeling of us there together in the middle of the gym was exactly what I wanted. I leaned against him and rested my head on his shoulder.

When the Mage showed up, no one really seemed to notice her. She stood hesitantly at the edge of the dance floor, and I had to turn and crane my neck for another look.

She'd come to the house in the woods looking wild and edgy, like Joan Jett or Siouxsie Sioux, but that version of her was long gone. Now she looked clean and young and shy. Like a girl. Just any ordinary girl, with lip gloss and soft, tousled curls. Her dress was grown-up and a little too big, like it had belonged to someone else.

Mike went to El, and his shoulders were tense, but his face was earnest and unguarded. The way he looked at her was so tender. Sure, he was still way too serious and he could be moody as hell, but he'd been nicer to me lately. I didn't really know who she was—what she wished for or why she liked him. But she did. Maybe all that really mattered was that she did.

Lucas was watching me as we swayed to the music, bending closer. When he kissed me, it was gentler and less awkward this time, and I felt my cheeks go a hot, flaming red, but I didn't care. I was there in Hawkins, with my hands on Lucas's shoulders in the middle of the dance floor, and for once, I was totally sure I belonged there.

ACKNOWLEDGMENTS

My gratitude belongs to:

My agent, Sarah Davies, who is wise, kind, sensible, and tireless. It's been ten years and I still count on you every step of the way.

My publisher, Michelle Nagler, for her vision, encouragement, and willingness to follow me down rabbit holes, and my intrepid editors, Rachel Poloski and Sara Sargent. Rachel got me started and Sara saw me through.

Krista Marino, for her continual faith in me and for remembering everything I like.

The whole *Stranger Things* team, for answering questions, sharing my love of the '80s, being generally and genuinely delightful, and creating an extraordinary world full of kind boys, fearsome monsters, and dangerous girls and then letting me dabble around in it.

And to David, who made this book possible, and Veronica, who sometimes made it impossible but in the most miraculous way. I love you both.

© Madalyn Yovanoff

Brenna Yovanoff was raised in a barn, a tent, and a tepee and was homeschooled until high school. She spent her formative years in Arkansas, in a town heavily populated with snakes, where sometimes they would drop turkeys out of the sky. When she was five, she moved to Colorado, where it snows on a regular basis but never snows turkeys. She is the *New York Times* bestselling author of *The Replacement*, *The Space Between*, *Paper Valentine*, and *Fiendish*. Her most recent novel is *Places No One Knows*. She lives in Denver.

brennayovanoff.com

@brennayovanoff
@brennayovanoff